HOUSEHOLDS, EMPLOYMENT, AND GENDER

A Social, Economic, and
Demographic View

HOUSEHOLDS, EMPLOYMENT, AND GENDER

A Social, Economic, and
Demographic View

PAULA ENGLAND
AND
GEORGE FARKAS

ALDINE
Publishing Company
New York

ABOUT
THE AUTHORS

PAULA ENGLAND is Associate Professor of Sociology and Political Economy, University of Texas at Dallas. Her current interests include gender inequality and occupational sex segregation. Dr. England has contributed to many journals and books and has served as Consulting Editor for the American Journal of Sociology.

GEORGE FARKAS is Associate Professor of Sociology and Political Economy, University of Texas at Dallas. His areas of specialization include population, the labor force and evaluation of employment/training programs. Dr. Farkas has served as reviewer, investigator, and project director on numerous U.S. Department of Labor research grants, and has authored articles for journals and books.

Aldine Publishing Company
200 Saw Mill River Road
Hawthorne, New York 10532

Library of Congress Cataloging in Publication Data

England, Paula.
  Households, employment, and gender.

  Bibliography: p.
  Includes index.
   1. Households—United States. 2. Cost and standard
of living—United States. 3. Women—Employment—
United States. 4. Sex discrimination in employment—
United States. I. Farkas, George, 1946–
II. Title.
HQ536.E54 1986   304.6   85-18628
ISBN 0-202-30322-5 (lib. bdg.)
ISBN 0-202-30323-3 (pbk.)

Printed in the United States of America
10 9 8 7 6 5 4 3 2 1

CONTENTS

IV   THE FUTURE

8   FUTURE TRENDS IN HOUSEHOLDS, EMPLOYMENT, AND GENDER

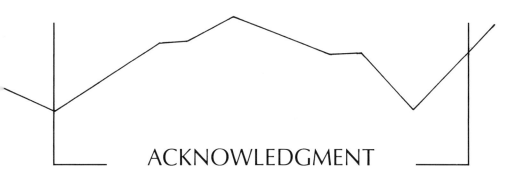

ACKNOWLEDGMENT

We are grateful for Beverly Duncan's detailed and sometimes skeptical comments, not all of which we responded to. We thank Barbara Bergmann for keeping us from error on one point and providing other thoughtful comments. We are also grateful for Dorothy Lutrell's speedy and careful typing of successive drafts under a tight deadline. We would each like to acknowledge the equal contribution made to this volume by the other.

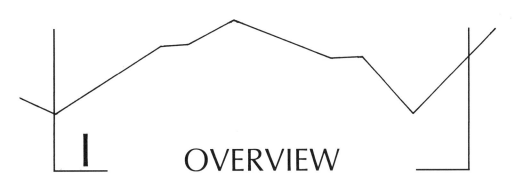

1 OVERVIEW

Consider the situation of a modern-day Rip van Winkle who fell asleep in the 1950s and awoke in the 1980s. The world left behind featured teenagers who went steady, cohabited little, and had an unambiguous sexual morality. This code contained a double standard, including "good" and "bad" girls. Women married early and specialized in homemaking and the rearing of several children. Only a minority of women worked outside the home and these were concentrated in "female" occupations. There was little divorce, even when marriages were unhappy, and couples planned to spend the "empty nest" and retirement periods together if death did not intervene. The civil rights movement had barely begun, the suffragist movement was almost forgotten, and gay had only one meaning.

Today, the proportion of 20- to 24-year-old women who have never been married is the highest it has been in this century. Childbearing is the lowest in United States history. One-half of recently contracted marriages are expected to end in divorce. Despite early retirement by men, only about one-half the marriages contracted in the 1980s will remain intact by the time of retirement. The early confrontations of the sexual, women's, and gay movements are history, although battles continue to be fought. Cohabitation is at an all-time high; premarital and extramarital sex are widespread. Female employment rates continue their strong upward movement. Employment among women with young children has more than doubled since the 1950s. Younger women are entering "male" occupations. During the 1970s women's proportion of new M.D.'s rose from 9 to 23%, and of new law school graduates from 6 to 26%. Women comprised 25% of the 1983 graduates of the Harvard Business School.

Events of the past 30 years have profoundly transformed arrangements governing love, work, and their routinization in households and employment; yet, some patterns endure relatively unchanged. During this period women have gained employment opportunities. This has reduced sex differentiation, although it has not equalized the roles or power of men and women. The strength of economic, moral, and legal constraints on marital search and divorce have also declined. These events have led to an unprecedented degree of uncertainty and instability in family and child-rearing arrangements, particularly in the links between divorced fathers and their children. Women who work outside the home have more power to leave an unhappy marriage; husbands who leave their employed wives are less stigmatized. Both sexes now proceed into marriage more cautiously, and with more information. With one-half of current marriages expected to end in divorce, some spouses keep an eye out for a better arrangement. With women contributing to earnings, one might expect men to increase the time they spend on child rearing and housework, although this has not occurred to a significant extent. With young women planning more continuous employment, more of them choose traditionally male jobs because discrimination has declined and male jobs offer more advancement. The goal of this book is to describe these trends and the patterns that remain constant amidst the change, and to provide an integrated framework for making sense of them.

The framework we offer seeks three levels of integration that we have found missing in previous studies. First, we integrate the topics of households and employment, showing similarities and causal links between household and employment arrangements. Second, we provide a conceptual framework that gives attention to both individuals' choices and to the structural constraints that limit and price available options. Finally, we provide an integration of economic and sociological views of employment, demographic behavior, and other household behavior.

Many of the same ideas can organize discussions of households and employment. In each case there is a period of search, followed by a contract, which is partially implicit and partially explicit. Both household and employment contracts are arrived at when the parties possess limited information from which to predict the benefits of the relationship, or future opportunities for alternative contracts. Each contract involves investment in the relationship that creates incentives for its continuation. In both spheres there are issues of power and bargaining over the joint gain due to the relationship. Although both marital and employment contracts are expected to last a long time, they can be terminated at the desire of either party, with ensuing issues of division or custody of the "product" from the relationship, and the search for a new relationship.

The topics of households and employment are also integrated by examining how change in sex differences in employment opportunities encourages change in sex roles at home, and vice versa. Despite much change, some areas of the system of gender roles are more intractable than others. The assignment of child rearing and housework to women, the sex segregation of jobs, and the sex gap in pay have been much more resistant to change than fertility, the double standard of sexual morality, female employment, or the volume of housework that is performed.

We believe that integrating both individual and structural views is necessary for understanding the changes and continuities of the postwar period. In one sense, the behavior we seek to explain results from the choices of optimizing individuals who search and bargain for arrangements that make them better off than their other available options, given their preferences and the costs of further search. We integrate this with the view that choices are constrained by structural arrangements that limit the contracts that are possible and the (pecuniary and nonpecuniary) prices of particular contracts. Such constraints include the array of available job slots, the distribution of power among groups, laws governing marriage and employment, and the collective consciousness of common morality and ideology. The former view is associated with neoclassical economics and sociological exchange theory, the latter with institutional economics and structural sociology.

The integrated view we develop draws from both economics and sociology and from the work of demographers in both disciplines. Our framework aims to escape the characteristic failings of each of the two disciplines—sociologists' lack of powerful and coherent theory and economists' predilection for making questionable assumptions and ignoring empirical findings that do not fit comfortably within their paradigm. Chapter 1 summarizes the remarkable changes that have occurred in the postwar period—as well as some striking continuities. Chapter 2 then presents a conceptual framework for understanding these relationships and their evolution. The remainder of the book expands upon this framework and applies it to explaining the relationships of household, employment, and gender in the postwar era.

1 POSTWAR TRENDS AND PATTERNS

I. INTRODUCTION

This is a book about changes and continuities in households, in employment, and in gender differentiation since the 1950s. The purpose of this chapter is to introduce the reader to our topic with a descriptive overview of the postwar trends and patterns. This chapter identifies many of the issues that later chapters will seek to explain in a more analytic fashion, using the framework to be discussed in Chapter 2.

II. HOUSEHOLDS AND MARRIAGE CONTRACTS

Business may be the business of America, but much of the work of America is performed in the household: birth; the acquisition of basic skills; the development of tastes and beliefs; love, nurturing and personality formation; decisions regarding education and training; decisions that affect nutrition and health; decisions about employment and occupational choice; sexual activity, household formation, marriage, and childbearing; spending, saving, and investment; intergenerational transfers and retirement decisions. The household may be viewed as a factory, the locus of production for an important portion of the nation's output. Many of these outputs—a well kept home, for example—are not traded in formal markets. Nonetheless they are produced at the cost of time and goods which might otherwise have been exchanged for money. Others of these outputs—socialized, educated youths—will find their labor priced in the next generation's labor market. Like a factory, the household involves production, a division of labor, distinct jobs, exchange, differentials in power, and contracts. One-half of our story concerns this household sector, the roles men and women play in its functioning, and the change it has undergone since the 1950s.

The employment relationship has always been a contract that either side might terminate when the benefits of doing so exceeded the costs. Since the

1950s we have moved toward a similar state of affairs in marriage. Prior to the enactment of no-fault divorce in many states in the 1970s, the letter if not the practice of the law treated marriage contracts substantially differently than other types of contracts; marriage contracts could not be terminated unilaterally or even by mutual agreement. Rather, they could be terminated only by the victim of a significant breach of contract. In concert with this legal situation, informal morality applied strong negative sanctions to the most common such breach, adultery. Further, all divorced persons were stigmatized for having "failed" at marriage. Women's economic dependence made divorce a frightful option for wives and children and a shameful option for husbands. Thus, strong social and economic forces discouraged the termination of marriage contracts. Divorce rates were low, with marriages lasting significantly longer than employment relationships.

The new marriage system is quite different. Most states have enacted "no-fault" divorce, which permits divorce upon demand by either party. In community property states this entails equal division of most tangible assets, without regard to fault. In many other states a similar outcome is achieved. Adulterers lose few friends as a consequence of their actions, although most spouses still perceive adultery as a grievous injury. Employed women know that they can support themselves and their children, albeit precariously. Thus, women dissatisfied with their marriages are more likely to divorce than ever before. The term "divorcee" is out of use, and rates of divorce have skyrocketed.

A key element of our story concerns the search for household and family arrangements, and their codification in the contract of marriage. Marriages can be viewed as partnerships for the production of "goods and services"— for example, affection and children—that are not easily acquired in other ways. Between 1950 and 1980 the economic and social arrangements affecting marital search and contracts changed so as to make the resulting match less stable. Associated with these changes have been the rise of living arrangements (such as cohabitation) which compete with marriage, extensions of the duration of marital search, lower fertility, and increased acquisition by women of skills that provide an income in the absence of marriage. In the remainder of this section we discuss the changes which have occurred in the household sector, relating these to changes in marital search and marriage itself.

A. The Search for Partners

In the 1950s, marital search was generally restricted to the high school years and the years shortly thereafter. The norm was to date during the later teenage years and marry in the early twenties. The transition from dating to marriage was usually marked by going steady followed by being engaged. Each stage brought greater sexual intimacy, usually stopping short of intercourse until, or just before, marriage. The socialization of females so estranged them from their sexuality that in order for males to have intercourse with a "nice girl," the likelihood of marriage had to exist. Thus, the choice of a mate was based upon little experience of potential mates, and little information regarding what living with this mate would be like.

As we see in Table 1.1, roughly 70% of women aged 20–24 were already married during the 1950s, and by age 30 almost 90% of women were married. A similar pattern held for men, with the proviso that males were expected to be at least several years older than their wives. This was consistent with a notion of women as more childlike and dependent than men. Reading down the columns of Table 1.1 we find markedly later ages at marriage as we move toward the present day. Between 1960 and 1980 the percentage of 20- to 24-year-old women who had not as yet married almost doubled, from 28 to 53%. The percentage of never-married 25- to 29-year-old women more than doubled, and even the percentage of never-married 30- to 34-year-old women almost doubled, from 7 to 12%. A similar pattern holds for men.

The extension of the period of marital search has coincided with the "sexual revolution" in the premarital period and the rise of cohabitation as a stage on the way to a (first or later) marriage. Table 1.2 shows that the percentage of (never-married) 16-year-old girls who had experienced intercourse went from 21% in 1971 to 38% in 1979. Among (never-married) 19-year-old women, the 1971 rate of 46% increased to 69% by 1979. Well over one-half of males this age had premarital sex even in the 1950s so the changes for men have been less dramatic. The increases in women's involvement signal an erosion of the double standard. Today, sexual in-

Table 1.1. Percentage of Women and Men Who Have Never Married, 1940–1982[a]

	Age of women (years)			Age of men (years)		
	20–24	25–29	30–34	20–24	25–29	30–34
1940	47.2	22.8	14.7	72.2	36.0	20.7
1950	32.3	13.3	9.3	59.0	23.8	13.2
1960	28.4	10.5	6.9	53.1	20.9	11.9
1970	35.8	10.5	6.2	54.7	19.1	9.4
1982	53.4	23.4	11.6	72.0	36.1	17.3

[a]Sources: 1940–1960: Masnick and Bane, 1980:129; 1970–1982: Saluter, 1983:2.

Table 1.2. Percentage Never-Married Women Living in Metropolitan Areas Who Had Experienced Sexual Intercourse, 1979 and 1971[a]

Age	1979	1971
15	22.5	14.4
16	37.8	20.9
17	48.5	26.1
18	56.9	39.7
19	69.0	46.4

[a]Source: Zelnik and Kantner, 1980: 231.

tercourse typically begins in the teenage years, and does not require talk of marriage. With first intercourse at its earliest age and first marriage at its latest age in this century, the sexual aspects of marital search extend across more years than ever before. Individuals are acquiring more intimate information about more potential mates, prior to marriage, than ever before.

Cohabitation is surely the method of selecting a marital partner that provides the most information about the potential marriage. Premarital cohabitation was considered immoral and was essentially unheard of in the 1950s. As recently as the late 1960s a college student living with her boyfriend could be expelled for the offense. Since that time such arrangements have proliferated and lost most of their stigma, particularly in the eyes of younger cohorts. Table 1.3 shows that the number of cohabitating couples more than tripled between 1970 and 1982. The increase among those under 25 years of age with no children was more than tenfold. In the 1980s, many youths cohabit at least once prior to marriage.

Table 1.3. Cohabitation: Number of Unmarried Couple Households, 1982 and 1970[a]

Year	Total	Age[b]		
		Under 25	25–44	45+
1982	1,863,000	374,000	713,000	776,000
1970	523,000	29,000	29,000	434,000

[a]Source: Saluter, 1983: 6. An unmarried couple household is one that contains exactly two adults, who are of the opposite sex and not related. Some of these households are arrangements such as an elderly man with a live-in female nurse. However, most of those under the age of 45 are thought to be "couples" in the lay sense of the term.

[b]Age is for the partner who is reported to "maintain the household."

Table 1.4. Percentage of Ever-Married Who Ever Divorce[a]

Year of birth	Percentage
1910–1914	15.8
1930–1934	26.0[b]
1950–1954	47.4[b]

[a]Source: Cherlin, 1981: 122.
[b]Projected.

B. Divorce, Marital Power, and Remarriage

Table 1.4 shows the projection that almost one-half of those born in the early 1950s can expect to experience divorce. The incidence of divorce has increased throughout the century, except for small dips during the 1930s and 1950s, and is as high today as it has ever been in our nation's history (Cherlin, 1981).

In the marriage system of the 1950s, few women saw divorce as a viable option even if they were deeply dissatisfied. Having invested heavily in a particular marriage, they had little ability to provide an income for themselves and their children outside marriage, and their children were a liability in finding a new marital partner. Men had greater power to divorce because of their financial independence of marriage, and their earning power was an asset in finding a new spouse. This power inequity led to social norms discouraging men from leaving their wives and children, but allowing men to exercise their disproportionate bargaining power within the marriage. For these people, the answer to marital dissatisfaction involved further adjustments within the marriage, especially by wives, and varieties of detachment without divorce ranging from separate hobbies and friends to adultery, especially by husbands.

Divorce has increased, despite evidence that men and women's satisfaction with the emotional and sexual quality of their marriages has actually increased. What has changed is women's ability to leave marriages they are dissatisfied with, and men's knowledge that women and children can manage without them. Women's options have increased because they have fewer children and most have jobs and earnings.

Yet, there is a paradox. Women's increased economic independence gives them the ability to leave marriages, but their earnings are still less than two-thirds of men's. Most divorced women are awarded modest sums of child support, which averaged about $2500 per year in 1981 (U.S. Bureau of Census, 1983). Less than one-half receive the full amount awarded, and many receive nothing. As a consequence, the per capita income of the home the average child is living in is declining. Thus, children are the clearest losers in a divorce-prone society. Furthermore, in addition to lowering the economic standard of living for children being raised by mothers who have not remarried, the rise in divorce has fostered a disconnection between vast numbers of children and their biological fathers.

Divorce may be high, but so is remarriage. Among older generations alive today, five out of six men and three out of four women have remarried after divorce, although the remarriage rate has been slightly lower in recent years (Cherlin, 1981).

One might expect that after the informative process of divorce, search, and remarriage, second marriages would be more durable than first marriages. However, this has not been the case in recent decades. The higher divorce rate for second marriages may reflect the strains of the "blended families" that often result when divorced women with custody of their children remarry. The legal and moral "rules" for blended families are just beginning to be negotiated. The new set of rules must deal with questions ranging from the responsibilities of stepparents for discipline to the boundaries between affection and quasi-incest.

C. Fertility and Household Work

In the old marriage system children were a major goal of marriage and, when economic conditions allowed, most couples began a family soon after marriage. This was not surprising since in the 1950s marriage and family were at the center of women's lives, and, along with sexual exclusivity, children were the defining characteristic of marriage. After the low fertility of the Depression and World War II, this family system produced the "baby boom," the great wave of childbearing that peaked in 1956 with age-specific rates consistent with the bearing of more than three children per woman (Cherlin, 1981). Figure 1.1 shows that fertility has declined ever since and is presently at an all-time low. Most couples in the present family system want no more than two children and voluntary childlessness is higher than ever before. Were present fertility rates to continue indefinitely, the United States population would eventually begin to decline in the absence of immigration.

In the 1950s, the marital division of labor was perfectly clear; men earned almost all the money and women did almost all the housework and nurturing of children. By the 1980s many more women are employed, more women consider their jobs as careers, and wives contribute a larger share of income. However, men's participation in household labor has been slow to adjust, even among couples with egalitarian sex role ideologies and similar incomes. Women still do most housework and child rearing; consequently, employed wives can be said to be holding two jobs. Women also continue

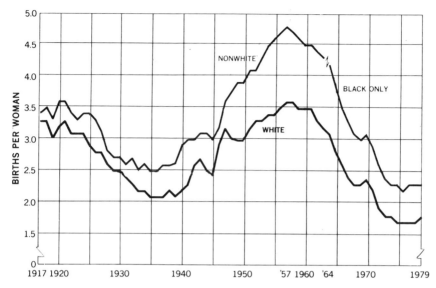

Figure 1.1. Total fertility rates for nonwhite and white women, 1917–1979. From Reid (1982:9). Total fertility rate for a given year indicates average number of children that would be born to women in the population if each woman were to live through her childbearing years (ages 15–44) bearing children at the same rate that women at each age in the given year actually did.

to specialize in the "emotional work" of relationships to a greater extent than men.

D. Consumption, Savings, and Retirement

During the baby boom years of the 1950s, couples began their families early, often before they had accumulated consumer durables such as a house, a second car, or a washing machine. In contrast, the common pattern of the children of the baby boom (who are producing the "baby bust") is to delay marriage, and after that to delay fertility until many such items have been acquired via the combination of husbands' and wives' earnings. Because of two-earner families, married baby boomers have thus far had higher family incomes at every stage of the life cycle than the cohort behind them. Yet, their individual earnings have been adversely affected by the recessions of the 1970s and 1980s.

A dramatic change in retirement between the 1950s and 1980s has been the progressively earlier retirement of men, made possible by changed regulations and expanded benefits provided by Social Security and Medicare programs, as well as by the growth of private pensions. Nonetheless, the fiscal crisis facing these programs may cause the baby boomers to fare less well in retirement than those presently retired.

III. EMPLOYMENT CONTRACTS AND GENDER

Employment can be thought of as a contract between employees and employers in which the investments in search and training made on each side of the relationship provide an incentive for both parties to keep the relationship intact. Of course, these investments characterize some jobs more than others, so some have much better developed contractual features than others. The resulting structure of different types of jobs is related to the characteristics of individuals in two ways. First, individuals with different characteristics are selected into differing kinds of jobs. Second, characteristics of the jobs mold the behavior of their incumbents. We will give particular attention to gender differences in employment experience, including differences in the contractual features of the jobs typically held by each sex.

Gender-specific employment patterns have undergone an incomplete revolution. Enormous change has occurred since the 1950s. More women are employed than previously, and they are beginning to move into "male" jobs. These changes have been important determinants of the household and family changes described above. Yet women are still employed less continuously than men, they are concentrated in "female" jobs, and, although their pay has increased absolutely, it did not begin to increase relative to men's pay until about 1980. These facts are consistent with a legacy of discrimination in employment and women's continued primary responsibility for home and children. Underlying these demographic patterns are billions of implicit contracts between individual husbands and wives, as well as between individual employees and employers, the nature of which provides the theme for much of this book. In this section we complete the task of summarizing postwar trends, turning attention to the employment relationship and differences between the employment experiences of men and women.

A. Labor Force Participation

The period from 1950 to 1980 brought a dramatic increase in the proportion of women in the paid labor force—from 34 to 52% (U.S. Department of Labor, 1983b). During the 1950s, young women were completing the postwar baby boom, each averaging over three children. But women whose children were in school or fully grown became the forerunners of a profound social change. Many of them reentered the labor force they had left to rear their children years earlier. In the 1960s both mature women and women of childbearing age increased their employment. By this time the typical pattern became employment before childbearing, a number of years at home, and then reentry into the labor force. This intermittent pattern has given way to more continuity in young women's employment in the 1970s and 1980s. Increased continuity comes from women spending fewer years at home—partly because they are having fewer children and partly because they are more apt to work when their children are young. Few in the 1950s would have believed that by 1980, almost one-half of women with children under 6 would be in the labor force. Of particular interest is that the bulk of the increase resulted from the employment of married women with children, and occurred during periods when male's real earnings were either rising or remaining stable.

During this same period, male labor force participation has decreased. Most of the decrease comes from progressively earlier retirement, but a part of it comes from an increase in discouraged workers, those who are no longer counted as unemployed because they have given up looking for a job.

B. The Sex Segregation of Jobs and the Pay Gap

As female employment rose in the postwar period, most went into occupations already sex-typed as female. The 1950s actually brought a slight increase in segregation (about 2 points on a 100-point scale), and the 1960s brought only a small decrease (about 3 points) (England, 1981). The decrease in the 1960s resulted primarily from more men entering teaching and social work, and more women becoming real estate salespersons, door-to-door peddlers, postal clerks, and ticket agents.

It was not until the 1970s that we have seen a significant drop in the level of segregation—a drop estimated to have averaged .75 point per year—cumulating to more than twice the level of decrease in the 1960s (Beller, 1984). Most of the decline during the 1970s was from women entering male occupations—particularly professional jobs—rather than from integrated occupations showing faster growth. The increased number of women becoming accountants, bank officers, financial managers, and janitors contributed heavily to this decline in segregation. Other male-dominated occupations that increased their percentage female by at least 10 percentage points during the 1970s include: computer programmers, personnel professionals, pharmacists, drafters, public relations professionals, office managers, buyers, insurance agents, real estate agents, postal clerks, stock clerks, ticket agents, typesetters, bus drivers, animal caretakers, and bartenders.

The desegregation of the 1970s was concentrated within certain occupational and age groups. Younger cohorts decreased their segregation more than older cohorts, although there was some decrease for all cohorts. Greater desegregation occurred within professional and managerial jobs than among blue-collar craftsmen, operatives, or laborers. Still, we must remember that even well educated young people are nowhere near going into jobs on a sex-blind basis. Supply-side forces of sex role socialization continue to combine with demand-side discrimination and structured mobility ladders to create and perpetuate a significant amount of segregation.

Title VII of the Civil Rights Act of 1964 embodied the first national legal prohibition of sex discrimination in hiring and placement. The Equal Employment Opportunity Commission (EEOC) was created to conciliate cases, and was later (in 1972) given the power to take cases to court. Shortly after the passage of Title VII, President Johnson issued an Executive Order requiring government contractors to engage in Affirmative Action. The Department of Labor's Office of Federal Contracts Compliance Programs (OFCCP) enforces this executive order. But Congressional and presidential discussion of the laws and the early actions of the EEOC focused almost exclusively on racial discrimination. Beginning in the 1970s, only after much lobbying by women's groups, did the EEOC take sex discrimination seriously. Table 1.5 shows the impact these laws and regulations had on firms' policies by the 1970s. The evidence suggests that these laws and regulations have caused many employers to permit women's entrance into formerly male preserves. These legal changes are an important part of the continued negotiation of how gender affects implicit and explicit employment contracts.

Although both men and women's real earnings rose between 1950 and 1970, the sex gap in pay failed to show a reduction until 1980. Between 1980 and 1983, the hourly earnings of full-time year-round women moved from 60 to 64% of those of men (Smith and Ward, 1984). While some of this pay gap results from differences in the length of job experience held by men and women, another large portion results from the segregation we have discussed above. Women are concentrated in occupations, industries, and firms offering lower earnings, less advancement, and less well developed contractual features.

Some commentators suggest that decreased job segregation will diminish the sex gap in pay. However, others suggest another complementary route to the same goal—raising the wages of traditionally female jobs. A new doctrine of "comparable worth" is being debated by the courts, federal agencies, and employers. Proponents assert that employers have engaged in

Table 1.5. Changes in Personnel Practices Resulting from EEO Laws[a]

Company programs and regulations	Percentage of companies
Have formal EEO programs	86
including Affirmative Action Plan	96
(of those subject to OFCCP regulations)	
Have had investigation or other action under Title VII	63
Have made changes in selection procedures for EEOC	
reasons	60
Testing procedures	39
Revised job qualifications	31
Application forms	20
Recruiting techniques	19
Have instituted special recruiting programs	
For all minority workers	69
For minorities in professional/managerial positions	58
Have instituted programs to ensure EEO policies are implemented	
Communications on EEO policy	95
Follow-up personnel or EEO office	85
Training sessions on EEO	67
Periodic publications of EEO results	48
EEO achievements included in performance appraisals	33
Have instituted special training programs	
For entry-level jobs	16
For upgrading	24
For management positions	16

[a]Source: Survey of firms by Bureau of National Affairs, cited in Freeman (1980: 337).

sex discrimination by keeping wages in women's jobs below those offered in men's jobs requiring comparable—although different—skill and education. For example, many firms pay secretaries less than janitors, and many counties pay nurses less than mechanics. In neither of these cases does the female job require less skill or training than the male job; the female jobs simply require different skills. It is too early to tell whether these efforts to recontract the relative pay of female jobs will be successful.

IV. GENDER IN THE OLD AND NEW SYSTEMS

Between the 1950s and the 1980s women's roles in households and employment have changed dramatically. Men's roles have also changed, but much less so. Nor has the overall system of gender differentiation changed radically; intact relationships between men and women still involve women shouldering major responsibility for the emotional and instrumental work of the household, while men take major responsibility for employment and earnings. As a result, men still have more power than women since their work yields outputs that are more readily exchanged in a wide variety of settings and relationships. While the characteristic differences between men's and women's roles have not changed, the proportion of their energies that women put into the household sector has declined. Since men have increased their household labor little, the net result is a reduction in the total volume of effort within the household sector. This is occurring simultaneously with an increased disconnection between children and their fathers after divorce.

Our remaining chapters explore the old and new systems in greater detail. In a final chapter we sketch possible directions for future changes in household and employment contracts, and their implications for women, men, and children. Among other projections, we discuss two major possibilities for change in gender roles. A first possibility is that the trends of the last 30 years may simply continue. If this occurred, women would direct increasing attention to employment and less to the household, but the decreasing volume of household work would still be assigned to women. As a consequence, women would continue to increase their power relative to men without ever closing the gap. Any negative effects of the decline of household labor would be compounded. Movement along the continuum from disciplined collective obligation to individual pursuit of self-fulfillment would continue. A second scenario is most compatible with feminist principles urging that husbands and wives share power, household work, and employment responsibility equally. While continuing women's advances in the world of paid employment, this would entail an increase in men's participation in the emotional and instrumental work of the household. This would reverse or at least halt the trend toward a reduction of investment in the historically feminine sphere of emotional ties, family, child rearing, and household labor, but it would do so in a way that would not reinforce power differences between men and women as a return to traditional patterns of sex differentiation would. While we have no crystal ball, we conclude with a discussion of the forces that can be expected to determine which of these visions best describes the future world of households, employment, and gender.

2 CHOICE, CONTRACTS, AND STRUCTURE

When I fulfill my obligations . . . , when I execute my contracts, I perform duties which are defined, externally to myself and my acts, in law and custom. Even if they conform to my own sentiments and I feel their reality subjectively, such reality is still objective, for I did not create them. . . . These types of conduct or thought are not only external to the individual but are, moreover, endowed with coercive power, by which they impose themselves upon him, independent of his individual will.

Emile Durkheim (1895)
The Rules of Sociological Method

The optimal marital decision at any moment would be the one that maximized the expected value of full wealth over the remainder of life, given the realizations up to that moment. . . . The approach to marital dissolution developed here should also prove useful in analyzing the dissolution of (implicit as well as explicit) contracts of indefinite duration between employees and employers. . . . The case for a common theoretical approach to all social behavior would be greatly strengthened if the same theory is applicable to employee turnover . . . as well as to marital dissolutions.

Gary Becker, Elisabeth Landes,
and Robert Michael (1977)
Journal of Political Economy

. . . if the speed of adjustment in auction markets is the speed of light, then that of contractual labor markets is 55 miles an hour. You wouldn't think much of a physicist who assumed that the national speed limit is the speed of light; you shouldn't think much of theories that assume markets clear at lightning speed. . . . (But) there is a general way to understand the phenomena. It surrounds the notion that implicit or explicit contracts are pervasive, are incomplete, are costly to negotiate or renegotiate, and therefore show a great deal of contract stickiness. . . . Important and commonplace examples include the workplace and family life.

William Nordhaus (1984)
American Economic Review

19

Exchange theorists begin with the self-interested actor faced with the problem of choice. They assume that the working out of these choices will generate
social structures. But the reverse is equally plausible. Social structure—
particularly the distribution of power in society—determines not only the terms
of exchange in a relationship, but the interests of the actors too. . . . Structures
shape behavior and attitudes in such ways as to fit the prevailing options.

John Wilson (1983)
Social Theory

I. INTRODUCTION

Between the 1950s and the 1980s an old system characterized by little
cohabitation, early marriage, high fertility, low divorce, continuous employment by men until a late retirement, intermittent employment by females,
and sex-segregated jobs has given way to a new system. The new system has
higher rates of premarital sex, out-of-wedlock births, and cohabitation, later
marriage, lower fertility, more divorce, earlier retirement by men, more
continuous employment by women, and—just recently discernible—
desegregation of jobs and lowering of the sex gap in pay. Yet common to
both systems is the assumption that child rearing, housework, and emotional
work will be undertaken primarily by women. The existence of these two
systems within a 30-year period raises two sets of questions. First, we need
to understand the determinants of the patterns common to both eras.
Second, we wish to comprehend the forces that have propelled us from the
old system to the new.

The goal of this chapter is to introduce the conceptual framework we will
develop throughout the book. We believe that an integrated view of
households, employment, and gender is best served by examining the
choices made by individuals as well as the structural constraints within
which they operate. Furthermore, we suggest the notion of implicit contracts
as particularly relevant for understanding the interplay of choice and
structure in households and employment. Long-term (but terminable) contracts are important because they govern many features of relationships in
both households and employment. These contracts are usually informal and
implicit rather than formal and explicit. This integrated framework
emphasizing individuals' optimizing choices, implicit contracts, and
structural constraints is based on the work of sociologists, economists, and
demographers within both disciplines.

II. CHOICES OF OPTIMIZING INDIVIDUALS

Our view of households and employment draws from both microeconomics and sociological exchange theory which focus on the choices
made by individuals who are striving to get the "best deal" they can. These

views recognize that such choices are made within constraints. For example, the microeconomic study of consumption and labor supply recognizes a "budget constraint" defined by wage rates and family wealth, but the sources of the constraints are not emphasized in this view, and, in any event, are presumed to arise from past interactions between optimizing individuals. These theories explain individual behavior in terms of the costs or benefits of different actions. Thus, they explain change as responses to alterations in these costs or benefits. An example of such reasoning is the finding in time-series analyses that increases in wages available to women have been a crucial determinant of the rise in female employment in the last several decades. Another example is the finding that the expansion of the benefits available from Social Security and private pension programs have led to progressively earlier retirement on the part of men.

This view assumes that individuals are rational and pursue their self-interest. Three provisos condition our acceptance of the assumption that individuals rationally seek to optimize their self-interest. First, we do not assume that individuals gauge self-interest exclusively in terms of money. Recently, many economists are joining sociologists in recognizing that nonpecuniary or "social-psychological" rewards enter the calculus of self-interest. Thus, when we talk about weighing the costs and benefits of various arrangements, these costs and benefits may be pecuniary or nonpecuniary. Examples of nonpecuniary rewards are the satisfactions of having children, of companionship with a spouse with common interests, or of leisure. Examples of nonpecuniary costs are the psychic disutility of being unattached while one is searching for a romantic partner, or the disutility many men attach to engaging in "women's work."

A second proviso is that we do not exclude altruistic behavior in the family from consideration. We discuss the elements of altruism involved in caring for children and one's spouse. The presence of such behavior does violate a narrowly construed assumption of self-interest, but is consistent with a more broadly defined notion of self-interest that includes the needs of others. Economists refer to this as including another's utility function in one's own.

Third, we do not assume that individuals make their choices with perfect information, as past generations of economists did. Rather, we draw upon economic "search theory," the central insight of which is that information is imperfect and costly to gather. This implies that the arrangement that is optimal after considering search costs may not be the one that would be optimal in a world of frictionless information. For example, even optimizing individuals generally do not wait for the perfect marital partner or job offer before entering into such relationships because the pecuniary and nonpecuniary costs of a protracted search are simply deemed too great.

III. CONTRACT THEORY

We speak metaphorically of "contracts" to suggest the importance of long-term considerations in the relationships within both households and employment. The recent development of a theory of implicit contracts in employment has injected a new realism into labor economics. We apply this notion of implicit contracts to marriages and other household cohabitational arrangements as well. We also add more sociological content to the theory of contracts.

On the employment side, the notion of contracts arose from attempts to account for observations that contradict standard neoclassical economic predictions. Foremost among these is the fact that, during recessions, when product and labor demand is slack, employers rarely cut wage rates. Rather, employers' responses to recessions are generally sluggish, and when they do respond, they usually do so by laying off relatively inexperienced workers rather than lowering wages. These arrangements contradict standard neoclassical economic predictions that assume employers and employees optimize profits and wages, respectively, in every short period. The fundamental insight of contract theory is that those employers who make large investments in screening and training workers will optimize profits over a longer period if they honor an implicit contract to increase workers wages and job security as they gain experience, thereby increasing their probability of retaining trained workers until they have made gains from their investment.

We refer to the contract as implicit, since many of the provisions are unwritten, and thus not formally binding. (Where there are unions, explicit contracts are also in effect, usually alongside well developed implicit contractual features.) However, the informal nature of contracts does not imply that compliance comes solely from a sense of moral obligation. Rather, the employer honors the contract when long-run benefits of doing so outweigh the costs. The workers' side of the contract is to take lower wages during the training period, stay with the firm afterward, and maintain an acceptable level of effort. They do this because of the benefits of remaining in a job if it is characterized by an upward trajectory of rewards. Thus, it is the structure of incentives on both sides that embodies the implicit contract. Of course, such contracts are sometimes broken—an extreme example is plant closings—and jobs vary greatly in the extent to which they involve such contracts.

In discussing employment and gender, we will develop implications of contract theory that help explain sex differentials in job placement and earnings. Personnel policies are geared to create long-term incentives by agreeing on the terms of the contract associated with a given job at the outset of the employment relationship. This implies that employers will match individuals and jobs on the basis of their predictions of the trajectories of the employees' performance—including turnover. Thus, statistical discrimination and sex-segregated jobs are more likely outcomes than would obtain under continual recontracting. Even when women increase the continuity of their employment, employers are still likely to segregate by sex until total convergence between typical turnover rates of males and females has occurred. In this way relatively small sex differences in turnover probabilities may be magnified into large differences in job distributions and earnings. Thus, jobs filled by females typically lack well-developed implicit contract features. Finally, contract theory focuses on the effects of arrangements with one set of workers upon the motivations of another set of workers. This reminds us that employers' dealings with female workers are influenced by the attitudes of male workers.

We also see marriage and other cohabitational partnerships as usefully analyzed via the metaphor of implicit contracts. There is certainly some truth to the conventional view that people stay in marriages because they feel a moral commitment to keep their marital vows. Such values are undoubtedly a more important part of the underpinnings of contractual relationships in marriage than in employment. But in marriage, as in employment relationships, the costs of search and early investments create incentives to make the relationship endure. It is this structure of incentives that embodies the implicit contract. The investments that create incentives for marriages to endure are those that are relationship-specific, the household analogs of firm-specific training in employment.

Relationships entail learning to get along with one's partner. We use the term "relationship-specific investment" to refer to the part of such learning that would be of little value in a subsequent relationship. The tremendous time and effort that is expended on rearing children is also an example of relationship-specific investment, since the gains from this activity will do little to enhance one's position in the "market" for a second marriage. Thus, partners have an incentive to stay together, even in the face of an opportunity to attract a more desirable partner. This is because terminating a relationship requires one to undergo search and relationship-specific investment again. Both partners to a marriage make relationship-specific investments, but we will argue that women make a larger share of these than men, and that this is an important aspect of gender differentiation. We add a sociological dimension to contract theory by using this to explain power differentials between husbands and wives, a subject ignored by economists.

IV. THE STRUCTURE OF CONSTRAINTS

Throughout the book we argue for the importance of the constraining structures within which choices are made. Yet it is "optimizing individuals" who are negotiating these structural realities, so our discussion integrates individual and structural views.

By "structure" we refer to aggregates. So, for example, we examine the effects of macroeconomic conditions on the changes in fertility levels represented by the baby boom and baby bust. In addition, we discuss the effect of macroeconomic "period" effects on the relative consumption levels experienced by the baby boom generation and the generation before them. But unlike some authors who define structure in terms of aggregates (e.g., Mayhew, 1980, 1981), we do not limit the notion of structure to material matters, but also include societal-wide values that create a sense of obligation in individuals as structural forces. An example of this is the hypothesis that the rise of an ethic of individual fulfillment has contributed to increasing divorce.

Most often, however, aggregates that we will consider to be structures are distributions of available slots, positions, or types of contracts. Here our usage is akin to that of the "new structuralism" in sociology. We refer to each such "slot" as a structural position. In this usage, a structural view of the employment system emphasizes the number of job slots of each type and the relationships between them, such as the probability of moving from one job to another. When we think structurally, we deemphasize the characteristics of the individuals who are searching for a position or bargaining within a position, concentrating instead on the characteristics of the positions themselves. Structural positions in employment—jobs—are defined in terms of the characteristics of the occupation, industry, or firm in which they occur. These characteristics often include the extent to which a job is characterized by long-term implicit or explicit contracts. In the household, roles such as full-time homemaker, sole breadwinner, or homemaker and part-time breadwinner are structural positions that differ in their implicit contractual features and other rewards. Just as aggregate occupational distributions change, the relative availability of particular household contracts has changed over time. Thus, the marital contract to be a full-time homemaker was more available in the 1950s than today.

Many of our discussions will involve the effects of particular structural positions on individuals. These refer to the consequences for individuals of being in a particular structural position. The consequences may include wages, wage trajectories (upward trajectories being a feature of implicit contracts in employment), and probabilities of upward mobility or unemployment. For example, predominantly male jobs in capital-intensive industries have better wages and better developed implicit contract features than predominantly female jobs in labor-intensive industries. One's structural position in the household (for example, whether a woman is a full-time homemaker or not) has implications for marital power and the probability of divorce. In both employment and the household, structural effects may entail the development of tastes, outlooks, or behavioral patterns arising from the "role molding the person." For example, jobs entailing more autonomy and self-direction encourage intellectual flexibility and a focus on internalized standards. In the household, the role of mothering develops empathic abilities.

When the focus is on the optimizing individual, forms of individual striving such as search or investment in human capital are seen to determine what structural position or contract type one achieves. One might ask, then, in what way the attachment of rewards to positions represent binding constraints, rather than merely effects of the investments those in the position have made. There are several answers to this question of how structural effects represent constraints rather than merely past choices. First, the sorting of individuals into positions according to their "qualifications" (or investments) is never perfect, given such things as imperfect information and discrimination. Thus, the reward levels that attach to positions are never a perfect reflection of the investments individuals holding them have made. In particular, empirical studies show effects of individuals' structural positions on their monetary rewards even after "selection bias" is removed by statistically controlling for individual characteristics. Second, the very fact that one has to change positions to attain a particular reward level represents a constraint, even if all positions are open to all. Finally, the constraining aspects of structure can be seen when we remember that the resources one had available for initial search and other investments were affected by the structural position of one's parents, something over which one had no control.

As Wilson (1983) points out (in the final quotation at the beginning of this chapter), there is an ongoing reciprocal relationship between structural positions and individual characteristics in both the household and employment. We will attend to both sides of this causal arrow in seeking to explain continuities and changes between the 1950s and 1980s. Like contracts, structures are rigidities representing the weight of past transactions in the present, and they make social change less fluid and more sporadic than would be the case without them.

V. SUMMARY

Throughout the book we will be discussing households and employment, with particular attention to gender roles and their change in these two spheres. We will point out parallels between household and employment relationships, and we will be concerned to examine the reciprocal links between these two spheres—how one's position in the household affects

affects behavior in employment, and how one's position in employment affects behavior in the household. Throughout, we will use the research and theory offered by sociologists, by economists, and by demographers from each of these disciplines. A key feature of our view is the notion of the (often implicit) contracts that characterize relationships in both the household and employment. These household and employment contracts, along with the choices and structural constraints that lie behind them, are the topics of the chapters that follow.

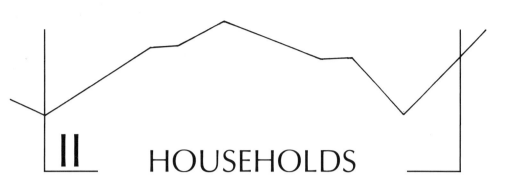

II HOUSEHOLDS

This section considers life within households, including their formation and dissolution, and the life-long processes of work, leisure, and reproduction within this sphere. We also examine changes in these activities between the 1950s and the 1980s. Chapter 3 deals with the search for a partner, long-term marital and other contractual relationships, power and bargaining within marriage, divorce, and the repetition of this pattern. Chapters 4 and 5 discuss those activities—household work and leisure, childbearing and rearing, consumption, investment, and saving—that occur within these ongoing relationships.

Our examination of these topics draws upon and expands the framework presented in Chapter 2. Thus it is useful to view household arrangements as contracts entered into after a period of search. By considering marriage as a contract, we do not refer to a written document or an agreement with completely enforceable provisions—these are rare or nonexistent—or do we imply that both parties enjoy equal power. Rather, the metaphor of contract refers to the fact that marital relationships endure over time, involving many informal as well as some legal obligations, and relationship-specific "investments." These investments are important in explaining the stability of relationships. Later, in Part III, we discuss certain parallels between household and employment contracts.

With households, as with employment, there is a reciprocal relationship between individuals' choices, on the one hand, and structural arrangements, on the other. Too often social scientists ignore one or the other side of this reciprocal relationship between individual and structural levels. Thus decisions about the search for a partner, bargaining within marriage, fertility, and consumption all occur within a web of structural realities. We call something "structural" when it concerns a larger aggregate than an individual, or when it is a characteristic of a position (e.g., a job or role) within a system of positions. Such structures endure irrespective of the actions of any particular individual. Examples of structural factors affecting households include norms of correct behavior and obligation toward one's spouse, the role one plays within the family division of labor, and the employment position or opportunities one has outside the household. Contracts within the household are strongly affected by the interplay between individual decision making and structural effects. Yet changing household contracts can also affect aggregate structural arrangements. In this section we give particular attention to the way in which the ongoing reciprocal relationship between individual and structural levels affects gender roles within the household.

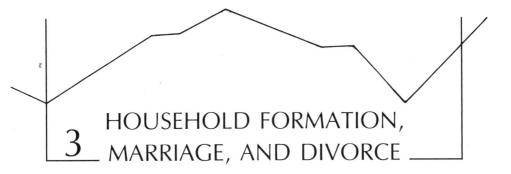

3 HOUSEHOLD FORMATION, MARRIAGE, AND DIVORCE

I. INTRODUCTION

Most individuals seek to find another person with whom to share life's intimacies, and most succeed. Thus, more than 90% of individuals marry at least once (Cherlin, 1981), and of those who do not, many enter into at least one long-standing, coresident relationship. Examples include homosexual couples, common-law heterosexual unions, or unmarried sisters sharing a home. (Although the following analysis often refers to marriage partners, much of it also applies to unmarried partners of various sorts. For a detailed comparison of heterosexual and homosexual couples, see Blumstein and Schwartz, 1983.)

Marriage and other long-term relationships involve search and contracts, two notions introduced in Chapter 2. We begin this chapter by presenting a model of how individuals search for partners. We then discuss how relationships can be analyzed as implicit contracts, the power dynamics of relationships, determinants of divorce, and remarriage patterns. We discuss how individual striving and structural patterns affect these processes. We also describe the rather different social worlds of the 1950s and 1980s.

II. A MARKET FOR PARTNERS

A. Individual Characteristics in Exchange

People do not always acknowledge the market aspects of finding partners. Rather, they think of a process in which one pursues short-term relationships until smitten by love, an eventuality often leading to a long-term commitment. Our analysis in no sense denies the importance of love. Instead, we suggest that love does not occur randomly; rather, individuals seek long-term partners possessing the characteristics they prefer. The market realities of this process dictate that an individual's ability to indulge preferences depends upon the demand for, and the availability of, the characteristics he or she desires, as well as the relative desirability of his or her own characteristics. This is analogous to labor markets, where one is more apt to find the job one desires if such jobs are relatively plentiful and/or one has characteristics that are highly valued by employers.

What is assumed in market models of mate selection? First, that individuals seek the best deal possible, subject to their constraints. Second, that the relative *desirability* of each potential partner can be summarized on a single scale (we will refer to this as the *D* scale) by taking a weighted sum across the relevant dimensions. The weights reflect the individual's judgment of the relative importance of the dimensions. Thus, if a man values beauty in a woman twice as much as he values being a good mother, beauty would figure twice as heavily in the overall *D* score he would give a prospective wife. Of course, individuals do not literally undertake numerical calculations of these quantities. Yet we believe that they do compare potential partners so as to yield behavior that is approximated by this market model.

What conclusions follow from such a market model of marital sorting? Let us take two dimensions affecting *D* as a stylized example. Consider the fact that our culture places a premium on beauty in women (Richman, 1977; Hite, 1981) and on earning power in men. This means that beauty is heavily weighted in the "formula" according to which the average man evaluates women, and earning power is heavily weighted in the "formula" by which the average woman evaluates men. Given these preferences for beauty in women and the earnings of men, exchanges occur in which money (or prospective earnings) is the currency in which one can "buy" a more beautiful woman, and beauty is the currency in which one can "buy" a higher earning man. In general, men with characteristics more valued for their sex will tend to be matched with women possessing characteristics more valued for their sex.

In markets for intimate partners, as in markets for jobs, the possession of desirable characteristics is not completely outside one's personal control. Just as individuals invest in their human capital by seeking education, credentials, and experience in order to strike better deals within the job market, so individuals may change themselves so as to increase their desirability to potential mates. Examples include striving to become a more interesting conversationalist, increasing one's earnings potential, losing weight, or undergoing psychotherapy. Each of these could be thought of as an investment in one's human capital for "marital production," that is, an increase in one's capacity to give pleasure to a marital partner. Such investment may well pay off in increased ability to attract a desirable partner. A theme running throughout this book is that human capital investment—broadly defined—is a key determinant of future life chances, but that such investment is strongly conditioned by the structural position one holds. Thus does social structure affect childhood socialization as well as the development of skills by adults.

Yet other characteristics valued in marriage and job markets are ascribed at birth, and subject to virtually no change thereafter. Examples include race, gender, social class background (defined by the social class of one's parents), and some aspects of body type. Sociologists refer to these as *ascribed* characteristics, while those under the individual's control are called *achieved* characteristics. Characteristics all along the continuum from ascription to achievement affect one's desirability in markets for partners.

An interesting feature of the market process is that having atypical preferences can be advantageous. For example, a man who has no preference for younger over older women may be better able to find a partner who is higher on other important dimensions of attractiveness. Similarly, a woman who is indifferent to the earning potential of her partner may be better able to find a man with exceptional qualities of emotional empathy. Such "compensating differentials" also arise in labor markets. Thus, a person who is atypical in enjoying dangerous work can thereby earn a higher wage. The higher wage arises precisely because the typical worker prefers avoiding danger.

B. Social Structure and Markets for Partners

Let us examine how the social structure—the system of roles and positions in the household or employment—affects the characteristics and the preferences for these characteristics that individuals bring to markets. Economists view preferences as "inputs" to market exchange. Yet the preferences themselves are influenced by social structural arrangements, and these structural arrangements are at least partly the legacy of past market outcomes. To illustrate this relationship, consider, for example, the case of males placing a premium on beauty in women, while women emphasize earning power in men.

How might such preferences arise? One explanation focuses on the social positions that men and women assume in adulthood. Thus, the premium placed by women on men's earning-power results from the tradition of female specialization in the home, while the husband is responsible for earnings. It has also arisen because of women's observation that employed women usually earn much less than men, so that relying on their own earnings has been a risky choice, even if they would prefer it. In a social system where the choice of a husband is identical to the choice of a living standard, women will weight men's earnings heavily in their desirability scale of potential partners. This is accentuated by women's view of children as an integral part of marriage, and their traditional concern for finding a man who will be a "good provider" for the resulting family.

From a structural point of view emphasizing roles and positions, it is less obvious why men weight physical attractiveness above abilities as home-maker, emotional confidante, or mother in the assessment of desirability, since the latter are the roles in which women have traditionally specialized. (We exclude, for the moment, the "role" of sex symbol.) Yet, here too, structural arrangements have an explanation to offer. Since the decline of the family farm and the end of child labor, wives' function as a producer of home goods and as a producer and manager of a home labor force have declined. This devalued homemaking skills, making women's status more subordinate. In addition, anticipation of female specialization in child rearing leads to a weakened empathic connection between the father and his future children. Thus, men become freer to indulge in weighting more "selfish" and less "functional" factors such as beauty more heavily in their preferences, since they give less attention than do women to the interests of their future children. Later in this chapter we consider the consequences of this fact for marital power.

C. Assortative Mating

In a marriage market with widely shared tastes, competitive forces will lead to a positive correlation between the D scores of mates. That is, individuals with high D's will be able to attract mates with high D's. However, since D can also be decomposed along each of its dimensions, we may also ask whether individuals tend to pair with those similar to or different from themselves on each of these constituent dimensions of D. This question of whether "likes" or "opposites" marry has been examined by both sociologists and economists. Marrying individuals with similar charac-teristics to oneself is referred to as marital homogamy, or positive assortative mating.

Becker (1981), a "new home economist," distinguishes between charac-teristics of spouses which are substitutes and complements in "home production." He argues that positive assortative mating will occur on traits where spouses are complements, that is, where two like partners comple-ment each other in contributing to the utility of each more than two partners whose traits are not alike. In contrast, specialization results where spousal traits function as substitutes for one another. The sociologist Winch (1958) used a similar notion of specialization and substitutes in proposing a theory of complementary needs in mate selection. (To avoid confusion one must remember that Becker's "complements" involve the *opposite* pattern as Winch's "complementary needs.") As an example of specialization, a skilled cook may prefer to pair with an individual who brings a different skill to the relationship, rather than another cook. The empirical question is whether most traits show a positive or a negative correlation between husbands and wives, and how these regularities are explained.

Empirically, many traits show positive assortative mating. These include educational attainment, social class background, physical attractiveness, and personality type (Duncan and Duncan, 1978: 208; Adams, 1979; Hendrick and Hendrick, 1983). However, even among these, those traits involved in gender role differentiation tend to show weaker positive (or occasionally negative) cross-partner correlations (Seyfried and Hendrick, 1973). Thus, earnings and physical attractiveness are less positively correlated across mates than are education or social class background. When a trait is preferred in either sex, but much more strongly in one than in the other, the cross-partner correlation is smaller than would be the case were the trait to be preferred equally strongly in each sex. These traits are involved in spousal specialization.

The positive assortative mating of individual characteristics can be explained in several ways. To begin with, many people display a preference for emotional attachment to individuals similar to themselves. The notion that similarity of roles contributes to empathy and thus emotional satisfaction within marriage has been called "role homophily" (Simpson and England, 1981). This helps explain positive assortative mating on family background and personality type. In such cases there is little marriage market competition across individuals of different types, since they are interested in different potential mates.

However, competition provides a second explanation of the positive correlation of certain traits. For example, we expect that most individuals rate physical attractiveness, emotional warmth, and charm as desirable. Positive cross-partner correlations on these characteristics are simply the result of the strong market position of the individuals possessing them.

A third explanation for the observed positive assortative mating on many traits (such as race, social class background, and educational level) involves the way one's structural position determines the search costs of meeting mates different than oneself. Individuals tend to marry those of similar social class background, race, and education partly because that is who they are most likely to meet at school, at social gatherings, in the neighborhood, and on the job. Geographical propinquity is an important determinant of marital choice (Adams, 1979). Geographical locations tend to be relatively homogeneous in social class, race, and education due to such factors as individual choice, discrimination in housing markets, and the use of zoning ordinances and other forms of local political power to create communities homogeneous in income and ethnicity. (Urban economists discuss this in terms of the "demand for neighborhood amenities.") Relatively homogeneous neighborhoods, schools, and workplaces are structural realities encouraging positive assortative mating via their effects on search costs. (A more general literature has measured the effect of the place of residence, school, or employment on a number of outcomes other than marriage. For debate on these "contextual effects" that "bring society back in" to the study of individual outcomes see Barton, 1968, 1970; Blalock, 1984; Hauser, 1970a,b, 1974; Farkas, 1974.) This process of search within socially structured markets for partners is our next subject.

III. THE SEARCH FOR A PARTNER

Search of one kind or another is an everyday activity. It occurs when we are running low on gas and keeping an eye out for a station that has posted a low price, when looking for a good cheap French restaurant, or when we seek to establish ties with a church after moving to a new city. Major life decisions also require search. Few individuals choose a college, career, house, or mate without some attempt to gather information and consider alternatives. By "search" we simply mean the activity of collecting information and weighing options. In recent years economists have developed a general theory of such activity. They have usually applied this theory to the study of job finding, but we shall apply it to the search for marital or other cohabitational partners. (See Becker et al., 1977, for a similar application.) After presentation of the theoretical approach, we will integrate it with sociological research on the empirical properties of such search.

A. An Economic Model of Search

Neoclassical economics is a coherent and elegant construction, but, prior to the advent of search theory, it ignored an essential element of everyday life—that decision making requires information, and that such information is costly both to acquire and to transmit. It was not that economists truly believed that individual decision makers are always in possession of perfect information. Rather, they regarded this as a useful assumption which simplified the analysis without affecting the final conclusions. The realization that information is costly to acquire and transmit, and that this does affect substantive conclusions is the basis for the development of search theory. The resulting analysis helps to account for a distribution of prices, rather than a single market price for a particular good, and shows how price depends upon search costs and benefits. [Seminal works on search include

Stigler (1961, 1962), Lippman and McCall (1976), and the literature cited there.]

Let us explain the model of search by making certain simplifying assumptions, and using the model to describe the situation of a woman looking for a husband. (These ideas also apply to a man looking for a wife or any person looking for some nonmarital cohabitational arrangement.) We rely on the same assumptions introduced in the market model (above), since search theory is simply an elaboration of this market model that adds the consideration of the costs of, and returns to, search. These assumptions are (1) that individuals are trying to maximize lifetime satisfaction (or "utility") by choosing the best available partner, and (2) that these individuals are able to summarize the relative attractiveness of each potential partner into a single desirability index, D.

A simple theory of search is then constructed by further assuming that during each time period of some fixed length, T, our searcher either receives or makes one offer of marriage. The cost of search in each period will be called C. These include out-of-pocket costs (e.g., direct costs of attendance at singles bars, and membership fees for clubs), the disutility of the search process (we will assume that the alienation and loneliness sometimes encountered during search can be valued at least approximately on a monetary scale), and the "opportunity costs" of search. Opportunity costs refer to the value of the activities foregone in order to spend time searching. To simplify matters, we will assume that the total of these costs of search, C, are the same for each period, T, in which our searcher meets and considers one potential partner.

We can envision the distribution of D scores of the men a particular woman is able to marry in a particular time period—that is, the men who would either offer her marriage, or accept her offer of marriage if she searches in the market during this period. (Recall that our time period is arbitrarily chosen, and that we have assumed no more than one marriage offer per period.) The exact shape of this curve is an empirical question,[1] but an example is shown in Fig. 3.1. This figure is interpreted as follows: During any particular time period, our searcher can find only one man, and she may be lucky (his D score is high) or unlucky (his D score is low). For any particular D (on the horizontal axis), the relative number of men at that D level who will make or accept an offer of this searcher is expressed by the height of the curve at that D score. One exception to this is the spike at the left of the curve. Of the men encountered during search, the height of the spike reveals the number who will not make an offer and will decline an offer if our searcher makes one. Thus, while their D scores are not all 0, we enumerate them at 0 because their nonoffer means that their existence in the pool of men our searcher meets does her no more good in finding a husband

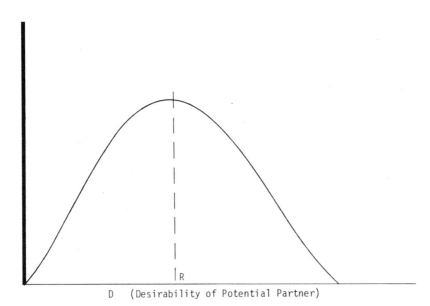

D   (Desirability of Potential Partner)

Figure 3.1. Distribution of *D* scores of potential partners who would make
an offer to or accept an offer from a particular searcher. *R* is the
"reservation-quality" partner. *R* may be at, above, or below the
mean of the distribution.

than does a man who is so undesirable his *D* score is 0. Of course, the men
our searcher meets are searchers themselves, deciding whether they are
interested in her on the basis of the desirability she has in their eyes. Thus,
the shape of the curve in Fig. 3.1, and, in particular, the extent to which it
includes high *D* scores, depends upon the searcher's own characteristics.
This formalizes the notion of "market position" introduced above; those
with higher *D*'s themselves face a distribution of willing *D*'s with a higher
mean.

An interesting question is whether our searcher actually knows the shape
of the curve—that is, her chance of securing a partner at each desirability
level—and also whether she knows the costs of search. The most realistic
assumption is that she begins searching with some vague idea of "how she
rates" with men, and what it costs her (in money, disutility, and opportunities for money and utility foregone) to search. However, with experience her
knowledge of these two quantities becomes more accurate. (Searching and
decision making while continually updating your information is sometimes
called a "Bayesian process." Thus a common simplifying assumption, and
one we shall adopt, is that the searcher possesses both pieces of information.

How will this information be employed? Will a woman seeking to maximize her lifetime happiness simply wait until she meets the first man whose D is at the mean of potential husbands available to her and then accept his offer or make him an offer? Or, regardless of the strategy she employs, will she inevitably end up marrying some man whose D is at the mean? Here is where the formal analysis of the search model comes into play. Such analysis suggests that the answer to these questions is "no."

The distribution of D's available to the searcher is not the only factor determining when she will stop searching, even under all the restrictive assumptions we have made. There are circumstances under which she will decide to accept an offer with a D less than her mean, or hold out for an offer above her mean. The reason for this has to do with search costs and benefits and is the core insight of search theory. Thus two searchers with the same preferences (how they assign D scores to the characteristics of potential partners) and the same market position (how many of each D category of men are willing to marry them) might, nonetheless, differ in that one will decide to marry a man with D score 70, whereas the other will hold out for an 80. These differences in behavior are explained by differences in search costs or benefits. Thus, one woman may have higher search costs because she lives in a rural area and has to travel farther to meet people. Or, more likely, one woman may simply experience the cost of being unmarried an additional year as higher than another woman who, because of support networks or personal psychology, is not bothered as much by being single. The point is that there is a trade-off between the quality of the partner finally selected and the time (and thus costs) spent searching. The person willing to bear more costs by searching longer will find a partner of higher quality. The person for whom search is extremely painful will settle relatively quickly for a partner of lower D, thus spending more of her lifetime with the enjoyment of at least some husband.

A similar analysis holds for the benefit side of search. Two searchers with the same tastes and market position may yet differ on the translation of D scores into lifetime happiness. Thus if these searchers differ on how long each expects the prospective marriage to last (due to age, health, one's own prior experience or that of parents or friends), the person expecting a longer duration should be willing to search longer. Similarly, if the individuals differ on the relative importance of D scores as predictors of marital happiness (because one thinks later happiness will be due to characteristics readily observed during search whereas the other believes more will be due to investments in the relationship she herself can control), those who give more importance to D scores should also be willing to search longer.

One implication of this analysis is that in the market for partners, being a rational "maximizer" does not typically involve seeking the highest D score.

That would be true in a world with no costs of search. However, once search costs are admitted, rational behavior requires weighing the costs of further search against the benefits to be derived from a relationship with a partner of a higher quality than one has yet been able to achieve.

Such strategic calculation leads to the notion of a "reservation quality partner" (defined in terms of D scores). The best strategy is to keep searching until the first partner with at least this level of desirability appears, and then to take him. This critical level of D can be shown to be that level at which the cost of continuing to search for one additional period exactly equals the expected benefits of this search. (These benefits are determined by the shape of Fig. 3.1, the expected duration of the marriage, and the reliability of the benefits from any particular D score.)

The "reservation quality partner" thus divides the distribution of D into two zones, one of acceptable, and one of unacceptable partners. This critical value need not be the mean D of the offers available to a woman—it may be above or below it. Its location will depend both on how she values additional increments to D and also on how she evaluates the costs of search. A similar analysis applies to the search for a job. In this case, familiar from recent labor economics, there is a "reservation wage," and one searches until finding the first job which meets or exceeds it. (Of course, this "wage" must take into account fringe benefits, working conditions, and other determinants of the desirabilty of a particular job.) The analysis of job search is analogous to that of marital search, with the searcher choosing a reservation wage after considering the costs and benefits of search. Similar analyses can be developed regarding search for such things as housing, other consumption goods, or a college to attend.

We have presented only the rudiments of a marital search model; this can be enriched and complicated by modifying the assumptions.[2] Our purpose has been merely to indicate how such models are conceived, so as to expand upon our common-sense understanding of the significant costs of search. For example, these costs of search help explain the assortative mating we discussed earlier, since it is usually "cheaper" to meet people within one's own geographical area, social class background, race, and educational level.

B. Search From the 1950s to the 1980s

Marital search changed significantly between the 1950s and the 1980s. During the 1950s, it was normal and expected to have found a marital partner by one's early twenties. Dating began in the teenage years, and going steady, engagement, and marriage followed in steady succession. Those not attending college often married their high school sweetheart shortly after graduation, while college students often married after college graduation. A typical pattern had the wife marrying an older male at the point of his graduation, and then herself dropping out of school to start a family. In this system the period of search was relatively brief, superficial (being carried out primarily through dates rather than living together), and involved few distinct partners.

Things are much different in the 1980s. Today age at marriage is significantly later, premarital sexual and nonsexual experience is more extensive, the number of serious relationships before marriage has increased, and cohabitation as a "trial" stage on the way to marriage is very common. Thus, search has been extended in duration, in the number of partners considered, and in the extent to which the information gathered is directly relevant to the later experience of marriage. Clearly, cohabitation provides such information much more accurately than did previous arrangements.

The "competitive market" feature of marital search—that is, the importance of possessing highly rated characteristics if one is to attract a desirable partner—was no doubt at least as important in the 1950s as it is today. Indeed, during the 1930s Waller (1937) analyzed the "rating-dating complex," finding a correlation between the prestige of the sorority and fraternity of dating partners, and a tendency for men with cars, spending money, and a place in campus activities to date women that were physically attractive and well dressed. The notion that some people "rate" a more "competitive" partner than others is, in essence, the notion that the aggregation of exchange behavior leads to a market price for various combinations of qualities. No doubt some version of this is as old as society itself, but which characteristics are thought desirable has changed between the 1950s and the 1980s. For example, the notion that college women should not be smart is undoubtedly less pronounced today than Komarovsky (1953) found for the college students of the 1950s.

Another change since the 1950s is a greater acknowledgment of the market features of search. Institutions such as classified advertising sections in magazines and newspapers, singles' bars, adult singles' groups within churches, and computer dating services have arisen to reduce search costs. Such institutions were virtually unknown 30 years ago. This is partly because with early, one-time marriage, search could be efficiently conducted within institutions—typically schools—whose main purpose was something other than marital search. (Yet, the recognition that colleges served this function was revealed by the now dated joke that women attended college to receive a "MRS." degree.) Now, with later age at first marriage, and more individuals in the market following divorce, other institutions have arisen. New York Magazine (March 19, 1984) reports that the volume of personal advertisements soliciting a partner in publications such as the *Village Voice* and the *New York Review of Books* almost doubled between 1981 and 1984. Such ads reduce search costs by coming to the attention of people who at least share a taste for the same reading matter, and also by the explicit specification of the qualities one desires in a partner. Anyone still skeptical of our presentation of the search for a partner in market terms might consider the extent to which this process is coming to resemble the search for a house or apartment.

The question arises as to whether individuals are always at least potentially in the market for a better partner, even while married. An analogous question is whether individuals remain in the job market even while employed. Some individuals undoubtedly do keep an eye out for a "better deal" while married, just as they scan job ads while employed, although the former is considered immoral by most Americans. Yet, for the most part, individuals remove themselves from markets for either partners or jobs until the termination or near termination of the current relationship. Some begin to keep an eye out for a better opportunity when they become sufficiently disenchanted with a relationship to cease investing in its future and merely "go through the motions" of minimal performance. Thus an important feature of the market for partners is that it is a market for a type of long-term contract (enduring relationship) rather than a spot market (a one-time transaction with a "new deal" every time the market shifts a little). This remains the case despite currently high divorce rates.

High search costs provide one reason that individuals do not change partners frequently. But a more important reason lies in the nature of marriage itself. This is because much of the satisfaction derived from marriage comes only as a result of large investments of time, emotion, and other scarce resources. Such investments yield their returns only in the fullness of time, and thereby provide one reason for long-term "contracting." It is to this long-term nature of marital and other cohabitational relationships that we now turn.

IV. MARRIAGE AS AN IMPLICIT CONTRACT

It is paradoxical that most marriage ceremonies include a pledge of love and loyalty to one's partner until death, yet about one-half of the marriages contracted today are projected to end in divorce. In light of this paradox, how should current marital understandings be described? They are not usually forever, even though at the time of marriage most hope or believe them to be. Are they then relationships that end the minute either party can get a better deal? Or are they contracts which fully specify behavior under every contingency, including breakup? More likely they contain features of both types, with social norms and ongoing bargaining figuring prominently in the arrangement. These issues can be clarified by asking whether marriages are more like exchanges in a spot market, contingent-claims contracts, or implicit contracts. We argue below that marriage and other long-term cohabitational arrangements are best viewed as implicit contracts, with many unstated agreements and means of enforcement. In Chapter 6 we also analyze the employment relationship as an implicit contract, drawing parallels between the contracts struck in households and in employment.

A. Spot Markets

Once an individual finds a partner, is s/he, nonetheless, still in a "spot market" for partners? For the most part s/he is not, and it is interesting to understand why. Until quite recently, orthodox economic theory saw all markets as spot markets characterized by frequent recontracting. For example, the price of shrimp at the local fish market changes from day to day. Customers may choose to buy beef during periods when shrimp prices are high. Even when a particular customer has traded with a particular fish merchant for many years, they have no explicit contract ensuring either the continuation or the terms of their relationship. Thus, when the price of shrimp is high the customer may refuse to buy, and when they are a bargain he or she may arrive too late to get any. In spot markets prices adjust to changes in demand or supply and market forces rule, unmediated by "personal relationships."

The ideal type of a spot market is an auction, although some other markets operate in a similar manner. These include stock markets, commodities markets, and markets for perishable groceries. Each of these involves millions of transactions between pairs of individuals or firms. Yet these pairs have made no investment in and have no commitment to the ongoing nature of their exchange relationship. Traders transact again with the same person only because they are offering the best deal available (taking search costs into account). Clearly such exchange relationships are quite impersonal. Indeed, in some markets (e.g., stocks), one never even speaks with one's trading partner.

If markets for partners and for the intimate services they provide had spot market characteristics, what would they be like? Most obviously they would tend to involve many short-term exchanges of specific services with many different individuals; each would last no longer than the arrival of an apparently superior "deal." Some individuals would cruise in singles' bars to exchange sexual services, while others would buy sex from prostitutes. Such markets exist. Other services often provided by marital partners can also be bought in spot markets less "personal" than marriage. These include food preparation, child care, yard work, and housework.

Yet these examples remind us that most people consider such arrangements to be inferior to marriage. That is, when it comes to household and intimate services, even ignoring the costs of constant search, a personal relationship is highly valued over impersonality. Perhaps surprisingly, there are ideas within economic theory which can illuminate this; they pertain to the distinction between investment in general human capital and in specific human capital.

By "human capital" economists refer to the stock of attributes in a person that can be put to use in serving some end. When that end is productivity on the job, attributes such as intelligence, strength, education, and skills are relevant. Similarly, we can think of those qualities helpful in person-to-person interaction as a form of human capital as well. These include the ability to provide empathy, companionship, sexual and intellectual pleasure, social status, or earnings. Individuals "invest" in human capital whenever they forego something desirable in the present to develop a personal attribute which will pay off in the future, whether in a job or household relationship.

With this notion of investment in mind, we can provide one answer to the question of why people search for long-term relationships rather than continually recontracting for new partners. The reason is that many of the highest-return investments within the household sector are to relationship-specific rather than general human capital. To call an investment relationship-specific means that it has value only within the current relationship, and would be of no benefit in a different one. Once such investments have been undertaken, both partners are likely to be better off within this relationship than they would be were they to have to start over with someone else. Of course, investments may be anywhere along a continuum from those useless in a new relationship to those whose benefits are completely transferable to a new relationship.

In paid employment, we call on-the-job training an investment in firm-specific (rather than general) human capital if the skills learned will not easily transfer to another employer and would be costly to teach to a new worker. This gives both the employer and the employee a vested interest in the continued employment of that worker with that firm. (For further discussion, see Chapter 6.)

Marital investments that transfer poorly to a new relationship include learning what shared leisure activities both partners enjoy, learning what division of labor is most efficient with this partner, decorating the house in a style both partners like, learning to fight and make up with this partner, learning this partner's sexual preferences, and developing relationships with in-laws. In addition, the tremendous investments of time, caring, and money that parents make in children bear fruit not only in the children's futures, but also in the satisfaction parents derive from the relationship. Investment in children with one partner contributes relatively little to improving one's relationship with a new partner. Thus, these and other long-term, relationship-specific investments mitigate against rapid turnover among partners.

In speaking of the employment relationship, Okun (1981) refers to the costs of search together with the costs of initial investment as a "toll" employers must pay when they hire an employee. This "toll" gives parties to both marriage and employment an incentive to make the relationship endure over time. This long-term nature of many household and employment arrangements is one reason we metaphorically refer to both of them as contracts. The various sorts of work and consumption that occur within these household contracts are the subjects of Chapters 4 and 5.

B. Contingent-Claims Contracts

We have suggested that marriage is like a long-term contract, so that individuals are not continually in a spot market for partners. What is the nature of this contract? The traditional marriage vow promising loyalty "in sickness and in health, till death do us part" suggests a contract, or promise, to remain in the relationship, providing love and other services, irrespective of future contingencies. However, the high divorce rate makes it clear that individuals often fail to honor such unconditional promises. This suggests that it might be useful for marriage partners to agree on a contract spelling out each side's rights and responsibilities under various contingencies. Such "contingent-claims" contracts are not unknown. Examples include inflation-pegged employment contracts and home mortgages. Insurance policies furnish a particularly important example: the company promises different levels of reimbursement depending upon the policy purchased and the details of the adverse event which occurs. Indeed, the desire to insure oneself against adverse future occurrences is a motive in most contingent-claims contracts. In the case of marriage, many informal understandings provide a form of insurance. And, written contingent-claims contracts do exist; prenuptial agreements are an example. Yet despite their seeming usefulness, contingent-claims contracts are rarely used within marriage, and it is instructive to examine why. Arrow (1974) lists five categories of impediments to contingent-claims contracting: legal restrictions, transaction costs, informational asymmetry, adverse selection, and moral hazard. We apply each of these to marriage.

There is a long legal tradition outlawing contracts which require involuntary servitude; in the case of marriage this prevents the enforcement of contracts specifying the contingencies under which one of the parties must remain within the relationship. The move toward liberalized divorce laws in most states since 1970 reinforces this state of affairs. Thus, marital contracts will be enforceable only where they specify performances or payments within the relationship or after its termination; they may not specify the conditions under which a person is obligated to remain in the relationship. Even some contractual payments at divorce might not be enforceable if they conflict with statutes such as those in community property states decreeing that all real property accrued during the marriage must be viewed as joint.

However, transaction costs provide an even more important check on the use of contingent-claims contracts within marriage. The costs of initially devising the terms of the contract might be thought of as the final stage of the search process, and thus as search costs. But transaction costs do not end when the deal is consummated because, to be meaningful, contingent-claims contracts must be enforced into the indefinite future, and attempts at such enforcement can be divisive. Suppose a couple has a contract specifying that if one partner ceases contributing an equal share of housework, the other is not obligated to share earnings. Or suppose, in a more sex-differentiated relationship, the couple has a contract stating that if the husband's earnings are not meeting expenses, the wife may seek employment, but must still retain responsibility for cooking, child care, and housework. Each of these contracts requires that the couples ascertain and agree on whether the specified condition has been met—whether someone is doing less than one-half the housework, or whether the husband's earnings are meeting expenses. What if there is disagreement about the share of the housework each is performing, or what constitutes necessary expenses? To avoid future haggling, the contract may have to be ludicrously specific. Even then, disagreements on interpretation of the terms are likely.

Another potential problem is that the information about whether the contingencies have been met may be more available to one party than to the other. This situation is known as informational asymmetry. Perhaps the classic example is adultery. Suppose a marriage contract specified that one partner's engaging in sex outside the relationship gave the other the right to leave the relationship and claim all of the equity in the house. With such a contract in place the partner committing adultery would hardly be likely to reveal it. So each partner has to either trust the other (in which case the contract is irrelevant) or incur great costs to find out if the contingency has occurred.

Such informational asymmetry is not only relevant because it makes enforcement difficult, but it also raises the issue known as "adverse selection." This is the propensity of "poor bets" to enter markets where they may be difficult to detect. Examples include the disproportionate tendency of those with a history of health problems to seek health insurance, and the disproportionate tendency of cars sold to used-car dealers to be "lemons." In the case of marriage contracts, one suspects that a partner desiring a contract specifying the ability to keep property brought into the marriage in the event of divorce is already contemplating leaving any time a better offer presents itself. Thus, one would probably find a more faithful partner among those not seeking such contracts.

Finally, contingent-claims contracts invite "moral hazard." This is the tendency of those who are insured against a risk to decrease their effort in preventing the insured-against event from occurring. For example, being insured against home theft may encourage carelessness in locking one's doors or make one less likely to install an alarm system. Similarly, a prenuptial agreement limiting one's loss in the event of marital dissolution might weaken the incentive to undertake those investments that help make the relationship last.

C. The Real World of Implicit Contracts

In the real world, marital and other cohabitational arrangements fall somewhere between the extreme flexibility and impersonality of spot markets, and the elaborate provision for all possible eventualities that characterize contingent-claims contracts. These "in-between" arrangements are called implicit contracts by economists, who first applied the notion to the analysis of the employment relationship. (See Chapter 6.)

"Implicit contract" is a term coined to describe relationships possessing two principal features: (1) informal understandings rather than explicit contracts regarding the obligations of the relationship, and (2) enforcement only through the disinclination of either party to incur either the bad reputation that would come from violating the understandings, or the costs of search and new relationship-specific investment entailed in starting over. Thus individuals act as though a formal contract were in effect, when in fact it is not. Yet by virtue of this informal understanding, transaction costs are decreased, a modicum of security is obtained, and options remain open for continued tinkering with the specifics of the agreement. Because they involve elements of both rational self-interest and social convention, such implicit contracts provide a vehicle for the integration of economic and sociological interpretations of behavior in both households and employment.

To describe the features of implicit contracts in greater detail, while comparing them to spot markets and contingent-claims contracts, Table 3.1

Table 3.1. Spot Markets, Implicit Contracts, and Contingent-Claims Contracts as Possible Arrangements for Marital Markets and Relationships

	Ideal type #1: spot markets	Real-world outcome: implicit contracts	Ideal type #2: contingent-claims contracts
Characteristics of markets	New market in each time period; different services may be traded with different persons	A market for long-term agreements specifying reasonable marital behavior	A market for explicit long-term agreements about the conditions under which various marital services will be performed
Allocation	Individuals strike their best deal in the market for partners each short time period; no risk spreading	One does not have a partner of exactly one's market value at all times; some risk spreading	Risk spreading perfect; individual gets predicted average market value for services over lifetime
Transactions costs	Search costs very high because of multiple transactions	Low because long contracts make search infrequent, and there is no explicit contract to negotiate and enforce; transaction costs that exist are informal bargaining within relationship	Very high because of all the contingencies that contracts must be negotiated to deal with, and the continual information gathering necessary to ascertain if contingencies have occurred
Incentive to make relationship-specific investments	Relatively low since relationship probably won't last long	High since relationship expected to be of long duration	Exact amount of investment undertaken that will yield amount of marital services specified in contract
Enforcement of contract provisions	None needed; when one can get a better deal elsewhere, one does so	Enforcement through incentives and informal pressure; search costs and relationship-specific investments provide incentives	High; may include fees for surveillance and lawyers

48

contrasts these arrangements as they might operate in the realm of marriage or cohabitation. [This table is adapted from an analogous table presented by Nalebuff and Zeckhauser (1981) for the employment relationship.]

The top panel of this table summarizes the characteristics of the three types of markets. On the one hand, spot markets provide constant turnover and recontracting: the time is eternally the present. (This would seem best for those with short time horizons.) On the other hand, contingent-claims markets are elaborately forward looking. (This is best for those with long time horizons and strong risk aversion.) Finally, implicit contracts are of medium, variable length. They combine some of the flexibility of spot markets with certain of the insurance aspects of contingent claims. That is, individuals are not completely locked into the terms of contingent-claims contracts agreed to in the past, yet there is at least an informal understanding and some incentives to provide security for the future. For example, it is usual to assume that if one loses one's job or becomes gravely ill, one's spouse will remain in the relationship and provide support despite one's lowered value in the marriage market. If markets for partners operated like spot markets, individuals would recontract for a new relationship the minute their marketability rose or that of their partners lowered. The widely accepted negative judgment of anyone who would leave their partner under such circumstances is evidence of the widespread use of implicit contracts within marriage. Yet the equally widespread judgment that there are limits to constancy—for example, that one should not be expected to stay with an abusive or mentally incompetent spouse—shows that market forces continue to be felt even within marriage.

The second panel of this table indicates that the different contract types also have varying implications for the allocation of partners. In spot markets, one always gets one's current market value; if you lose your job or become ill, you might expect your partner to look elsewhere. With a contingent-claims contract one is guaranteed one's long-run average market value as it can be predicted from one's characteristics at contracting time. This will sometimes be above and sometimes below one's actual market value at future time points. In this "bet," which resembles that involved in insurance policies, the "winners" are those who suffer a loss in market value and must invoke the contract, while the "losers" are those who turn out to have no need of the contract, and instead find themselves with a partner less valuable than a spot market would provide. The important point, however, is that the risk is spread and all are protected against extremely negative outcomes. On this dimension, as others, implicit contracts fall somewhere between the extremes; there is some, but not complete, risk spreading and insurance, and one is permitted to move toward one's best spot market partner, but not without cost.

Moving down Table 3.1, the third and fourth panels exhibit two further reasons that marriages are conducted as implicit contracts rather than either striking the best deal currently available as in spot markets, or "locking in" one's best long-term prospects through contingent-claims contracts. These reasons are that implicit contracts involve lower transaction costs, while providing the opportunity and incentive to invest in the relationship. We have already spoken of search and other transaction costs. Obviously these costs are high if one is either in the marriage market continually or trying to make or enforce a contract specifying rights and obligations across many eventualities. These costs go beyond out-of-pocket expenditures such as for dates or divorce lawyers to include opportunity costs—time and emotional energy spent on search, contract negotiation, or contract enforcement that could have been spent earning money, enjoying leisure, or in unpaid but important work at home. It is commonly observed that even in the highly competitive business world, many transactions depend more on trust and reputation than on explicit contractual provisions. This is precisely because the costs of negotiating and enforcing these contracts are so high. Thus it is hardly surprising that in the more personal world of marriage, partners avoid these costs through the use of structured incentives and more informal understandings.

The fourth panel of this table reminds us of the reciprocal relationship between the investments people make in relationships and the long-term nature of the resulting implicit contract. On the one hand, such investment is important in increasing the duration of familiar relationships by making them more comfortable than new ones, even where the latter offer the initial excitement of falling in love. On the other hand, it is just the implicit promise of a long-term relationship which makes extensive investment a wise decision.

The bottom panel of Table 3.1 summarizes contract enforcement across the three types. Spot markets require no enforcement because there is neither an explicit contract nor an expectation that the relationship will endure any longer than it remains optimal for both parties. Thus spot market relationships are self-enforcing (Arrow, 1974). By contrast, the difficulties of enforcing contingent-claims contracts are an important reason for their relative scarcity. Finally, implicit contracts are enforced by informal means, directed toward maintenance of effort within the relationship. Such enforcement is partially achieved through the incentives provided by relationship-specific investment and a desire to avoid transaction costs. The fear of gaining a bad reputation as a partner also has a disciplining effect. This is not only because of the internalized, Durkheimian force of society's moral code, but also because a bad reputation as a partner might lower one's ability to attract a new partner. This is likely to be even more important in the employment relationship, where a reputation as a "good worker" or a "good employer" is often of paramount importance.

V. BARGAINING AND POWER

Harmony does not always prevail within relationships, even where there is substantial love, trust, and commitment. Partners often have different preferences regarding issues which affect them both. This gives rise to the on-going bargaining and negotiation that we think of as the give-and-take of relationships. The long-term nature of marriage is one of the reasons for such bargaining. If marriage were a spot market, one would simply leave the minute one was displeased and could attract a more promising partner. Thus there would be only limited occasions for bargaining. On the other hand, if marriage were a contingent-claims contract, almost all bargaining would occur "up front," when the contract was first negotiated. Later negotiations would concentrate on issues of interpretation and enforcement. However, because marriage is an implicit contract, bargaining and negotiation is a constant feature, typically conducted with a combination of exhortation and offers of exchange.

Exhortation is the attempt by one partner to convince the other to begin or cease doing something simply because it displeases the first partner, because it "isn't right," or because others will disapprove. Offers (and threats) of exchange provide further incentives, taking the form of "If you do (or do not do) X, I'll do (or not do) Y." Sometimes the offers and the terms of exchange are unspoken, but this need not decrease their effectiveness. They may involve actions to be taken within the relationship, but they may also involve the threat of leaving. Thus relationships make their way through situations of conflict and changed external marriage market possibilities. This raises two questions. First, do men or women generally have more bargaining power in heterosexual relationships? And second, what are the sources of such differential power?

A. Defining and Measuring Power

In order to empirically study who has more power, researchers have had to grapple with defining and measuring power. This has proved difficult. Max Weber defined power as the probability that an actor will be able to realize his or her objectives even against opposition (Giddens, 1971). Sociologists studying marital power have usually adopted this definition and attempted to measure power on the basis of individual responses to survey questions. These surveys typically take one of two approaches, each of which emphasizes the outcomes of couples' decision-making processes. The first approach begins by identifying a number of decision-making areas.

Within each of these, the respondent is asked to report who usually makes the final decision governing this matter, with possible responses being "husband always," "husband usually," "half and half," "wife usually," "wife always." An early study using this method was that of Blood and Wolfe (1960). These authors studied the following eight decision-making areas: what job the husband should take, which automobile to purchase, whether or not to purchase life insurance, where to go on vacation, what house or apartment to choose, whether or not the wife should begin or quit work outside the home, what doctor to use, and how much money the family can afford to spend per week on food.

Several problems arise with this first method of research on family power relations. To begin with, since husbands and wives typically specialize in different areas of household management, any global measure of marital power (summed over all decision-making areas) is sensitive to which areas are chosen for study. Further, the researcher may misjudge the importance of different areas, and spouses may themselves differ in this assessment, so that weighting areas to compute a global measure becomes problematic. A related difficulty is that even when an area is important to both individuals, the fact that one makes all the decisions need not indicate that the other is not achieving his or her desires. For example, husbands may be quite content to let wives make most decisions regarding child rearing. If this is the case, husbands' lack of decision making about child rearing does not indicate a lack of ability to realize their desires, and it should not lower their score on marital power.

In response to these criticisms, as well as to the observation that the outcome of actual conflicts should provide insight into the power balance, a second research strategy has arisen. In this work, the individuals themselves are asked to identify areas of conflict, and then report who usually "wins" (Heer, 1963; Scanzoni, 1970; Bahr, 1974; Scanzoni and Scanzoni, 1981: 441). In order of decreasing frequency, these areas are reported to be what to spend money on, issues concerning children, and issues of leisure time spent with kin and friends (Blood and Wolfe, 1960: 241; Scanzoni, 1970: 157; Scanzoni and Scanzoni, 1981: 484). One suspects that sexual behavior is another potential source of difficulty, although individuals rarely volunteer this, perhaps because of embarrassment (Scanzoni and Scanzoni, 1981: 484). Surveys asking about sexual behavior often discover that men would prefer sex more often (Hite, 1981; Blumstein and Schwartz, 1983), while women complain of lack of emotional closeness accompanying sex, and lack of orgasms (Hite, 1976).

Other sociological approaches to marital power have included laboratory studies in which couples are observed making a decision or solving a disagreement. Judges watching the interaction assess power by noting who interrupted more, who was more persuasive, or who seemed to get their way. The essential point is that each of these operationalizations of power attempts to measure the successful pursuit of self-interest (what economists would call utility maximization) where partners differ in preferences.

Economists have ignored the issue of power within marriage. For example, Becker's (1981) "A Treatise on the Family" makes no mention of power, although he does analyze the seemingly "sociological" issue of altruism within the family. Power is not mentioned because, as defined (above) by sociologists, power has no place within the conceptual scheme of neoclassical economics. The difficulty becomes clear once we recognize that the sociological notion involves one partner deriving more utility from the relationship than the other one does. That is, if the husband has more power, we mean by this that he usually "gets more of what he wants" than the wife, at least in those areas where spouses' preferences conflict. Yet this statement violates the assumption, long accepted by economists, that interpersonal utility comparisons are meaningless. That is, economists believe that there is no way to know if the utility one person gets from consuming any given item is lesser or greater than the utility a second person gets from consuming the same item. A similar argument holds for marital decision making. (See, for example, the standard microeconomics text by Hirshleifer, 1976: 54–64. For an unusual dissenting opinion, see Simon, 1974.) Yet there is a possible area of rapprochement between sociologists and economists in conceptualizing power. It centers on the notion of marriage as a bilateral monopoly and the resultant need to resort to the logic of game theory.

Economists call a market monopolistic when there is only one seller of a particular good or service. In this situation, or in the related case of oligopoly (i.e., few sellers), "market power" *is* defined; it consists in the ability of the seller to affect the price of the good or service, causing it to deviate from the value it would display under competition. This is possible because the "atomistic competition" of the market is not present. Market forces and a determinate market solution are replaced by bargaining and an indeterminate solution affected by political and sociological considerations (Scherer, 1980). In a situation containing elements of monopoly, economists do acknowledge power, although they do not define it to imply that those with more power necessarily have more utility.

What does monopoly have to do with conflict and bargaining within marriage? We have analyzed the choice of a partner as a market phenomenon. This market is competitive rather than monopolistic since there are generally many men competing for each woman, and vice versa. Yet, once extensive relationship-specific investments have been made by a couple, they pass into a situation of "bilateral monopoly" in which each holds monopoly power over the other. That is, after couple-specific investment, both partners are likely to be better off within the relationship than if they reverted to the market for partners. The difference between the gains from the relationship to a given partner and what he or she could obtain outside the relationship is the "surplus" (sometimes called "economic rent"). After relationship-specific investment has occurred, competitive market processes cannot determine the distribution of this surplus because there is no alternative partner with whom one has already made these relationship-specific investments. Thus, each partner can be said to have bilateral monopoly power over the other, and the surplus is divided between them on the basis of other than strictly competitive market terms.

The study of such "bargaining over the surplus" takes us into the realm of game theory, which becomes relevant when the number of potential parties to an exchange is small, ensuring that each has at least some monopoly power over the others (Schotter and Schwodiauer, 1980). Empirical studies of bargaining suggest that the better one's alternatives outside the relationship, the harder one will bargain within it. Thus, a person whose investments have been more relationship-specific will be disadvantaged in bargaining power in comparison to the person whose investments yield benefits more portable to another relationship. Social notions of fairness are important as well, moving bargainers toward some normatively determined point of agreement; any negotiator who attempts to get more than this may end up with nothing at all (Raiffa, 1982).

Discussions such as these provide a bridge between the sociological and economic perspectives on marital power. Economists may still not accept the notion that one party "gets more of what s/he wants" than the other. However, when slightly reworded, conclusions from sociological studies of decision-making power within marriage are consistent with game theory and studies of decision making in nonmarital contexts under bilateral monopoly. In the following section we review the findings of the sociological literature on marital power, providing an interpretation that draws in part on these economic and game-theoretic concepts.

B. Determinants of Marital Power

Whatever their method of measurement, sociological studies have typically found that husbands have more power than wives, and that this male dominance is stronger when the wife is exclusively a homemaker than when she is employed outside the home. (For United States' findings see Heer, 1958; Kligler, 1954; Glueck and Glueck, 1957; Blood, 1963; Blood and Wolfe, 1960; Heer, 1963; Scanzoni, 1970; Bahr, 1972; Duncan and Duncan, 1978: 205; and Blumstein and Schwartz, 1983. For cross-cultural support from other industrialized societies, see the literature cited in Scanzoni, 1979b. For anthropological findings see Sanday, 1981, and Chafetz, 1984.)[3] Many sociologists write as if it were obvious that the partner bringing in more money will have greater power (e.g., Scanzoni, 1972, 1979). We think that this hypothesis requires further explanation, and suggest an integrated interpretation drawing on the economic theory of contracts, more general microeconomic and sociological theories of exchange, structural reasoning regarding how placement within "slots" affects individual behavior, and cultural reasoning that stresses the importance of tastes or values. The remainder of this section is devoted to presenting this integrated interpretation.

A key observation is that men typically make fewer relationship-specific investments than women, accumulating instead resources which are as useful outside as within their current relationship. Thus, while both men and women work at the relationship-specific issues of learning to get along with the other person, women are usually the expressive-emotional specialists, focusing heavily on personal relationships and empathic understanding. (See Parsons and Bales, 1955; Balswick and Peek, 1971; Hill et al., 1979; Gilligan, 1982; Kessler and McLeod, 1984; Kessler et al., in press.) Of course, some of these efforts are potentially useful in future relationships as well—examples include skills at listening, pleasing, and compromising. Yet much of the investment in these emotional skills is by its very nature specific to the particular relationship. In addition, women typically take the major responsibility for child rearing, heavily investing their own time for the future benefit of the children, but also for the benefits of the particular marriage. Thus women's effort is skewed toward investments which are most valuable within the particular relationship.

The relationship-specific nature of learning to get along with a particular husband can be seen by questioning what value such learning has for the woman if she becomes divorced. Furthermore, what good are kin links with the current husband's family (links she has invested time and emotion in) once she is divorced or when she is remarried? And, especially, are the children, in whom she has invested so much, an asset in finding a new partner? More likely they are a hindrance. Of course, the earnings of employed women are something they can transfer out of the relationship. They can live on these earnings, and use them to support their children (usually a necessity given the large proportion of fathers that pay no child support). Such earnings may also be a bargaining chip in finding a new partner. While many men expect to support their wives financially, the prospect of supporting another man's children often decreases their interest in marrying. A woman with her own earnings ability can at least partially offset this disadvantage. Yet, even women with earnings seldom earn as much as their partners. (Determinants of the sex gap in pay are discussed in Chapter 7.) Thus, whether employed outside the home or not, wives tend to accumulate fewer resources that are of value outside the current relationship.

While women are taking major responsibility for the instrumental and expressive work of the household, men are advancing their careers. Even blue-collar men not getting promotions are accumulating years of seniority that usually increase their earnings. A husband's increased earning power will, of course, benefit the man's wife as long as the relationship persists, but it continues to benefit the husband should he leave the relationship. That is, earning power is "liquid," readily transferable to a new life. A divorced man can live on his earnings, purchase some of the domestic services his wife was providing, and his earnings are a resource that improve his "rating" in the market for new partners.

What is the significance for marital power of the more relationship-specific nature of women's investments? We suggest the apparent paradox that women have less power within relationships precisely because their investments are more heavily focused on these relationships. This is because bargaining power derives not only from contributions to the relationship, but also from one's alternatives outside the relationship. Both game theory (Raiffa, 1982) and exchange theory (Waller, 1951: 190–192; Thibaut and Kelley, 1959; Heer, 1963) suggest that an individual's bargaining power within a relationship decreases the more that their gains within the relationship exceed what they could get outside the relationship. Thus we may imagine individuals calculating their "surplus" by subtracting benefits without the relationship from those within it. Where the surplus is large, the desire to remain in the relationship is strong, and this leads to a willingness to compromise rather than to hard bargaining. Since most husbands have better alternatives outside the relationship than do wives, they are subtracting the benefits of the relationship from a larger number. Thus, other things being equal, they have a lower motivation to remain in the relationship. This gives them more bargaining power within it.

Our emphasis on men's relatively good alternatives outside their current relationship might lead one to ask why men do not simply leave their wives to take advantage of these alternatives rather than using their position to bargain within marriage. Obviously, some divorces or other breakups do occur because men (and sometimes women) seek "greener pastures" elsewhere. As suggested in our discussion of implicit contracts, informal contractual agreements and the prospect of search and transaction costs all provide motivation to work things out within the relationship so long as there is at least some "surplus." Bargaining is one way to increase one's share of the surplus. Of course the same is true for women, but they typically have less bargaining power. In short, the bilateral monopoly caused by relationship-specific investments and search costs gives men more monopoly power than women, although both partners have some.[4]

The discussion thus far has emphasized the structural positions men and women occupy within the economy and marriage, and the consequences for bargaining within marriage. We have said little about cultural factors such as norms, values, and tastes, although they are implied by some of this discussion. We turn now to a closer examination of these issues.

The most obvious explanation of male dominance is that it is a social norm, inculcated in successive generations via childhood socialization. As economists (who never use the word "norm" except in its statistical sense) would say, men and women have a "taste" for male leadership. That such an ideology does in fact exist is evidenced by the Biblical proviso that wives obey their husbands, an admonition that continues to appear in some marriage ceremonies. While such norms clearly do exist, it is almost tautological to use them to explain male dominance. Rather, if the role of cultural values in the determination of power relations is to be clearly understood, it is important to examine the differential valuation placed on the goods and services typically provided by men and women, given their structural positions within the marriage. For it is this valuation which is relevant to power differentials coming out of exchange in marriage.

We suggest that three cultural standards define the valuation of the resources men and women typically exchange. These are the double standard of aging, the attachments women form to children, and the importance placed on empathy and emotional nurturance within marriage. By the double standard of aging we refer to the fact that men prefer younger women, while women prefer men either their age or older than themselves. This is related to the twin facts that physical attractiveness is extremely important in most men's criteria for evaluating women, and that our cultural standards define beauty partly in terms of youthful looks. These tastes imply that as women age, they become decreasingly attractive. For married women, two implications follow. First, their attractiveness to their husband, one of the "resources" they are providing to the relationship, declines in value over time. This should decrease their bargaining power, since it decreases the husband's marital surplus. Second, their ability to attract a new mate declines over time, decreasing their own options outside the marriage, and thus also decreasing their bargaining power within it. We do not suggest that this cultural value is totally exogenous to the structural arrangements of marriage and the labor market. Indeed, we predict as women's wage rates increase, they will come to be judged less by their physical beauty. However, although it may have arisen as a consequence of women's financial dependence, this cultural emphasis on female youth and beauty will likely maintain some life of its own within a changing world.

We argued above that women's child-rearing role places them at a marital power disadvantage, since the benefits of these relationship-specific investments are not easily transferable to single life or a new relationship. Yet this presumes certain tastes and values which were left implicit in the discussion: for example, that women will wish to keep the children in event of divorce, that men will not mind the loss of their children so much that it greatly reduces the benefits from forming a new relationship, and that men who are prospective new partners of a divorced woman will feel little attraction to living with (and possibly supporting) another man's children. At present, each of these is a fairly safe assumption, although exceptions exist. Each is also a cultural value that could in principle be otherwise, and did not arise in a vacuum devoid of structure. We suggest that the "taste" of women for emotional attachment to children, while largely a result of childhood socialization, also comes from the experience of mothering itself (Chodorow, 1978). Thus, women's structural position within marriage encourages a taste that places women at a disadvantage in marital power because it reduces their options outside the marriage.

There is another way in which women's greater emotional attachment to children may disadvantage them in bargaining with men, even in the relationship with the father of their children. We have talked of men and women exchanging financial support for domestic work. This language suggests that men receive the benefits of women's domestic work. However, in the case of child rearing, the direct recipients are the children, not the husbands. A husband will feel benefited by child rearing only to the extent that he empathizes with the children so that their well-being partly defines his own. But precisely because women nurture children, they are the ones that develop greater empathy with children, and define their well-being more in terms of the children's. Thus, the husband's lesser attachment to children implies that many of the wife's contributions are only weakly perceived as benefits by the husband, and thus add less to her bargaining power than they would if he were as attached to children as she is.

A final matter concerns the valuation of empathy and emotional nurturance from one partner to the other. These days a certain degree of reciprocity is expected. Yet prior to the 19th century neither men nor women expected much in the way of such emotional exchange within marriage. Rather, such activities were the exclusive province of women and children, and women looked to their children and to women friends for such empathy (Cott, 1977). Scanzoni (1979b: 26–32) argues that in this period women were viewed as the property of men, partly as a consequence of their financial dependence, and partly because men did not receive or appreciate their socioemotional functions. The rise of the importance of love and emotion within marriage, with men learning to desire some of the benefits of what women were already specialists in, has undoubtedly strengthened women's position within marriage. Yet the fact that men are socialized to have less of a taste for these "emotional services" than are women limits the bargaining power women can gain from providing these services.

Let us summarize our view of marital power. Marriage and other household arrangements operate as implicit contracts. The common set of informal understandings (arising from sex role socialization and the reality of labor market discrimination against women) assigns men and women to different roles within marital relationships. The resulting division of labor generates unequal bargaining power because women undertake greater relationship-specific investment than men, while men accumulate resources (primarily earning power) which easily transfer to another relationship. The difference in partners' alternatives outside the current relationship generally, leads to greater male bargaining power within it. This male advantage decreases when women are employed, although it seldom disappears since women seldom have equal earning power.

The fact that employed women have more marital power than homemakers suggests that women have increased their marital power between the 1950s and 1980s, as more have become employed, and that we should expect further increases in women's marital power if the sex gap in pay diminishes. However, the relative bargaining power of husbands and wives is also affected by how their contributions to the marriage are valued. The double standard of aging and men's lesser attachment to children are "tastes" that work to the disadvantage of women's bargaining power within marriage. The increasing emphasis on love and emotion within marriage has operated to women's advantage, since they typically specialize in providing empathy and emotional nurturance. The future of power relations within marriage will be affected by changes in these values over time.

VI. THE INCREASING DIVORCE RATE

Despite the fervent hopes of brides and grooms, approximately one-half of currently contracted marriages are expected to end in divorce. Yet our recently increasing divorce rate is not a new phenomenon. The proportion of marriages ending in divorce has been rising at least since 1870, and the rate of increase has increased steadily as well (Cherlin, 1981: 23).

Beginning with more recent history, the 1950s exhibited a slightly lower divorce rate than would have been predicted by extrapolation from the long-term trend. This lowered divorce rate (which continued in effect for those couples married during this period) appears to be associated with the high fertility of these "baby boom" years (Preston and McDonald, 1979). The long-term increase in divorce then resumed in the 1960s and continued through the 1970s, bringing the United States divorce rate higher than ever before. However, there is evidence that this rate has leveled off in the 1980s, while still remaining at quite a high level. This was predicted by Preston and McDonald (1979), who note that several features of the 1970s may have produced an unusually large increase in divorce, but predict continued, although slower, rates of increase in divorce:

> Marriages formed in the mid- and late 1960s were clearly subjected in later years to an extreme reversal in aggregate economic circumstances, probably matched in severity only among marriages formed in the late 1970s. Post-marital economic difficulties were probably exacerbated by a changing age structure of the labor force. Furthermore, many of the marriages were con-tracted during a period of rapid wartime mobilization. Finally, the widespread liberalization of divorce laws during the 1970s should be expected to exert a short-term, period-specific effect on divorce rates. All of these factors suggest that divorce rates in the mid-1970s are above trend and can be expected to reduce—but only to a cohort trend line whose upward thrust has itself been extraordinarily present. (Preston and McDonald, 1979)

But what explains the persistent upward trend of divorce within this century? Three factors are typically singled out: first, a shift in values emphasizing individual fulfillment over a sense of obligation to past com-mitments to others; second, the claim that marriage offers relatively less to each spouse than was previously the case; and third, that general increases in wages as well as women's increasing employment have increased women's ability to leave an unhappy marriage, allowed men to leave knowing their wives can support themselves, and increased economic benefits to men from leaving. We will consider each of these in turn. In doing so, we adopt the general "benefit-cost" approach that is consistent with sociological exchange theory and microeconomic perspectives. That is, we suppose that individuals decide to remain in or leave a marriage by comparing the benefits and costs of staying to the benefits and costs of leaving. However, we do not apply this approach narrowly; rather, we explicitly acknowledge that structural position may affect the goods and services that partners offer one another, and that many of these services may be social-psychological in nature.

A. Changing Values and Increased Divorce

Members of the unusually divorce-free cohort married in the postwar years often lament the lack of commitment to their marriages shown by younger cohorts, suggesting that an increased tolerance of divorce "ex-plains" the increased divorce rate. Indeed, values have certainly changed. Survey data analyzed by Thornton (1983) asked women if they agreed or disagreed with the statement that "When there are children in the family, parents should stay together even if they don't get along." In 1962 51% disagreed; by 1982 this had risen to 82%. Yet changing values may be *caused by* changing behavior rather than vice versa; the rising divorce rate may have led to easier acceptance of divorce.

Issues of causal order such as this are not easily resolved. However, we take the view that wide-ranging economic and constitutional change have reciprocal links with change in general sets of values, and that these in turn affect actions and attitudes across a range of more specific issues, one of which is divorce. Thus the increasing emphasis on individual fulfillment (partly a consequence of affluence) combined with a declining emphasis upon group obligation (partly a consequence of urbanization) appears to have contributed to the increased divorce rate. Weiss (1975) calls this an "ethic of self-realization," where individuals give overriding importance to goals of personal growth, fulfillment, and self-expression. (See also Stone, 1982, on individualism, and Lesthaeghe, 1983, on effects of secularization on divorce in Europe. Both are cited in Preston, 1984.) Our free-market economy encourages individualism rather than group loyalty because the supporting ideology stresses competition and individual achievement, and commercial advertising encourages an ethos of self-indulgence rather than obligation. With Preston (1984), we speculate that a rise in values emphasizing individual fulfillment has contributed to the rise in divorce through encouragement of desires that many marriages cannot satisfy.

B. Declining Benefits from Marriage?

A second explanation for rising divorce is that structural change has made marriage less satisfying to either husbands or wives. If this were the case, and if the benefits and costs of being single were unchanged from times past, rising divorce (and delayed marriage) would be a plausible outcome. Thus we wish to know whether the "gain," "utility," or "satisfaction" individuals subjectively perceive within marriage has declined over time. (We use these three terms synonymously.)

A major difficulty is the lack of studies asking married couples the same questions, but decades apart. However, one unusual study undertaken in the late 1970s (Caplow et al., 1982) interviewed couples in Muncie, Indiana, the same town Lynd and Lynd studied in their classic "Middletown" (1929) and "Middletown in Transition" (1937). In some cases Caplow et al. compare field notes on a particular topic at the two time periods; but in a few cases they actually report responses to the same questions asked 40 or 50 years earlier. They find that the satisfactions of marriage have increased substantially over this time period.

Caplow *et al.* summarize the Lynds' description of marriage in the 1920s as follows:

> The Lynds' portrait of the average marriage in Middletown was a dreary one, especially for the working class. Marriage for many husbands meant weariness from trying to provide for their families, numerous children, and wives weary from doing other people's washing. . . . For many wives marriage meant poverty, cruelty, adultery, and abandonment. . . . Married life was disappointing, but the prospect of a divorce was even more painful. They forgot their discouragement by focusing on day-to-day living and by ignoring the question of whether it was worth the effort. . . . Decisions about the children, the house payment, and the food budget were quickly dealt with in a bickering fashion, and, with those problems disposed of, couples often lapsed into "apathetic silence." The Lynds reported that many times during their survey of wives, the interviewer had a difficult time terminating the interview. The women seemed hungry for someone to talk to. (Caplow et al., 1982: 114–115).

In more recent times a number of factors have changed for the better. Thus, even within the troubled economic climate of the 1970s, real income and wealth was much greater than during the 1920s. We can infer that this reduced the stress placed on marriage from cross-sectional studies which show greater marital dissatisfaction and higher divorce within lower income strata (Blood and Wolfe, 1960; Gurin et al., 1960; Renne, 1970; Scanzoni, 1970; Miller, 1976; Norton and Glick, 1979). Furthermore, by the 1970s there was a noticeably increased emphasis on conversation, shared leisure time activities, empathy, and companionship within marriage, although wives still voiced complaints of unsatisfactory communication and empathy from their husbands. In 1924 the Lynds asked wives "What are the thoughts and plans that give you courage to go on when thoroughly discouraged?" Not a single one mentioned her husband as a source of reassurance. In response to the same question in the 1978 survey, 7% of wives mentioned their husbands and 16% mentioned family (which may have referred to husbands as well as other family members).

The trend to later marriage, often preceded by cohabitation, should also lower dissatisfaction with marriage, and hence divorce. One reason for divorce is that at least one spouse is surprised by the characteristics of the other. Becker (1981) phrases this as a matter of inadequate information in marriage markets. Couples who live together before marriage gain much better information about the characteristics of their future partner. Thus, increases in cohabitation provide a mechanism by which marital satisfaction may have increased.

The final, and perhaps strongest piece of evidence on marital happiness is Thornton and Freedman's (1983) study of public opinion poll data for 1957 and 1976. They find that between these years, the percentage of individuals saying that their marriage was either very happy or above average increased from 68 to 80%.[5]

Despite this evidence, some still assert that in recent years marriage has become less satisfactory, often identifying women's employment as the culprit. Indeed, both cross-sectional and time-series data support a correlational and perhaps causal link between women's employment and divorce. The question is whether the link between these outcomes is explained by a decline in the "satisfactions" or "gain" from marriage as claimed by some writers. (The contrasting argument that the major effect of women's employment on divorce has occurred because employment increases options outside the current marriage, is discussed in the following section.)

Sociologists and economists have both offered arguments along these lines, although they use different vocabularies. A "role differentiation" theory of marital solidarity can be traced to Parsons' application of functionalism (1949, 1955) to the family. Functionalism "explains" the existence of phenomena (such as low rates of women's employment) in terms of their functional contribution to some larger system (such as the family or society), and emphasizes that individuals internalize the norms and values that are consistent with functional requisites. Particularly in earlier decades, functionalists argued that a division of labor by sex is functional for the family as a unit, and when women are employed, particularly in full-time careers, tension is created. One can infer that in this view the dissatisfaction caused by such tension becomes the proximate cause of increased divorce.

A similar argument is offered by the "new home economics" (Becker et al., 1977; Becker, 1981). The argument is that women's employment has reduced the joint gain (and thus, presumably, satisfaction) from marriage because when wives are employed there is less specialization between husband and wife and such specialization increases joint gain. One can see the similarity between this notion of specialization and the functionalists' emphasis upon role differentiation. The difference between the theories is that the economist's ultimate reference is to individuals striving to maximize their utility, not to the needs of institutions which are met through individual internalization of the appropriate norms.

For Becker and his colleagues, variations in the divorce rate are to be explained by variations in the size of the "joint gain" from marriage. The argument hinges on the distinction between traits or roles that complement and substitute for one another in "household production." Parallel to this is the distinction we discussed earlier between traits on which there will be positive and negative assortative mating (i.e., a positive or a negative husband–wife correlation). For example, two ballroom dancers complement each other; thus, marriages will be more satisfactory to the extent that there is positive assortative mating on the basis of this skill. The same could be said about an interest in staying home to read and discuss books.

On the other hand, where one spouse having the trait or role can substitute for the other not having it, negative assortative mating and specialization within couples produces more gain from marriage. Thus a woman desiring to be a homemaker does better to pair with a man whose earnings allow her to stay out of the labor force than with a man who likes homemaking and does not want to be employed. Since the female domestic role and the male employment role constitute the major form of specialization within marriage, Becker argues that women's employment has decreased the gain from marriage, and thus increased divorce. His is a theoretical argument; he does not provide empirical evidence that marital satisfaction has decreased.

How might we theoretically account for the finding that marital satisfaction has increased even as specialization and role differentiation have decreased within marriage? Even if we grant that the efficiencies of specialization produce some joint gain in marriage as in firms, it is still possible that there is a countervailing force which increases marital satisfaction when spouses play similar rather than different roles. Simpson and England (1981) argue for a theory of "role homophily," which states that empathy and companionship, two major predictors of marital satisfaction, are enhanced when spouses undertake similar roles. When their roles are similar, spouses can understand one another better, and they enjoy each other's company more because of their common interests. Thus marriage may be more satisfying when husbands and wives both work outside the home, and share domestic responsibility as well. In Becker's terminology, domestic work and paid employment may function partly as complements, not solely as substitutes. While an attempt to test this empirically yielded equivocal results,[6] it does help explain why marital satisfaction has not declined as wives have increased their employment. Another plausible explanation is that women's employment has increased as fertility has declined, and children in the household have been shown to decrease marital satisfaction, even as they offer some alternative satisfactions (Campbell et al., 1976: 325). Finally, the rise in family incomes that occurred up until 1970 undoubtedly improved marriages. Yet, if marital satisfaction has not declined in recent years, what explains the apparent link between female employment and divorce? We consider this below.

C. Divorce, Women's Economic Independence, and Male Economic Benefits

There is strong evidence of some sort of link between women's employment and divorce. Both have increased during this century, escalating their pace of increase after 1960 (Cherlin, 1981). In addition, cross-sectional analyses show that women are more apt to divorce if they are employed (Cherlin, 1981: 53), and employed women are more apt to divorce if they have relatively high earnings (Ross and Sawhill, 1975: 57) or high potential earnings (Cherlin, 1978). Both husbands and wives are more apt to have thought of divorce if the wife is employed (Huber and Spitze, 1980). The explanation comes back to our earlier discussion of the divorce decision resulting from a comparison of one's situation within and without the marriage. Thus, rather than marriages being less satisfactory when wives are employed, it may be that the financial independence women achieve from employment permits divorce in situations where marital dissatisfaction arises from nonemployment-related reasons. With more women employed, they are more able to support themselves outside of marriage, and men are less apt to have to face the shame of leaving a family destitute in order to divorce. In addition, nonpecuniary features of wives' employment experience provide information and contacts which make leaving a marriage a less frightening possibility. We suspect that these factors explain why increases in women's employment have increased divorce despite the lack of decreasing marital satisfaction.

Since most divorced men make very small or no child-support payments, men usually derive economic benefits from divorce. The income they have to spend on themselves goes up after a divorce because they are sharing less of their income than previously. The magnitude of this gain has increased as male wage levels have increased in the postwar period (Preston, 1984). This means that men in unhappy marriages had an increasing economic motivation to divorce, at least through 1970 when (as we shall see in Table 7.2) average earnings stopped growing.

VII. THE PROCESS REPEATED

Rather than representing the "end of the family," currently high divorce rates simply insert new stages into the life cycle, so that for many, marriage is sequential rather than for life. Approximately five out of six men, and three out of four women who divorce also remarry, and about one-half of these do so within 3 years (Cherlin, 1981: 29). The experiences of adults and children after a divorce often entail three periods: a period after the separation or divorce in which adjustments are made to the change in household composition, a period of search for a new partner, and a period of remarriage—involvement in a new contract. Since remarriage is itself subject to divorce (the rates are actually slightly higher than for first marriage), some individuals repeat the process more than once.

A. Household Composition

When divorce or separation occur (or when unmarried cohabitors break up) one household becomes two. In roughly 90% of the cases, the mother gains custody of any children (Gersick, 1979). Thus, in the absence of remarriage or a new cohabitational arrangement, the result is one household containing a single male and one household with either a single female or a woman living with her children.

On the average, the effect of divorce is to raise the per capita income of men and lower that of women and children (Hill and Hoffman, 1977; Hoffman, 1977; Espenshade, 1979a). This is because men's earnings are much higher than those of women, and most fathers contribute relatively little to their children's support following divorce (U.S. Bureau of Census, 1983). As noted by Preston (1984), this "disappearing act by fathers" is an important cause of rising child poverty:

> What happens to the father after the divorce? . . . Fifty-two percent of children with a nonresidential father had not seen him in the past year and an additional 16 percent had seen him less than once per month. Fewer than half of the fathers made child support payments. . . . Some of the children abandoned by their natural fathers will of course come to live with other adult males who support them, but this does not happen as often as commonly believed. . . . The upshot is that economic circumstances usually deteriorate for women and children following divorce and separation . . . the ratio of income to needs rose 30 percent for men who became divorced or separated and still remained in that state but declined by 7 percent for the women in this category . . . (Preston, 1984: 443).

One wonders whether women have fully considered the economic situation they face in the event of divorce. Of course, the per capita income decline following divorce is probably less, on average, than during the 1950s, when women's employment opportunities were more restricted, and family sizes larger. Yet in either period, the economic hardships of divorce suggest either (1) that women do not realize how high the economic price is, (2) that they are so dissatisfied with their marriages that they are willing to pay even this high price, (3) that they anticipate remarrying relatively soon, or (4) that men are more likely to be the ones insisting upon the divorce. Unfortunately, little research presently permits us to choose among these hypotheses.

Economic difficulties are not the only ones faced by the newly divorced or separated. Emotional distress is typically great for both adults and children, and is experienced as depression, a disorganized household routine, and other manifestations of loss (Weiss, 1975; Hetherington et al., 1977, 1979; Pearlin and Johnson, 1977; Wallerstein and Kelly, 1980). Over time, divorcees also experience loss of formerly joint friends, and women with custody of their children often become socially isolated (Bohannon, 1970; Hetherington et al., 1977, 1978). However, there are few reliable longitudinal studies of the long-term effects of divorce on the physical and emotional health of adults. Goetting (1981) reviews cross-sectional studies showing a positive correlation between divorce and lower mental and physical health. However, few studies have controlled for factors that determine selection of couples into divorce, such as family income. Since divorce is more common in lower-income families, and low income is itself correlated with poor health, the relationship between divorce and poor health may not be causal.

As for children, there is mounting evidence that they suffer from psychological trauma right after their parents are divorced (Hetherington, 1979; Hetherington et al., 1979; Kellam et al., 1977). Studies offer conflicting evidence on longer-run effects. Some have found higher rates of suicide (Furstenberg and Allison, 1984; Furstenberg and Seltzer, 1983; Fuchs, 1983) and lower school achievement (Hetherington et al., 1983; McLanahan, 1983) among children of divorce. Yet advance press releases from seven studies sponsored by the National Institute of Mental Health do not show children of divorce doing any worse than other children on achievement tests in school, bullying behavior, or arrest (U.S.A. Today, December 20, 1984).[7] Even when children of divorce seem less well off, it is hard to tell if the breakup or father-absence itself is what has done the damage. Conflict occurring while marriage is still intact but on its way to divorce may be at least as damaging as the trauma of the divorce itself and the loss of the father (Herzog and Sudia, 1973; Renne, 1971; Rutter and Madge, 1976; Raschke and Raschke, 1979; Zill, 1978). Marriages that end in divorce are no doubt more conflict-laden than others. Thus, in comparing children who have experienced a divorce with those who have not, we miss a true picture of what would have happened to those children involved in the divorce had it not occurred, but everything else, including the conflict, had remained the same. However, one thing at least is clear: current divorce rates entail an unprecedented disconnection between children and their fathers. And there is evidence that children who see their father more frequently adjust better to divorce (Wallerstein and Kelly, 1980).

B. The Search for a New Partner

At some point most divorced persons seek a new cohabitational or marital relationship. Indeed, the vast majority remarry. Looking for a new partner with whom to establish a long-term relationship proceeds via the process of search in marriage markets described above. Of course, the resources and liabilities brought to this market by divorced men and women may now be different, as may their search costs.

By comparison with their status prior to marriage, divorced women often find themselves disadvantaged within marriage markets. They are both older and thus typically judged less attractive, and they also often have children. Men, in contrast, are devalued less for aging and seldom have custody of their children. This may explain why a somewhat lower proportion of women than men ultimately remarry. Evidence on the age issue comes from findings that the older the groom, the greater the age difference between his wife and himself (Goldman et al., 1984). Since older males are overrepresented among divorced men remarrying, this finding suggests that the age gap between brides and grooms is greater in remarriages than in marriages.

Other things being equal, quicker remarriage occurs among younger women (National Center for Health Statistics, 1980) and among those with fewer children (Glick and Norton, 1979: 19). Other characteristics positively correlated with quicker remarriage for women include good health, being without a job or reporting low job satisfaction, lower educational level, and lack of access to transfer payments providing support for the unmarried (Mott and Moore, 1983). In light of the market model presented above, two principles appear to explain these findings. First, personal characteristics which function as assets in this market will speed remarriage. This principle is illustrated by the more rapid remarriage of younger women, those with fewer children, and those in good health. Second, personal circumstances which raise the benefits of marriage relative to being single will speed remarriage. This second principle is illustrated by the more rapid remarriage of women without a job, with low job satisfaction, and with low education (and thus low earning power). These women are most in need of a partner's income, so the relative gains from marriage are larger for them. This principle is also illustrated by the contrasting case of women with access to transfer payments that are not "portable" into marriage. Such women will perceive higher relative benefits from remaining single.

Divorced men face a substantially different situation than do women. Their increased age is less of a disadvantage in marriage markets: given its usual association with economic and career success as well as increased personal authority, being older than most never-married men may actually be an asset for the divorced man. Furthermore, such men have less economic need to find a partner. However, casual observation suggests that divorced men often have greater emotional needs for remarriage than do their female counterparts; their concentration on employment has left them in need of a wife to provide an emotional life off the job. This may be an important cause of the rapid remarriage of divorced men.

There has been relatively little research on which men remarry most rapidly. However, cross-sectional evidence shows that unmarried men display lower than average education and earnings (Duncan et al., 1972). This is, of course, consistent with the notion that men of low socioeconomic status are in a relatively weak position in marriage markets.

C. Second Marriages

With currently high rates of divorce and remarriage, almost one-half of Americans entering adulthood in the 1970s and 1980s can be expected to experience a second marriage at some point in their lives. How do these second marriages fare?

Findings are mixed, at least partly because this is a new area of research, and partly because social change in this area has been rapid. White (1979) found that remarried women were less happy than those still on their first marriage, whereas the opposite was true for men. She interpreted these findings to indicate that women's position in remarriage markets is more disadvantaged than men's (relative to each sex's position in first marriage markets), leading women to settle for a less satisfactory mate on the second marriage. However, this interpretation must be questioned given Glenn and Weaver's (1977) finding of no difference between the satisfaction expressed by those in first and second marriage for either sex.

We do know that second marriages have a somewhat higher divorce probability than first marriages (Cherlin, 1981). Cherlin (1978) argues that this is because remarriage is "an incomplete institution" in which the norms have not yet been regularized. This is particularly the case for relations between stepparents and stepchildren. In the absence of established conventions, confusion and conflict arise over parental discipline, financial obligations, incest taboos between stepbrothers and sisters, and a host of other issues. One might summarize this situation by noting that we lack established conventions regarding the full nature of the implicit contract governing the "blended families" of second marriages. The higher divorce rate of second marriage may also be influenced by the fact that those with a high proclivity to divorce are, of course, disproportionately represented in second marriages.

VIII. SUMMARY

In this chapter we have focused on the formation, negotiation, and termination of household units. Although we have spoken repeatedly of marriage, most of our analysis applies to other cohabitational relationships as well. We have presented a view of how individuals find household partners that emphasizes market features, search costs, and the structural and cultural realities which condition them. The market features of search imply that one's own characteristics determine the characteristics of the partner one is able to attract. Yet, this market process occurs within a structural reality that differentiates the resources and thus characteristics individuals are able to bring to marriage markets, and within a cultural setting influencing which characteristics of male and female partners are most valued. To this market model we add the notion of the material and psychological costs of searching for a partner. These costs lead optimizing individuals to pair with less than the "highest-rated" among willing partners. The prospective search costs involved in finding a new partner also help explain why marriages are generally not terminated the moment disenchantment sets in.

We analyzed marriage as an implicit contract, a concept borrowed from labor economists who have recently used it to characterize employment relationships. The term "implicit contract" refers to a relationship in which there is no formal contract, but in which partners stay together because of the informal incentives provided by such things as the desire to benefit from relationship-specific investments made early in the relationship. Yet we pointed out that women usually make greater relationship-specific investments than do men—these include the emotional work of empathizing with a partner or rearing the children of a particular partner. Men's structural position in the marriage more often involves investment in earning power that is not relationship-specific but readily transferable to a new relationship. This provides one explanation for the sociological finding that husbands generally have more marital decision-making power than their wives, and that this sex gap is less pronounced when the wife is employed.

We considered explanations for the rise in divorce that has characterized most decades of this century. One likely factor is the rise in values emphasizing individual fulfillment. Also, women's increased employment has promoted divorce, not because it has created more dissatisfaction with marriage, but because it has made it financially possible for women to leave unhappy marriages. It has also released men from the shame of knowing that their families would be completely destitute if they divorced. In addition, rising male wages have increased the economic benefits of divorce for men.

We concluded by examining the aftermath of divorce—initial adjustments, the search for a new partner, and cohabitation and/or remarriage. Although divorce is more financially feasible for women now than previously, even today women and children generally experience a substantial fall in income after a divorce. This results from women's relatively low earnings, and typically low child-support paid by fathers. As for noneconomic effects, after the initial emotional trauma ·for adults and children, long-term negative effects may or may not occur. Since remarriage rates are high, an increasing proportion of adults and children will spend time in a "blended family" containing a natural parent, children, and a (usually male) stepparent.

NOTES

[1]Several things will affect whether the distribution of D scores of men (or women) making or accepting offers to a hypothetical searcher is normally distributed. One

factor is whether the characteristics that (in weighted average) go into the searcher's calculation of D are themselves normally distributed. Many human characteristics are distributed approximately normally, but all are not. The distribution of earnings, for example, is skewed to the right, and this might be a factor contributing to D. Also the shape of the distribution one faces may depend on one's own D score in the eyes of the average prospective partner. The higher one's D is, the higher the D of the people who will find one above their reservation D. Because of ceiling and floor effects on D, this will affect the shape of the distribution of the D's one faces.

[2]The simple search model can be complicated in several different ways by changing its assumptions. We can specify either that offers not accepted immediately are lost, or that the searcher can return to previous offers (i.e., sampling without and with recall). The number of offers received per time period can vary. Search can be random, or people can be assumed to investigate the "best" opportunities first. The intensity of search can be fixed or varied over time. The maximum duration of time spent searching can be fixed ahead of time, or be open-ended. The searcher can be indifferent toward risk or be risk averse. Individuals may have different discount rates that determine their propensity to defer gratification. The distribution, D, of the individual's potential offers can be fixed, or may shift over time. The individual may fully know this distribution at the outset of search, or may update knowledge during search. The wealth of the searcher (including such human capital variables as mental health) may be fixed or declining as search continues. The searcher may currently have a partner, or be alone. Each of these (and other) variations can be analyzed mathematically. For our purposes the important finding is that in almost all cases the optimal strategy has the "reservation quality partner" property. In addition, this quality level can be calculated in a simple "myopic" fashion—the searcher need only find that level of quality at which the costs of giving up such a partner and continuing to search tomorrow exactly balance the gains from continuing to search until a higher valued partner is found.

[3]The positive correlation of women's employment or earnings with their marital power is found in nearly all studies. Those that do not find it are usually including many relatively mundane decision areas in the measure of power, areas for which we would expect men to take increased responsibility when their wives are employed, but which may not really increase their utility (Bahr, 1974: 173–174). However, men's socioeconomic status (measured by income, occupational prestige, or education) is not consistently found to correlate with their marital power (Blood and Wolfe, 1960; Komarovsky, 1962; Scanzoni, 1970). In particular, lower blue-collar husbands make more unilateral decisions than do more skilled blue-collar workers. The lack of consistency in these findings may be explained by the crude methodologies of the studies, which do not use multivariate analysis to separate out the net effects of husband's earnings, wives' earnings, husband's education, and wife's education. In particular, we suspect that education has a liberalizing effect on the egalitarianism of men, while male income (with which education is highly correlated) increases men's marital power.

Waite (1981) suggests that the correlation between wives' employment and marital power may not indicate a causal relationship but rather result from selection bias. That is, having a powerful demeanor may lead women to exercise more marital power and to be employed as well. This is possible, but we doubt that marital power stems from personality factors alone.

[4]Our analysis has utilized much economic logic regarding opportunity costs and how they are affected by specific versus general investments. However, most economists would stop short of our conclusion that these factors lead men to have more power than women, unless power is defined behaviorally to exclude utility

from the definition. One reason for this is the assumption that interpersonal utility comparisons cannot be made. Economists would also raise the question of why women do not change their roles in relationships if they perceive them to be less desirable than men's. One answer to this is that there are strong social pressures against married women eschewing the role of specialist in relationship-specific investments such as child rearing and emotional work. Economists concede that utility may be reduced for those who face "barriers to entry" into some roles; that is similar to a "monopolistic restriction." But we think that the question of the rewards to women's domestic roles can not be reduced to a question of whether women have access to traditionally male roles; we do not believe that women's domestic roles yield relatively low utility only because women are pressured not to enter male roles. We will make a similar argument in Chapter 7—that the exclusion of women from predominantly male occupations is not the only factor generating the low wages of women's jobs.

[5]An increasing divorce rate can, in itself, raise cross-sectional satisfaction averages through removing a disproportionate number of unhappy marriages from the population of married persons. Thus, it is conceivable that this is all the finding of increased average satisfaction means, and that a research design that properly adjusted for this "population mortality" would find no change or a decrease in marital satisfaction. Although this is possible, we doubt that the finding of increased marital satisfaction is entirely an artifact in this sense, for reasons discussed in the text. These include the fact that fewer married couples have children in the household than previously, and that family incomes are higher than they were in the 1950s.

[6]Some studies have found a positive correlation between wives' employment and either husbands' or wives' satisfaction with their marriages. (For wives see Burke and Weir, 1976; Ferree, 1976; Simpson and England, 1981; for husbands see Simpson and England, 1981.) Other studies have found a negative correlation (Gover, 1963; Michel, 1970; Bean et al., 1977). Still others have found no correlation (Blood and Wolfe, 1960; Campbell et al., 1976; Booth, 1977; Glenn and Weaver, 1978; Wright, 1978). The positive effects on both men's and women's perceptions of their marriages found by Simpson and England (1981) have disappeared or changed signs under changed procedures for missing values in further analysis by Frank Howell and Paula England (unpublished). Thus the direct empirical evidence supports neither the role differentiation, the Beckerian economic, nor the role homophily theory unequivocally.

[7]Among the investigators in these studies are Thomas Langner of Columbia University, Nicholas Zill of Child Trends, Inc., Martin Levin of Emory University, and James B. Taylor of University of Kansas.

4

REPRODUCTION
AND PRODUCTION
IN THE HOUSEHOLD

I. INTRODUCTION

There is an important truth to the observation that the industrial revolution removed the workplace from the home. However, it is important to remember that although many activities involving subsistence and exchange have been removed from the home, a great deal of real, unpaid work continues to be performed there. Indeed, the "new home economics" views the household as a little factory whose output includes meals, physical and emotional health, and socialized children and whose inputs are the labor of household members and capital goods bought in the market (such as the house or apartment, furniture, appliances, and books). Sociologists, too, have seen some usefulness in this perspective. (For discussions of the new home economics see T. W. Schultz, 1974; T. P. Schultz, 1981; Becker, 1981. For a description of the new home economics by sociologists see Farkas, 1976; Berk, 1980; and Berk and Berk, 1979, 1983.)

Yet many scholars have not treated household labor as "production." There are a number of reasons for this. Some sociologists and anthropologists have distinguished between production and reproduction, and then defined all household work as belonging to the reproductive sphere (e.g., Chafetz, 1984). Within economics, domestic work has long been excluded from computations of the gross national product, at least partly because the resulting output is not traded in explicit markets, and is thus difficult to value in dollars. A further argument along these lines is that it is sometimes difficult to tell when activities are work and when they are leisure. For example, is the time a parent spends reading to a child work or leisure? Finally, since most household labor is performed by women, scholars may have unwittingly absorbed the sexist devaluation of the traditionally female activities entailed in the disinclination to call them "work."

Despite these issues, it is obvious that hard, socially necessary, and

73

important work is performed in the household, and that this work is regulated by an implicit contract arising out of a marriage market and involving ongoing exchange. As discussed in Chapters 3 and 6, these arrangements have counterparts in the arrangements governing employment for pay outside the home. That is, marriages involve a market for implicit contracts, as well as bargaining within the contract, just as employment does. Furthermore, both activities occur within a social context involving norms and structural positions.

Thus, we shall treat the household as a little factory, without worrying at this point over the practical difficulties of measuring the factory's "output." The factory analogy is metaphorical, designed merely to suggest a point of view, and thus call attention to input constraints of time, money, and skill; the decisions about tradeoffs which must be made; and the individual and societal importance of the resulting outputs. Since one of the principal such outputs is children, we begin by examining the determinants and trends in childbearing, known to demographers as "fertility." This is followed by a consideration of the work of rearing children, and the other emotional and instrumental work of the household.

II. FERTILITY

Why do couples want more or fewer children? Demographers have come to see fertility as a choice—albeit one determined by biological, social, cultural, and economic factors, some of which are beyond an individual's control. Thus economic demographers speak about desired family size as the "demand" for a certain quantity of children (T. P. Schultz, 1981). This has been expanded to the notion of the demand for children with particular, costly characteristics (such as a college education), referred to as different levels of "child quality." Thus there is a quantity/quality tradeoff, since with limited resources, one can invest more in each child only by having fewer children. These notions have been used to describe both variations in fertility across couples at the present time, and the historical decline in fertility that has accompanied economic development (Becker, 1981; T. W. Schultz, 1981; T. P. Schultz, 1981).

One might expect that childbearing was not under individual control prior to the development of modern contraceptive devices. Yet although advances in contraceptive technology have certainly increased individual control over fertility, demographers are certain that some such control has in fact been exercised for centuries. Thus, historical studies show that fertility declined dramatically before even primitive means of contraception such as the condom were widely available (van de Walle and Knodel, 1980; Becker, 1981: Chapter 5). Apparently, fertility control has long been achieved through rhythm, withdrawal, or abstinence (either within marriage or via delayed marriage). Indeed, there is evidence that in hunting and gathering societies child spacing was practiced to avoid a woman having more than one child small enough to require being carried (Lee, 1972). Evidence for the United States shows that the century-long reduction in fertility has been largely a decline in desired family size (Cherlin, 1981).

Thus, two sets of questions arise in seeking to understand how fertility has varied across time and across population subgroups. First, how do cultural and socioeconomic conditions determine individual tastes regarding the benefits and costs of childbearing? Second, how do these conditions affect the price of, the income available for, and the gain from each child? As elsewhere in this book, we adopt a benefit-cost approach to decision making, but with the proviso that nonmaterial benefits and costs (such as the emotional gratification of intimacy) are to be accounted for, and that the structural context of decision making must be considered.

A. Benefits, Costs, and the Demand for Children

Underlying the demand for children are the tastes or cultural values that determine how adults perceive the rewards of childbearing. Surveys conducted in different nations have enumerated these (Hoffman, 1975; Hoffman and Hoffman, 1973; Arnold et al., 1975; Hoffman et al., 1978; Hoffman and Manis, 1979). After factor analyzing responses to an open-ended question concerning the "advantages or good things about having children," researchers have identified eight nonmaterial motives for having children. As summarized by Espenshade (1979b) these are: (1) adult status and social identity, (2) expansion of the self, tie to a larger entity, and "immortality," (3) morality (subordination of narrow self-interest to a higher goal through sacrifice for someone else), (4) primary group ties, affiliation, and the emotional security of a family, (5) stimulation and novelty, (6) creativity, accomplishment, and a feeling of competence, (7) power and influence over the child's life, and (8) social comparison or competition. As for the material benefits of children, they include subsistence work (e.g., housework or family agriculture) when the child is young, and a source of income when the child is an adult and the parents require help in their old age (Leibenstein, 1963; Lindert, 1978).

The costs of childbearing are also both nonmaterial and material. The former include emotional worry over the child's present and future well-being, the demands of child care, frustration if the child does not behave or "turn out" as hoped, and the opportunity cost of being "tied down" and unable to participate in social and leisure time activities (Arnold et al., 1975). On the material side there are also both direct and opportunity costs of childbearing (Espenshade, 1979b). Direct costs include out-of-pocket expenses for food, clothing, housing, medical care, toys, and schooling. Opportunity costs include the consumption foregone because of the expenditures just listed, the savings and investment foregone for the same reasons, and the foregone earnings of the primary child caretaker—almost always the mother—if she has not been employed outside the home because of the children (Lindert, 1978).

Social psychologists and economists alike have emphasized these benefits and costs in seeking to model fertility behavior. Economists have tended to explain fertility change in terms of changes in the price of satisfying the tastes discussed above, or in the income available to satisfy these tastes, rather than in terms of an exogenous shift in the distribution of the tastes themselves. From this viewpoint a change in the average desired number of children is not explained as an exogenous cultural shift in the value placed on children, but rather as a shift in either the income available to indulge parents' tastes for children or in the price of indulging these tastes for children. These "income" and "price" effects (T. P. Schultz, 1981) are the textbook building blocks of the microeconomic theory of demand for any good or service. Accordingly, applying them to fertility involves treating the demand for children just like the demand for some other good or service. The propositions involving these two effects are that other things being equal, a rise in one's income will increase the number of children demanded, and other things being equal, an increase in the price of children will decrease the number demanded.

While at first glance this economic approach may appear to be unrelated to sociological explanations, it is in fact similar to what is often called the structuralist position within sociology. Structuralists generally explain changing behavior in terms of changes in the constraints individuals face due to the aggregate socioeconomic situation or their position within it. The similarity between neoclassical economic and structural sociological approaches to fertility is sometimes obscured by economists' use of language emphasizing "choice" (assuming that different choices will be taken if constraints change), whereas structuralist sociologists emphasize the constraints themselves (also assuming that different choices will be taken when the constraints change). When seeking to explain the time trend of United States fertility, both economic and sociological demographers point toward changing economic conditions as generating the price and income affects that in turn affected fertility. Although there may also have been shifts in values, they seem more a consequence of shifting economic conditions than a prime mover themselves. This is particularly the case when it comes to explaining the "demographic transition," that long-term decline in birth and death rates which accompanies economic development. However, before treating this long-term fertility decline, we focus on a recent, major deviation from this trend, the postwar baby boom.

B. The Postwar Baby Boom

The century-long decline in United States' fertility was briefly and dramatically interrupted by an unexpected upsurge in fertility between 1946 and the early 1960s. The entire society has been profoundly affected by this phenomenon, dubbed the "baby boom."

Demographers expected fertility rates to rise temporarily while couples who had been apart "made up for lost time" after the war. Unexpected, however, was the continued elevation of these rates through the 1950s, much longer than can be explained by pent up demand for children that was unmet during the war. Two competing sets of explanations have been offered for this phenomenon; they are typically referred to as cohort versus period effects.

The explanation in terms of cohort effects sees the baby boom as an increase in the fertility of a group of individuals, called a cohort, born during the same time period, that resulted from a particular experience they shared during the earlier portion of their life course. This cohort explanation is nicely summarized by Cherlin (1981: Chapter 2), drawing on the work of the economist Easterlin (1961, 1968, 1978, 1980) and the sociologist Elder (1974). Both authors see the baby boom as a response to membership in those birth cohorts which grew up during the economic Depression of the 1930s.

Easterlin focuses on relative cohort size as a determinant of income and tastes. He points out that fertility was unusually low during the Depression, as couples delayed marriage and childbearing in response to lowered incomes and depressed future prospects. Thus, the cohort of individuals born during the 1930s was relatively small in number. When the men of this cohort entered the labor market of the 1950s, their relatively small number made job competition weak and wages accordingly higher than they would have been if the supply of entry-level labor had been greater. Their situation was further aided by the vigorous postwar economic expansion. Thus, via the "income effect" described above, we would expect the demand for children to have increased.

Easterlin believes that changing tastes were also relevant. He argues that a cohort's notions of affluence and consequently their tastes for material goods are influenced by the material conditions of their childhood. Since this cohort was raised during the hard times of the Depression and War, their demands for material goods were relatively modest. Thus, they were particularly likely to invest significant portions of their increased income in children rather than goods. This cohort, with a higher propensity to spend income on children, experienced an unusually large rise in income relative to that of their own childhood experience. The result, according to Easterlin, was the Baby Boom. This cohort-based story can be extended to predict the family-size choices of the Baby Boom members themselves. Their income during their early work years (the 1970s) was depressed because of the large size of their cohort, and also because of the stagnant economic times of the 1970s. This undoubtedly contributed to the "baby bust," the lowered fertility these individuals chose during the 1970s and 1980s (Easterlin, 1980).

Elder (1974) analyzed over-time data on a sample of individuals raised during the Depression. He found that they were apt to have had a father who was unemployed at some time, and that the resulting psychological distress and family disruption led them to place an especially high value on family life when it became their turn to be parents. He also found that families in which a father became unemployed in the 1930s were apt to send their sons out to get a job while increasing the amount of housework allocated to daughters. So these cohorts received early reinforcement of sex-differentiated tasks, and a belief in the possibility of needing to rely upon one's children to contribute to family economic security. These experiences help explain why the Depression cohorts developed tastes for the sex role traditionality of relatively large families, women staying home, and low rates of divorce.

The cohort-based explanations of Elder and Easterlin can be termed "structural" in that they focus on people's rational responses to exogenous shifts in external socioeconomic conditions over which they have little control. These structural cohort explanations seem quite compelling so long as they concentrate on the cohorts raised during the Depression. But a problem arises since they fail to explain why even women born as early as 1911 (who were already adults when the Depression began but still within the childbearing ages at the start of the baby boom) and as late as 1942 (and were thus raised during a period of prosperity and economic expansion) all showed heightened fertility during the Baby Boom years. If, rather than an effect for selected birth cohorts, the fertility of all birth cohorts passing through their childbearing ages during a particular time period rose, then we must see this as a period rather than a cohort effect, and seek another explanation.

Demographers have attempted to statistically estimate the relative strength of cohort and period explanations of fertility, female employment, and other phenomena (Mason et al., 1973; Farkas, 1977; Fienberg and Mason, 1979; B. Duncan, 1979; Pullum, 1980; Smith, 1981; Clogg, 1982). Perhaps surprisingly, the conclusion seems to be that where fertility is concerned, period effects predominate. That is, most of the variation in annual age-specific fertility rates is explained by assuming period-specific effects, which raise and lower all cohorts in a similar manner (Pullum, 1980; Smith, 1981; Namboodiri, 1981). Further, the fertility rise (baby boom) and decrease (baby bust) occurred similarly for all race, ethnic, and social class groupings (Rindfuss and Sweet, 1977; Sweet and Rindfus, 1981.)

Demographers are thus faced with a puzzle—an intuitively compelling cohort story that does not fit the data, and an intuitively empty period story that seems to have statistical support. The structural, cohort explanation accounts for high fertility within the relatively small cohort of individuals reared during the deprivation of the Depression. Yet the statistical data show that it was not only those cohorts whose childbearing behavior accounted for the elevated fertility of 1946–1960. However, the data are silent concerning the features of this period that affected all potential mothers so strongly. The economists' price effects are not terribly helpful here, since there was no dramatic decline in the "price" of a child during this period. [Lindert (1978) does, however, point to the potential significance of the income tax deduction for dependents, which first became important as more families faced significant tax rates in the postwar period.] The income effect provides a more promising explanation, yet the pace and magnitude of economic growth in the postwar period can not easily account for the timing of the relatively sharp "up and down" swing of the baby boom and bust fertility rates. We are thus left wondering whether tastes or values changed exogenously during this period, and then shifted again after about 1960. Yet the hypothesis that values affecting fertility move in one direction for a century, reverse direction for about 14 years, and then resume their long-run trend itself requires further explanation.

Our speculation is that the answer to this puzzle involves a cohort effect (via cohort size, the associated relative income effect, and the taste effects of having been reared during the Depression) having initially compounded the period effect of the pent up fertility demand associated with the War. Then, in the manner of cultural contagion, the demand for larger families spread to cohorts other than those that began the baby boom, creating a "fad" that was a genuine "period" shift in tastes. This effect was then strengthened by a postwar pronatalist ideology shaped by the felt need to get "Rosy the Riveter" back into the home so as to make room in the civilian labor force for the returning male soldiers. All cohorts vividly recalled Depression conditions, and many feared a renewed Depression if males did not find employment.

As for the "baby bust," it appears that fertility decreased after 1960 because other aggregate, structural conditions increased female employment opportunities and wage rates, and thus the opportunity cost of children. This "price" effect is surely one of the major causes of continued low fertility in the United States today. Also the development of the birth control pill and IUD may have accelerated the fertility decline of the late 1960s and early 1970s. Between 1965 and 1973, the proportion of married women's births in the preceding 5 years that were unplanned dropped from 65 to 37% (Pratt et al., 1984). As noted above, currently low fertility can be viewed as the continuation of a more than century-long downward trend, a trend only briefly interrupted by the baby boom. Let us consider the sources of this long-term trend.

C. The Long-Term Demographic Transition

The postwar baby boom surprised demographers who had become accustomed to the downward movement of fertility over time as described by the theory of the demographic transition. This refers to the movement of populations from a regime of high mortality and fertility, typically in balance with one another so that there is little population growth, to a regime of low mortality and fertility, also in balance with one another, and thus producing low rates of growth.

The usual sequence is approximately as follows. In preindustrial times and places, women had very large families, infant mortality was high, life spans were low, and total population fluctuated around a low average. With economic growth, urbanization, industrialization, a rising standard of living, and improved public health and medicine, mortality rates began to decline. Total population consequently grew. As mortality fell and more infants survived to maturity, parents began to realize that fewer births were required to achieve a given family size, and they began to limit their fertility. So fertility declined also, and eventually came back into line with mortality, slowing total population growth.

Yet much real world variation exists around this stylized view. In particular, the fertility decline, the pace and extent of which is such an important determinant of total population growth, has proceeded irregularly across countries and time periods. Thus, the determinants of this decline constitute a central issue for demographers. A particular anomaly has been why the historical trend is not toward increased fertility with economic development, since viewing children as something that is "purchased with income" suggests that increasing income would increase the demand for children just as it increases the demand for many other goods.

This observation has provoked extensive debate, which has been more or less resolved by two observations: First, the income effect would only be observed if other things were held equal, whereas many other determinants of the benefits and costs of childbearing have in fact been changing. Second, when considering couples' childbearing decision making it may be important to consider the "quality" as well as the quantity of children they desire, since limited resources imply a "quality/quantity tradeoff." We discuss each of these in turn.

Economic development brings changes in the benefits and costs of childbearing, since, to take one example, the shift from rural and agricultural to urban and industrial life decreases the material benefits of children. On the farm, children are useful hands, but they are less productive in the city, particularly after passage of laws prohibiting their paid labor and mandating their schooling. Under these conditions, children become an economic liability rather than an asset. Also, in a mobile urban society, children are less apt to support their parents in old age. This is at least partly because fathers no longer determine the inheritance of income-producing land by their children (Goode, 1979; Folbre, 1983). At the same time, governmentally run social security systems decrease the reliance on children for income in old age (Hohm, 1975).

As for the cost side of childbearing, a large portion is accounted for by the opportunity cost of the mother's time. In most societies women have primary responsibility for small children (Chafetz, 1984), but across societies there is wide variation in the extent to which families must forego the direct product or earnings from women's work during the childrearing period. In agrarian societies women can often easily combine child rearing with home and farm production. As long as women remain on the farm, economic development seldom has a strong negative effect on fertility (Coggswell and Sussman, 1979). In contrast, where the home is separated from the site of employment, and female employment is on the rise, fertility tends to decrease. Thus, we see the negative causal effect of female employment on fertility in contemporary United States' data (Lazear, 1972; Waite and Stolzenberg, 1976; Cramer, 1980; Hout, 1978) and the frequent finding that cross-nationally, the employment and fertility rates of nonrural women are inversely related (Coggswell and Sussman, 1979).

Butz and Ward (1977, 1979a,b) have elaborated this notion of the opportunity cost of fertility. They present a time-series analysis showing that an interaction effect between female employment, the female wage rate, and fertility can explain both the overall trend and the changing counter-business-cycle movement of fertility during the postwar period. They observe that in recent years fertility has declined during business cycle upswings, which appears to be the opposite of what the "income effect" would predict. Yet, as Butz and Ward point out, since it is largely mothers rather than fathers who forego employment when a baby is born, a rise in male income should increase fertility via the income effect, whereas a rise in female wages has the opposite effect. Thus, when the business cycle swings upward, and the wages and employment opportunities of both men and women increase, two opposing effects on fertility come into play. (Cross-sectional analyses showing these opposing forces include Mincer, 1963; De Tray, 1973; Willis, 1973; and Ben-Porath, 1973.) The relative size of these effects is then the empirical question determining whether good economic times increase or decrease fertility.

On this score, Butz and Ward present compelling evidence that the price effect (the female's wage rate opportunity cost of childbearing) has become stronger over time and is now more decisive than the income effect of husband's wages. This is because the effect of the female wage rate on a woman's fertility is only relevant to those women who are employed. If a woman plans to stay home for another 10 years with her first child, a change in her potential wage is unlikely to affect whether she will go on to have a second child. Thus, the higher the female employment rate, the stronger will be the negative effect of an increase in female wages on fertility. (This is the interaction effect mentioned above). Rising female wage rates affect fertility in two ways. First, they induce more women to enter the labor force, which will reduce their fertility. Second, this larger proportion of females who are employed increases the sensitivity of fertility to continued increases in the female wage rate. Consequently, Butz and Ward attribute much of the increase in female employment and the decrease in fertility from 1960 to the early 1970s to rising female wage rates during this period. Their model also helps explain why increases in wages during the 1950s resulted in fertility increases. The explanation is that during the 1950s, there were still too few women in the labor force for the (opportunity cost) price effect to offset the income effect of husbands' earnings.

In addition to the opportunity cost of childbearing, there are also out-of-pocket costs which can themselves be quite substantial. These may go beyond the necessities of food, clothing, and shelter to include expensive schooling. This leads to the notion of the quantity/quality tradeoff in childbearing, introduced by Becker and Lewis (1973) to explain the long-term decline in fertility in the face of rising income. Blake (1981) employs United States survey data to show that for any given level of parental economic and educational resources, having more children reduces the educational attainment and intellectual ability of each child. Thus there is a trade-off between at least these types of quality and quantity in children. (Whether there is also a trade-off between other kinds of quality, such as emotional health, and quantity, is not yet known.) Economic development increases the demand for a schooled labor force as well as the rate of return on investment in children's human capital. Such investments are paid for by parents in dollars (for schooling, books, or transportation to school), in children's earnings foregone, and in the opportunity cost of parent's time. These increased returns to human capital investment encourage parents to invest more in their children, but at any income level, they must have fewer children in order to do so. Thus, the demand for increased human capital investment leads parents to trade-off quantity for quality in their childbearing decision making. While they have fewer children, they provide greater "inputs" to the "production of child quality" for each child. The labor involved in making these inputs falls largely on women. They engage in this labor employing material and social resources provided by themselves and the children's father if they live with him or otherwise receive resources from him. It is to the rigors and results of this child rearing that we next turn our attention.

III. CHILD REARING

A. Human Capital for Future Earnings

Parents must give up something in order for their children to complete formal education or otherwise learn skills that will increase their earnings as adults. In the United States and other industrial societies, parents are making an investment in the human capital of their children from which the children rather than the parent will reap the material returns. This illustrates Becker's (1981) point that considerable altruism prevails within families. Yet in a broader sense, we can see parent's investments in their children's education as providing nonpecuniary rewards for themselves. Such rewards include, but are not limited to, the satisfaction of having successful offspring.

When, in 1979, T. W. Schultz was awarded the Nobel Prize for a lifetime of work on human capital, agriculture, and economic development, it marked the acceptance of what at first had been a controversial idea—that the development of human skills can be viewed as a form of investment. That is, present consumption (or competing investments) are foregone in order to reap a later reward, much as in the case of investment in capital equipment. However, in the case of human capital investment, the resulting increased productive capacity inheres in the person rather than in a piece of machinery or a building.

Early work in this area focused on the return to schooling and on-the-job training (Schultz, 1960, 1961, 1963; Becker, 1964). More recently, human capital studies have been merged with the new home economics by conceptualizing many child-rearing activities as investment in humans (T. W. Schultz, 1974, 1981; T. P. Schultz, 1981; Becker, 1981). Becker (1981: Chapter 2) broadens the concept of human capital to include stocks of skill relevant to either paid employment (which he calls "the market") or to household production. Indeed, we could broaden the concept even further to consider all aspects of socialization discussed by psychologists and sociologists as forms of human capital investment. (For estimation, by an economist, of the financial returns to "affective human capital," see Filer, 1981.)

The deliberateness implied by the term "investment" seems a bit strained to a sociologist's ear. One reason for this is that many of the parental behaviors which enhance the ultimate earnings of children are not consciously undertaken for this purpose. Rather, they are at least partially the unintended consequences of actions taken to further parental goals unrelated to child rearing. For example, parents with a college degree may produce children who speak with proper grammar simply because the children grow up hearing their parents' grammar. The same can be said about the books present in the home, a taste for "high-brow" leisure-time activities, or the level of job status and affluence the youth learns to aspire to. With such a list in mind, it is clear that investment in children's human capital must be viewed as a multifaceted activity, only portions of which are undertaken with a clear notion of their economic returns. Thus, we agree with the new home economics that in some cases parental investment in their children's human capital depends upon the parents' tastes, their income and wealth, the price (including opportunity cost) of such investments, the total number of children (quantity/quality trade-off), and the rate of return they or their children can expect to realize. However, we desire to integrate this economic framework with a structural sociological view in which such economic concepts as income, price, and taste effects are themselves seen as reflecting the structural position of the parents. This corrects the tendency of some economists to see variation in "freely chosen" (exogenously determined) tastes as the ultimate determinants of income inequality, despite the fact that this view is not required by the assumptions of their paradigm.

Sociologists have long been concerned with how parents' child-rearing practices affect the earning power and other attributes of their offspring. Their efforts have differed from those of economists in attending to a more diverse array of behavioral and attitudinal variables linking child-rearing practices with outcomes. Some of these links are direct, whereas others are indirect, acting via their effect upon the quantity and quality of schooling the youth receives. (For reviews of this literature see Kerckhoff, 1972; Gecas, 1979.)

Yet a more significant difference between the economic and sociological perspectives flows from the latter's emphasis on how adults' experiences in the workplace affect their child-rearing practices (Kohn, 1969). This view is consistent with the view of "social structure and the individual" in sociolo-

gy. The latter focuses on how parents' structural position within the economy (the characteristics and requirements of their job) alters their personal
characteristics or resources, thus affecting their conscious and unconscious
"investments" in a child's human capital, and influencing the child's
eventual structural position and earnings. We see conceptual harmony
between this older tradition and the more recent "new structuralism" in
sociology (discussed in Chapter 6) which examines the direct effects of
structural position on adult's earnings rather than the indirect effects of
parents' structural position on their children's earnings via socialization
practices and resources.[1]

Using this approach, let us examine the determinants of parents' inputs
that affect children's earnings. As noted above, one of the most important of
these is the economists' "income effect," the propensity to purchase more of
most goods (called "normal goods") when income is higher. Here the
child's human capital is simply one more good, the "purchase" of which is
under the parent's discretion. Parent's income positively affects the nutrition, health care, reading material, and overall standard of living provided
for children, and each of these has been shown to positively affect school
performance (Wray, 1971; Jencks et al., 1972; Leibowitz, 1974, 1977;
Lindert, 1977; Murnane, Maynard and Ohls, 1981). Family income also
affects the socioeconomic mix, crime rate, public school quality and other
characteristics of the neighborhood the youth grows up in (Tiebout, 1956;
Jencks et al., 1972), whether private primary and secondary schooling will
be purchased, and the amount and quality of higher education that will be
financed by parents. Each of these affect the youth's ultimate earning power
(Featherman and Hauser, 1978; Jencks et al., 1972). In short, the higher the
parents' income, the greater the human capital investment in their children
and the better the outcomes achieved by these children. As we discuss in
Chapter 6, the parents' structural position in the economy partially determines such income.

Yet the "income effect" does not exhaust the ways in which class
position is perpetuated from parent to child. Independent of income,
parents' "tastes" for their children's characteristics also affect those characteristics, and these tastes, rather than being exogenous and randomly
distributed, are influenced by the parents' structural position and thus job
experiences. This is the essence of the "structural" argument made by
sociologists such as Kohn (1969). He argues that working class people hold
jobs that allow them little self-direction, requiring obedience to specific
behavioral regulations rather than encouraging self-direction. Thus working
class parents infer that their child's well-being is advanced by teaching them
the kind of behavioral conformity required in the parents' (and presumably
the youth's prospective) jobs. This may indeed serve the child well if he or

she ends up in a job permitting little self-direction. However, the lack of emphasis on internalized self-direction and educational achievement works against upward mobility. Even neighborhood schools reflect these differing class structures, with working class schools emphasizing obedience and respect for authority while middle class schools place greater emphasis on self-direction (Bowles and Gintis, 1976).[2]

In addition to these income and taste effects, there is also a "price" effect on investment in children's human capital. As noted above, this involves both out-of-pocket costs and the opportunity cost of the mother's time, with the latter cost usually the higher. Children's school performance is positively influenced by the educational level of, and the number of hours of interaction with, the mother (Leibowitz, 1974; Taubman, 1977; Olneck and Wolfe, 1980; Murnane, Maynard and Ohls, 1981). The amount of time mothers spend with their children involves two conflicting forces. First, as the mother's educational level rises, so too does the extent to which the cognitive stimulation she can provide exceed that provided by a hired caretaker. This makes the gain from foregoing employment greater for highly educated women. Second, as women's educational level rises, so too does their market wage rate, making it more expensive for them to stay at home. This means that the price (in the form of opportunity cost) of staying home with children is greater for more highly educated mothers. As women's employment opportunities and wage rates rise, particularly among younger cohorts, we can expect the latter effect to predominate, leading hired child care to expand to ever earlier years of childhood. Studies to date have not shown any deleterious effects on the cognitive development of children from being cared for in day care rather than at home (Hoffman, 1975; Stewart and Fein, 1983). This may be because the added cognitive inputs from interacting with other children offset the loss of hours of interaction with the mother.[3]

If inputs of mothers' time are likely to be smaller in the years ahead, might not other inputs to children be expanded? After all, average family incomes rose considerably in the 1950s and 1960s, and slightly since 1970, and some of this increased income has undoubtedly been spent on children. Further, fertility has been declining since 1957, so inputs per child can rise even in the absence of growth in family income.

Yet there is a countervailing development which has had dramatic negative effects on the resources devoted to many of the nation's children. This is the high divorce rate among couples with children, coupled with the fact that many divorced fathers contribute little or nothing to the financial or emotional support of their children (see Chapter 3). Thus, children are increasingly disconnected from the support normally provided by their father. A further factor in this disconnection is the increase in out-of-wedlock births, which rose from 5% of all births in 1960 to 18% of births in 1980 (Preston, 1984). In his Presidential Address to the American Population Association, Preston (1984) points to the decreasing financial support for, and human capital investment in children, as a serious social problem. The government has done little to ameliorate this increasing disconnection between fathers and their children. The average payment level under AFDC actually lost ground to inflation during the 1970s, after growth during the 1960s (Preston, 1984). Since 1980, the Reagan administration and Congress have sharply cut back programs benefiting poor children, including AFDC, WIC, and Medicaid, while leaving programs for the elderly—the other major group of dependents—virtually untouched. (This point, which is stressed by Preston, is examined further in Chapter 5.) Federal legislation to aid states in garnishing the wages of delinquent fathers was passed in 1984, but its impact remains to be seen. Finally, inputs to children via the public school system appear to have declined since the early 1970s. Although per capita expenditures on schools have increased, teachers' salaries have declined in real terms, as has their performance on standardized tests. Yet such measures of teacher "smartness" are among the few characteristics of schools (other than the socioeconomic mix of their students) affecting student performance (Hanushek, 1981, Murnane, 1981). During this same period, student performance on standardized tests such as the SAT has declined, as has the proportion of youths graduating from high school. Overall, Preston (1984) makes a forceful case for the notion that living standards of children and investments in children have declined since 1960.

B. Reproducing Gender Roles

In addition to producing young adults able to earn a living in the next generation's marketplace, the household also serves as a locus for the reproduction of gender differentiation within each new generation. What defines the distinct roles assumed by males and females as adults, and the individual skills and characteristics that harmonize with these roles? Men's roles have centered on paid employment and a position of authority within the family. Women's roles have centered on child rearing and other domestic work, with outside employment responsibilities increasingly added over time. In the world of paid employment, jobs have been strongly sex segregated for a long period of time (see Chapter 7). Male roles have emphasized preparation for paid employment; they have thus focused on mechanical, technical, and mathematical skills involving objects and abstractions, emotional individuation, and physical and emotional toughness. For females there has been greater emphasis on homemaking skills: verbal ability, nurturing, altruism, emotional connections to others, and physical attractiveness. While the boundaries of these roles have blurred substantially since the 1950s, particularly by allowing women to acquire "male" traits, the broad outline of these differences is readily discernible among today's adults and children.

Gender differences are socially produced at least partially via intentional inputs of time and resources for particular types of learning that are given to one sex and not the other. This intentional form of sex role socialization is described by reinforcement theory in psychology and by Becker's (1981) notion of "efficient investments" within the new home economics. Yet equally important are the "externalities" created by the example of the gender-differentiated lives led by adults. Children take lessons from these even when there is no specific adult intention to impart gender roles. These more subtle forces for gender role reproduction are analyzed by cognitive development theory in psychology and by recent reinterpretations of psychodynamic theory. We discuss each of these in turn.

Psychological reinforcement theory shares one underlying premise with the new home economics—that individuals respond to rewards. When applied to the reproduction of gender roles, the notion is that parents and adults reward different kinds of behavior in males and females. There is certainly data to support this view, although Maccoby and Jacklin (1974: Chapter 9) emphasize that the amount of differential reinforcement mothers present to small children is much less than might be imagined. Men seem more committed than women to passing on the regime of gender roles in that they engage in more differential reinforcement of male and female children's behavior than do females (Maccoby and Jacklin, 1974; Stockard and Johnson, 1980: Chapter 8). Such differential reinforcement of male and female roles also seems more extreme within blue-collar, working class families than within the homes of professionals or managers (Rubin, 1976: 125–126; Goode et al., 1971; Kohn, 1969). The question as to why adults engage in such differential reinforcement is usually not examined by psychologists; sociologists have viewed such behavior as simply reflecting the adults' own internalization of society-wide gender roles.

By contrast, Becker's explanation focuses on efficiency and biology. He sees the process as one of investing in different kinds of human capital for male versus females, and believes that this occurs for the same reasons that a sex-based division of labor generally exists within families. These reasons center on the claim that a division of labor between employment and domestic work is more efficient than shared roles, in the usual sense that specialization is efficient if the scope of activity is sufficiently large. This, however, does not require that women rather than men specialize in household work—merely that one party in each family do so. On this score Becker argues from biology as it interacts with rational responses to biological sex differences. While we do not think biological sex differences should be ignored, we think Becker overstates their importance.

To begin with, Becker observes that women specialize in nursing and rearing children because of their biological advantages in doing so, and that efficiency considerations then lead them to specialize in those household activities which complement these. However, while it is difficult to dispute women's biological advantage for nursing, one can dispute how compelling an explanation this provides for women's monopoly over homemaking in the postwar period. In fact, during the 1950s and early 1960s when employment rates among mothers of young children were still low, breastfeeding was discouraged by doctors and practiced by less than one-quarter of mothers (Pratt et al., 1984). Today nursing is recommended by doctors and is practiced by more than one-half of mothers, despite higher female employment rates (Pratt et al., 1984). Becker also follows Rossi's (1977) essay on "A Biosocial Perspective on Parenting" in arguing that women have a biological advantage in all aspects of child rearing, yet this remains a subject of intense debate. (See, for example, Signs, Summer, 1979.) Thus he may overstate the case for biological comparative advantage.

Becker does acknowledge differential investments of parents in male and female children, but he ties these directly to biological differences via a kind of "statistical discrimination" (see Chapters 6 and 7). In this view, sex differences in means on various traits are biologically produced, but there are always individuals whose genes are atypical for their sex. Since parents are unable to identify these children early on, they decide that it is efficient to engage in statistical discrimination by socializing all children in accordance with what is average for their sex. Again, Becker is undoubtedly overstating the case for real rather than imagined biological contributions to parents' decisions to engage in differential socialization.

Psychological theories of cognitive development have explained gender differentiation in children as resulting from the children's observation of the gender roles of adults and other children around them (Kohlberg, 1966; Kohlberg and Zigler, 1967; Stockard and Johnson, 1980: 191–196). In this view, children first learn to distinguish males from females, identify with their own gender, and find it inherently rewarding to behave in ways they observe adults of their own sex behaving. The underlying learning is cognitive in nature, and not always a response to rewards extrinsic to the behavior itself (as reinforcement theory would suggest). One observation in support of this view is that, at least among preschoolers, cognitive sophistication is positively correlated with sex-typed behavior (Kohlberg and Zigler, 1967), suggesting that it is through a cognitive process that gender roles are learned. A striking implication of this view is the causal primacy it places on adult behavior that is gender-differentiated but not specifically directed at childhood socialization. This implies that social change will begin with adults changing the everyday practice of their gender roles, rather than changing the deliberate actions they take in the service of childhood socialization. Deliberate reinforcement is simply too small a portion of the gender role inputs received by children to be decisive.

Recent revisions of psychodynamic theory begun by the sociologist Chodorow (1978) have also contributed to our understanding of the reproduction of gender roles. Chodorow argues that a key aspect of childhood socialization flows unintentionally from the fact that women are almost always the primary caretakers of young children. This means that females are reared by a same sex person, whereas males are reared by a person of a different sex. As a result, males become more individuated than females because defining themselves as a male requires separation from, rather than identity with, their caretaker. Since male role models are relatively remote for a small boy surrounded by women, he may come to define maleness as the opposite of femaleness, producing the psychological roots of disdain for females. In contrast, among females, such separation is not required. This allows females to retain more permeable psychological boundaries that encourage emotional closeness, empathy, and altruism. Chodorow sees this orientation toward emotional connection to others as one root of women's desire to mother and to focus on the emotional work of relationships. (For clinical and ethnographic evidence supporting this pattern, see Rubin, 1979, 1983. For discussion of how this revision of psychoanalytic theory alters the Freudian view, see Stockard and Johnson, 1980: 201–223.) Such a perspective is consistent with evidence that women both expend more effort on listening and developing emotional empathy with men, and are less satisfied than are men with what they receive from their partners in this area (Scanzoni, 1970, 1975, 1977; Rubin, 1979, 1983).

Gilligan (1982) describes sex differences in moral reasoning which fit nicely within this perspective. She notes that males with a highly developed moral sense tend to see ethical conduct in terms of not coercing or violating the boundaries of other people. In contrast, female ethical development emphasizes responsibility to others. The gender difference in underlying assumptions is one of individuation and the permeability of boundaries between people. Like older psychodynamic formulations, this new view is difficult to test empirically since the asserted independent variable—a female primary caretaker—has been virtually a constant across time and societies (Chafetz, 1984). Yet if Chodorow is correct, those psychological sex differences related to individuation-connectedness will be altered only by a move toward equal sharing of parenting between men and women. To switch back to the vocabulary of economics, we conclude that if Chodorow is correct, a division of labor in which women do most of the child rearing is an investment, perhaps unwitting, in the male dominance and sex differentiation of the next generation.

IV. EMOTIONAL LABOR

When considering household work, we typically think of child rearing, or of physical housework such as cooking, cleaning, and yardwork. The emotional (as opposed to physical) aspect of the work of child rearing is also usually acknowledged; we think of making a child feel loved and secure, or correctly interpreting the meaning of a child's occasional unusual behavior. However, emotional work involves more than children—it also occurs between adult partners—yet the work involved in these efforts is less often acknowledged. One explanation for this oversight is that such work often occurs in conjunction with leisure, such as a talk at the dinner table or in bed at night. Such efforts are undertaken with mixed motives: for their beneficial effects on the "recipient" partner, for the associated satisfaction gained from aiding someone close to you, and for the intrinsic satisfaction of the closeness involved. Yet such mixed motives also exist in employment outside the home, where intrinsic satisfaction is sometimes as important as the wage. (For a discussion of emotional work in paid employment, see Hochschild, 1983.)

How should emotional work be defined? We refer to efforts made to understand others, to have empathy with their situation, to feel their feelings as a part of one's own. So long as these have an opportunity cost, that is, they require one to at least momentarily forego a more pleasurable state, they can be regarded as a form of work. Defining emotional work in this way links the concept to discussions within several different theoretical traditions.

Sociologists have long distinguished between instrumental and expressive tasks in families and other groups. Expressive tasks relate to group solidarity; instrumental tasks are those undertaken for a goal outside the immediate relational system. Instrumental actions are directed toward some product as a means to an end; expressive actions are concerned with the emotional quality and motivation of the group (Stockard and Johnson, 1980: 173–176). Emotional work is also related to the issue of individuation versus emotional connectedness discussed above (Chodorow, 1978; Rubin, 1979, 1983). Such work presumes some permeability of the boundaries between oneself and the other and requires both the inclination and ability to unearth and experience the feelings of another. Further, emotional work seems a prerequisite to altruism, a concept Becker (1981: Chapter 8) has used in his "new home economics" of the family. Altruism is defined within economic theory as taking another person's utility function as part of one's own.

Whether conceived as expressiveness, as "being emotional," or as role permeability, women specialize more in this work (both within the household and in employment) than do men. As noted above, this may occur via childhood socialization because females separate less from their female primary caretakers and because cognitive learning and reinforcement create these as other gender differences in children. In addition, women's performance of emotional work may arise because they are expected to parent and in so doing acquire the emotional abilities needed for the job, and because women have less power than men in household and employment interactions and thus develop empathic responsiveness as a survival technique. Perhaps because women attend more to empathy within marriage than do men, an "empathy gap" often develops, with women being typically less satisfied than men with the emotional quality of their marriages (Scanzoni, 1970, 1975, 1977). For example, studies of the process of communication between men and women show that topics of conversation introduced by men more often guide the conversation because women ask questions to continue to elicit a story once it is begun, whereas men are more apt to interrupt or to offer a minimal response that does not encourage the woman to continue the topic (Kramarae, 1980; Pfeiffer, 1985; Thorne and Henley, 1975).

Becker's (1981) exposition of the economics of the family is of interest here because his concept of altruism seems related to the concept of emotional work, yet he does not mention this as an area of specialization for women. By an altruist Becker means an individual whose utility function depends positively on the well-being of another individual. Of course, this notion of altruism is not entirely encapsulated by what we have called emotional work. However, altruism does presuppose sufficient empathy to genuinely understand what contributes to the well-being of another family member—and that, we argue, requires emotional work. In addition to emotional work, altruistic behavior also entails transfers of income or labor from oneself to another. Becker argues that altruism is common within families because people have an incentive to select those with whom they have a mutually altruistic relationship as marital partners, and because altruism is more efficient in families than firms because of the families' smaller size. His other point about altruism is sometimes called the "rotten kid theorem" but applicable to spouses as well. He argues that, in the presence of an altruist, it will be in the self-interest of a selfish beneficiary to be altruistic toward the altruist on any matters that affect the production of income or other services by the altruist. This formulation permits Becker to define a single family utility function based on the altruist's preferences that everybody in the family is led to wish to maximize. Yet even as sympathetic a reviewer as Ben-Porath (1982: 54) has pointed out that the altruist will induce the whole family to cooperate only if the altruist has the last word about the production and distribution of goods and services that are altruistically given. Put another way, altruism can generate altruism and thus a single utility function (in which interpersonal utility comparisons need not be made) only if the altruist has power but does not use it selfishly.

This raises one of the difficulties with Becker's formulation. He never specifies which spouse will be the altruist. Indeed, although Becker refers to the altruist as "he" and the beneficiary as "she" throughout the discussion, he claims that specifying gender is not at all necessary to his argument. The altruist could be any family member. In addition, there can be, although there need not be, more than one altruist. However, Becker's model requires that the person who has the greatest power to withhold resources also be inclined to altruism. Yet the empirical evidence we have reviewed on gender differentiation reveals that men have greater authority whereas women have more of the emotional permeability that leads one to empathize to the extent of bringing someone else's utility function into one's own. Thus a major part of Becker's model, the single family utility function, is on shaky empirical ground. Accordingly, research that examines distributional conflict and power within the family is warranted.

We are not arguing that altruism is absent within families. If it were not present, young children might die in the contemporary United States where they are economic liabilities. Considerable love and altruism exists between spouses as well. Yet we believe that a model of either complete selfishness or complete altruism is unrealistic for both the household and employment. Rather, we have advanced the notion of implicit contracts between individuals whose interests sometimes diverge. Unfortunately, this in-between set of arrangements produces less in the way of theoretically determinant results than models that assume either complete altruism or complete selfishness of each individual. Thus women's greater tendency to internalize others' feelings is partly a preference they indulge, given their socialization, partly the glue that makes relationships better for both parties, and partly a disadvantage when bargaining with a more detached spouse who also has greater resources that can be withdrawn from the relationship. On the other hand, the altruism of two people with equal propensities for empathy undoubtedly increases the utility of both. However, the gender differentiation of roles in families of origin and procreation makes it unlikely that men and women will be equally matched on this propensity. Thus, the emotional work performed by women within relationships is often a source of their disadvantage as well as reward.

V. HOUSEWORK

While the home is often seen as the locus of affect and emotion rather than of instrumental work, a good deal of such work is performed at home. Meals are prepared, clothes washed, floors swept, lawns cut, children bathed, appliances maintained, and so on. Overall, the volume of such work per capita appears to have declined as female employment outside the home has accelerated in the postwar period. Yet, women's responsibility for such work has changed very little over this period (Miller and Garrison, 1982).

Vanek (1974) used time-budget data to show that despite the growth of labor-saving devices, the number of hours spent on domestic work by homemakers not employed outside the home remained virtually unchanged between 1920 and 1970. It seems likely that cultural norms for "good homemaking" simply expanded to fill the time made available by increased efficiency. We suspect, however, that these new standards were only partially internalized, with many individuals being aware that more of women's hours were spent on tasks that were considered dispensable by their mothers. Two observations lend credence to this view that much of the work done by full-time homemakers has been viewed as dispensable. First, as we will discuss in Chapter 7, female labor supply has been quite responsive to the wage rate available to women. Second, the adjustment to increased female employment has been to decrease total housework, rather than to increase by much the husband's participation in such housework (Farkas, 1976; Berk and Berk, 1979; Robinson, 1980; Geerken and Gove, 1983). This latter finding also suggests strong resistance to male participation in housework. Indeed, even among unmarried, cohabiting couples, who might be expected to be in the vanguard of gender role change, women are responsible for the great majority of housework (Stafford et al., 1977).

This failure of males to increase their housework participation more than trivially remains one of the major puzzles of research in this area. Since the assignment of domestic labor to women is part of an allocation of labor across housework and paid employment outside the home, one might expect that as women's participation in paid employment increases, so too would men's participation in housework. Yet very little such adjustment has actually occurred. For example, Geerken and Gove (1983) report that in 1974 wives were overwhelmingly responsible for cleaning the house, preparing meals, doing the dishes, and caring for children. If we take one task, doing the dishes, as an example to illustrate the extremity of women's primary responsibility, we find that only 2% of husbands were solely responsible for this chore, only 5% were primarily responsible, and fully 64% claimed that they never did the dishes. However, husbands were primarily responsible for maintaining the house and yard, and responsibility for bill paying was roughly evenly divided.

Four factors have been proposed to explain men's relatively low participation in housework (Coverman, in press). First, the new home economists' notion of efficient labor allocation; second, sociological exchange theory's emphasis on the resources each spouse brings to the relationship explaining their power to avoid housework; third, the sociological notion that sex role tastes or ideologies, which may vary by social class, determine the extent to which men do housework; and fourth, the "common sense" view that housework is allocated to men only when practical necessity requires it. We consider each of these in turn.

A. Household Efficiency and the New Home Economics

The new home economics applies microeconomic reasoning to household decision making. However, as noted above, although economists typically assume that each person is rationally maximizing his or her individual utility, most new home economists have assumed that families make decision to maximize the well-being of the family as a whole (Becker, 1981). Thus, since conflicts of interest are ignored or are considered to be overridden by altruism, efficiency in attaining the family's (agreed-upon) goals becomes the only consideration. (One exception is the work of economists Manser and Brown, 1979, who look at couples' bargaining over their individual preferences.) It is therefore presumed that work will be allocated on the basis of the tastes of family members, and their relative productivities at different tasks. Thus, for each spouse, there is a computation (at least implicitly) of the value to the family of the work they could do at home versus the wage the person could command in paid employment. As a consequence, specialization may develop because men typically command higher wage rates in the marketplace, whereas women are more productive at home (Becker, 1981: Chapter 2). So the decision that men will perform little housework occurs jointly with the decision that they will spend more hours in paid employment. This view predicts that the relative potential wage of husbands and wives will be an important predictor of their division of labor. In couples where the wife's wage is close to that of her husband, wives will be engaged in more employment and the husband in more housework than in situations where the husband's wage is much greater than his wife's.

To test this model, researchers have examined whether male housework really does respond to husband/wife relative wage rates. Both Farkas (1976) and Coverman (in press) explicitly tested this hypothesis; neither found much effect. It appears that, contrary to at least this prediction from economic theory, most men perform little housework, even when their wife's wage or potential wage is as high or higher than their own.

B. Exchange Theory, Power, and Housework

Sociological exchange theory employs a different logic to arrive at conclusions similar to those of the new home economics. Exchange theory (sometimes called resource or bargaining theory) posits that partner A will have more power than partner B if A brings more resources to the relationship (in comparison to what B would have absent the relation) than B brings to the relationship (in comparison to what A would have absent the relationship). While spouses may use their power altruistically, exchange theorists find it unrealistic to follow Becker (1981) in assuming that altruism always prevails within marriage. Thus, since much of housework is viewed as unpleasant (Berk and Berk, 1979), it is reasonable to suppose that the person with less power will do more of it, since they have more to lose from the dissolution of the relationship. Wages are a measure of resources that one provides to the relationship and withdraws if the relationship dissolves. Thus, their failure to predict husband's housework contradicts this theory's prediction, just as it contradicts that of the new home economics. While wages do increase women's marital power as we discussed in Chapter 3, it appears that women either do not, or cannot use this increased marital power to get men to do housework.

C. Gender Role Ideology and Class Subcultures

A third hypothesis is that male reluctance to engage in housework results from a traditional sex role ideology whose strength varies by social class. One way to test this is to see whether men giving more egalitarian responses to questions about sex roles do in fact perform more housework than other men. Coverman (in press) analyzed data in which men responded to the following questions: First, "how much do you agree or disagree that it is much better for everyone involved if the man earns the money and the woman takes care of the home and children?" Second, "how much do you agree or disagree that a mother who works outside the home can have just as good a relationship with her children as a mother who does not work?" The author fails to find the hypothesized negative relationship between traditionality of response and the amount of houswork men performed. Corroboration of this finding is provided by Geerken and Gove (1983) who find no relationship between men's housework and their score on a scale of sex role ideology constructed from a longer list of similar questions. However, the issue is still in some doubt since Stafford et al. (1977) and Perrucci *et al.* (1978) do find that men with less traditional gender-role ideology perform more housework.

Many authors have written about distinct social class subcultures that differ, among other things, in the traditionality of their sex roles. A variety of ethnographic studies have found that working class individuals hold more traditional sex role values and expectations than do members of the middle or upper classes (Elkin and Handel, 1978; Gans, 1962, 1967; Rainwater, 1970; Rubin, 1976). Similar notions have emerged from psychological and sociological studies of childhood socialization (Rabban, 1950; Kohn, 1969; Goode *et al.* 1971; Rubin, 1976). The thrust of these studies is that while all classes place greater emphasis upon employment-relevant achievement for boys, and emotional sensitivity for girls, this gender-based differentiation is more pronounced within the working class. Some dissenting research finds few class differences in gender socialization (Hartmann, 1981; Beer, 1983; Coverman, 1983). The dissenters stress that where gender roles are concerned, there may be greater class differences in attitudes than in actual behavior. Accordingly, this area continues to be one of some debate.

Studies investigating the link between social class and gender roles have measured social class in a variety of ways, including husbands' or family income, educational level, or the autonomy parents are able to exercise at the workplace. How might these aspects of class difference affect gender differentiation? One line of reasoning emphasizes education. The notion is that a higher educational level may promote a less traditional view of the world and greater questioning of role assignment based exclusively on sex. Another argument stresses the differential autonomy and mental effort involved in jobs at different levels within the class hierarchy. Working class jobs possess little autonomy and are subject to the supervisor's authority; they typically neither require nor permit complex judgments. Long periods in such a job lead to a relatively rigid rather than flexible view of the world (Kohn, 1969; Kohn *et al.*, 1983). Such a view is more likely to endorse rigid sex differentiation than a blurring of male and female roles. However, social class appears to be more strongly correlated with the traditionality of the gender roles parents teach their children than with the amount of housework adult males do.

D. Situational Factors and Men's Housework

A "common sense" view holds that most couples assume the wife is responsible for housework except where circumstances make this impractical. Thus an event, such as the birth of a child, which drastically increases ·the home work load, may lead to greater male participation in housework since now the woman simply cannot do it all, particularly if she is employed. This view is supported by research showing that the presence, number, or youth of children affects how much housework men do (Farkas, 1976; Berk and Berk, 1979; Geerken and Gove, 1983; Coverman, in press). The "situational nature" of this adjustment is illustrated by Berk and Berk's (1979) detailed analysis of which tasks are performed by each spouse at different times of day. They demonstrate that the principal adjustment after childbearing is that fathers take on some child care (usually the least onerous forms such as playing with children) in the evening after dinner when the wife is doing the dishes. Thus it appears that the adjustment is made because the husband is available, playing with children is relatively pleasant, and the wife can not do both the dishes and child care at once. Further support for this view comes from the finding that husbands increase their participation in housework slightly in response to an employed wife (Beer, 1983; Berk and Berk, 1979; Blood and Wolfe, 1960: 65; Coverman, in press; Duncan and Duncan, 1978: 207; Ericksen et al., 1979; Gecas, 1976; Geerken and Gove, 1983; Huber and Spitze, 1981: 180; Slocum and Nye, 1976: 92; Weingarten, 1978). (However, a minority of studies find husbands of employed women doing no more housework than other husbands. See Ferber, 1982; Szinovacz, 1977; Vanek, 1974; Walker and Woods, 1976.)

Closer examination of the housework done by men with employed wives provides further support for the "situational" view that the men are simply picking up the chores which become virtually impossible for their wives to perform. In this vein, Berk and Berk (1979) report that much of the elevation of the average amount of housework among men with employed wives comes from husbands of women who work an evening shift. These men often get dinner or do the dishes. However, they rarely undertake these chores if they have an employed wife who is home in the evening—even though she may work the same number of hours he does. Also, studies which have measured the actual hours of men's housework participation usually find only a slight difference in the hours put in by men with and without employed wives. Studies focusing on the tasks husbands are in charge of find that the main effect of the wife's employment is to increase the number of tasks men are *sometimes* in charge of. Again, this suggests that men perform housework mainly as a response to the unavailability of their wives.

E. From the 1950s to the 1980s

Let us try to provide an integrated view of these findings on the household division of labor, and summarize what they suggest about the home worlds of the 1950s and 1980s. In the 1950s, between one-quarter and one-third of married women were employed, and those who were generally had little career commitment. Thus, it was hardly surprising that women performed most of the housework. Today, over one-half of married women are employed, and many of these show strong career commitment. This has led to a large reduction in female housework, but only a small increase in male housework. What explains this resistance to change? It appears that neither the relative earning power nor the relative education of husbands and wives predicts husbands' housework, as considerations of efficiency or power might suggest. Further, while there may be some class subcultural differences in sex role attitudes, they seem not to be manifested in husbands' housework. Rather, husbands are induced to marginally increment their housework only by situational exigencies such as the wife's unavailability. Thus, it seems that women's housework role has been institutionalized to the point that it has virtually taken on a life of its own, unresponsive to household variations in potential efficiency, male power, or ideology. This illustrates the "lumpiness" of social change that we presented as a feature of the world of implicit contracts. Such contracts amalgamate packages of exchanges between individuals into indivisible "bundles" not fluidly responsive to changes occurring outside them. Yet this same "lumpiness" implies that if change does get rolling within this sphere, it might pick up speed dramatically. The only evidence of this so far is the greater housework performed by younger men (Coverman, in press) and the greater responsiveness of housework to other variables among younger men (Farkas, 1976). If these are cohort effects, they may herald the social change to come. But, for now, most employed wives are holding down two jobs.

VI. SUMMARY

This chapter has considered the reproduction of humans, the work of rearing them, and other work that goes on within the household. We considered the pecuniary and social-psychological benefits and costs to parents of having children, and how economic development has modified these benefits and costs to produce a decline in fertility. Focusing on the postwar United States, we examined both cohort and period explanations of the postwar baby boom. We concluded that what began as a response by the cohort born in the Depression to their relatively advantageous economic situation in the 1950s later became "contagious," elevating the fertility of all cohorts for a period. We presented the reasons for the steady decline in average number of children per woman in the United States since 1957. Here, as elsewhere in the world, fertility has declined even while male incomes have risen. This would be expected to increase fertility. However, this "income effect" has been offset by a "price effect" that increasingly predominates. As women's real wage rates have risen, more women have moved into paid employment. Once employed, women's wage rates are an "opportunity cost" of time spent at home raising children. As this opportunity cost has increased, fertility has declined. Also, increasing demands for an educated labor force have led parents to face a quality/quantity trade-off, leading to lowered fertility.

We suggest that discussion of parents' investments in the earnings-relevant human capital of their children should be embedded within a structural perspective. In this view, parents' structural (job) positions affect the investments they are able and inclined to make in their children via effects of their jobs on the income available for investment, on the price (often in opportunity costs of a mother's wages) of investments of parents' time, and on their tastes and behavior patterns. Between the 1950s and the 1980s a major change has occurred in investments in children. The high divorce rate coupled with fathers' minimal or absent child-support payments means that less income is available to children than previously.

Another aspect of child rearing is the reproduction of gender roles. We discussed the ways in which differential reinforcement and teaching of boys and girls, cognitive learning, and psychodynamic processes all contribute to reproducing gender differentiation across generations. We concluded that changes in the gender roles currently practiced by adults (such as shared participation in parenting), rather than changes in deliberate socialization practices, are most likely to lead to the adoption of more egalitarian gender roles by their children.

The household is the locus for other emotional and instrumental work as well. We examined the roots and consequences of females' specialization in emotional work, requiring empathic skills. Such work involves altruism, a concept used in Becker's new home economics. We question Becker's contention that the presence of one altruist gives families a single utility function. This would only be the case if the person specializing in altruism also had the most power; but, in fact, women often specialize in emotional work and altruism, while men have more power.

Finally, we considered housework. We noted that women are performing fewer hours of housework as their paid employment rises. Yet men have increased their housework participation only marginally. Men's participation in housework seems to be little affected by their earnings relative to their wives' or by their sex role ideologies. Rather, they increase their housework primarily in response to situational factors such as a wife who works through the dinner hour and simply cannot cook dinner. Thus, the resistance to changing men's participation in housework illustrates the "lumpiness" of social change typical of institutions characterized by implicit contracts.

NOTES

[1]Recently some sociologists have made a distinction between "structural" and "individual" perspectives (e.g., Beck et al., 1978; Kanter, 1977). This distinction is concerned with whether the proximate explanation of some outcomes lies in characteristics of the individual or, rather, in effects of the job position one holds (effects that are net of, or interact with, individual characteristics). This useful distinction has made some researchers forget that a demonstration that one's structural position affects one's own and one's children's individual characteristics is further evidence of the power of structural arrangements, not an abandonment of the structural view. Rather than choosing between structural and individual views, we see a need for an integrated view that comprehends the reciprocal relations between individual and positional characteristics in both individual and aggregate data.

[2]Other discussions of class differences in socialization are found in Gans, 1962: 244–247; Kerckhoff, 1972; and Gecas, 1979. Most disputes over class differences in orientations and behavior center around whether such differences have positional roots or are merely cultural in origin. Yet even the empirical reality of some commonly asserted class differences, such as present time orientation and deferred gratification, have been questioned (Gecas, 1979).

[3]Those few studies finding deleterious effects of day care are more apt to find them for boys than girls. Boys seem to be more sensitive than girls to a wide variety of environmental effects. One criticism of studies showing no difference between children cared for in day care centers and at home is that only good quality day care centers are examined in such studies. Further research is needed on how various characteristics of day care centers affect children. (On these points see Stewart and Fein's 1983 review.)

CONSUMPTION, SAVINGS, AND RETIREMENT

I. INTRODUCTION

Households are the decision-making unit for much of the consumption and saving which occurs within the economy. This chapter focuses on the life cycle trajectory of these outcomes. We relate these to the earnings of household members. Annual earnings in the long run can be combined in a kind of averaging to estimate the "permanent income" of the household, and there is evidence that households respond to their knowledge of this permanent income by borrowing and saving in any particular year so as to even out their consumption across years with unusually low or high earnings. However, the resulting "smoothing" of consumption is far from perfect, and we examine how the amount and timing of childbearing and household composition change affect consumption and savings. This discussion provides a link between social demography and macroeconomic performance.

We also examine retirement, when individuals are primarily engaged in consuming the income from previous saving, rather than investing to increase future earnings. Attention is given to the great improvements in the economic well-being of the elderly which occurred betwen 1950 and 1980. Finally, we consider how the baby boom and bust cohorts have fared economically in their preretirement life cycle stages, and the issues facing the social security and private pension systems as these cohorts move toward retirement.

II. CONSUMPTION AND SAVING

A. Permanent Income and the Life Cycle

We begin with some definitions. Income refers to the stream of money received in a particular time period. One type of income is earnings, which refers to the salary or wages from a job or net receipts from self-employment.

By contrast, unearned income includes interest on savings accounts, dividends, and other returns on investment. Savings are the positive difference between current income and current consumption. Dissaving is a negative difference, representing either a spending of savings or borrowing. Assets are either financial holdings arising from savings, or durable goods that have been purchased. Thus, earned and unearned income, saving, and dissaving are flows over time; assets are stocks at any one point in time.

When a household is formed (through a youth leaving the parental household to live alone, a marriage, a divorce, or the beginning of some other cohabitation) members have some idea of the income trajectory they can expect over the remainder of their life cycle. Their ability to make better than random predictions about this trajectory stems from several factors: that earnings are higher for those with more education and training, that inheritances can be anticipated, and that one can observe the typical wage trajectory of the job one holds or is training for. Thus, personal characteristics, investment in oneself, and the place one has achieved or is achieving within the structural positions of the economy permit an approximate calculation of one's permanent income.

The life-cycle permanent income hypothesis (Friedman, 1957; Brumberg and Modigliani, 1962; Mayer, 1972) suggests that individuals strive to keep levels of year-to-year consumption relatively constant. To this end they save money during years of unusually good earnings so as to use these funds to maintain a constant standard of living during years of poor earnings. In its idealized form, never actually achieved in real life, this constant standard of living, expressed in real terms (i.e., independent of inflation) is the "permanent income" one could identically consume every year given one's lifetime earnings (see Barro, 1984: 93). To compute this, one would need to anticipate the household's earnings in each future year, which would in turn require assumptions about schooling, childbearing, household composition change, and other variables that cannot always be anticipated. Yet to the extent that individuals are able to make rough predictions about such things, the "consumption smoothing" of the hypothesis provides a model of how households may seek to behave.

To what extent is this hypothesis consistent with the evidence? It does help explain why annual fluctuations in national consumption are smaller than annual fluctuations in national income. In this regard, the permanent income hypothesis has helped provide theoretical underpinnings for the aggregate consumption function, an important building block of macroeconomics. Further, the theory predicts a higher propensity to consume (percentage consumed rather than saved) out of permanent than out of transitory income. That is, when your income rises in a permanent manner (perhaps because you enter a better paying profession) a higher percentage will be consumed than when it is only a transitory gain (e.g., a one-time windfall from a lottery). Empirical evidence generally supports these predictions (Barro, 1984: 94–95).

Yet, the permanent income hypothesis cannot tell the whole story.This is partly because national economic conditions and individual life events are inherently difficult to predict. It is also because credit markets are "imperfect," and may not permit individuals to borrow enough to fully invest in themselves or to fully smooth out their consumption stream. Thus, low-income people may be unable to finance the full extent of human capital investment that might be theoretically justified by their potential future earnings, and medical students and others may be unable to borrow sufficiently to maintain a standard of living early in life that is commensurate with what they will have later. (Obviously, risk is an important factor here, and there is an interesting literature dealing with it; see, for example, Arrow, 1971.) Recent studies show that changes in the demography of the household, such as fertility, divorce, or children leaving home, are major determinants of changes in families' income, consumption, and savings. It is to this that we now turn.

B. Childbearing, Savings, and Consumption

Demographers have long suspected that population change—in particular, fertility trends—are important determinants of the aggregate level of economic activity (Coale and Hoover, 1958; Easterlin, 1968; Lindert, 1978; Simon, 1977; Smith and Ward, 1980). Fertility will affect the economy because the number and timing of births helps determine the time allocation of spouses, particularly whether women are employed, as well as needed and desired patterns of consumption, saving, and asset accumulation. Of course, the fertility rate also determines the number of workers and consumers in the next generation, a potentially important determinant of economic functioning at that time.

One of the principal ways that childbearing affects family income and consumption is by shifting the mother's time away from paid employment and toward the work of child rearing in the home. However, this effect is weaker today than in the 1950s, since the employment rate of mothers in the United States (in particular, of mothers with young children) is at an all-time high. Family consumption patterns are also affected. There are direct expenditures on the child's food, living space, clothing, medical care, education, and so on. However, an additional effect of childbearing is the shift toward goods which are complementary with children and time in the household. Thus, expenditures on restaurant meals, movies, and expensive vacations may decline, while expenditures on family game rooms, cable television, and family sports and camping equipment increase.

Since both income and consumption patterns are affected by childbearing, the net effect on saving and asset accumulation is an empirical question, one which has been addressed by Smith and Ward (1980). They find that the largest effects of fertility on household financial status occur when children are born early in marriage. In this case, female earnings are often dramatically reduced when male earnings have yet to rise substantially, and family acquisition of key durable goods (such as a house, car, and appliances) has just begun. Families typically adjust to their reduced income by lowering their consumption, using up savings, and taking on increased debt. In this way they are able to continue to accumulate key durable goods. A net result is dissaving, since decreased consumption is usually insufficient to fully offset decreased earnings.

Very different results occur when children are born later in marriage. In this case, the family has already acquired many of the basic durable goods, and the amount by which female earnings are reduced also tends to be lower. This is probably because when children are born later the mother is better established in her job by the time of birth. Thus, the opportunity cost of each month or year spent at home with the new baby is higher for these women. They are also more apt to have developed a taste for employment. For these and other reasons, such women return to paid employment more rapidly after the first birth (Shapiro and Mott, 1979; McLaughlin, 1982). The combination of a higher average income, a smaller reduction in income, and more durable goods already acquired makes the household financial adjustment much easier. It is largely accomplished through reduced consumption, and there is typically no dissaving; in fact, a slight increase in family savings usually occurs after the birth (Smith and Ward, 1980: 253–256).

These findings have a number of implications. First, they remind us of the important relationship between family formation and rates of saving and investment. This goes beyond financial asset accumulation to include human capital investment. To take one example, the negative economic consequences for both mother and children of out-of-wedlock teenage childbearing, particularly among young, poor, urban women, are becoming increasingly well known (Card and Wise, 1978; Freedman and Thornton, 1979; Hofferth and Moore, 1979; Millman and Hendershot, 1980; Farkas and Olsen, 1983; Hogan et al., 1984; Moore et al., 1984).

Second, these results are consistent with the findings from a 15-year study of a representative sample of 5000 American families. This study, conducted at the University of Michigan, shows that changes in household composition rival unemployment as one of the two most important determinants of household income change (Duncan, 1984). The most frequent such event is the breakup of a marriage or other cohabitational arrangement. In this case, one household becomes two, usually with little transfer of income between the two after an initial property settlement. Since men usually have higher earnings, while women usually keep the children, the effects of the breakup on per capita household income are typically negative for women and children but positive for men (Hill, 1983; Duncan, 1984).

Finally, these results add another dimension to the study of change between the 1950s and the 1980s. The pattern of early marriage and childbearing characteristic of the baby boom years is a sharp contrast with the current baby bust in its implications for households' finances. Thus, because of delayed childbearing, couples currently in their twenties and thirties are today faring much better financially than they otherwise would have fared. Below, we continue our brief tour through the life-cycle stages by examining two important successors to childbearing and childraising—the empty-nest and retirement.

III. AGING AND RETIREMENT

A. The Empty Nest

The "empty nest" refers to the period immediately after the children have left home; it typically occurs somewhere between the ages of forty and sixty. Most couples now own (are paying off a mortgage on) a home, and financial assets are larger than previously. As the children leave, couples—the wife, in particular—gain increased leisure. For both men and women, marital and life satisfaction rise at this stage (Burr, 1970; Rollins and Feldman, 1970; Rollins and Cannon, 1974; Glenn, 1975; Lowenthal et al., 1975; Maas and Kuypers, 1975; Spanier et al., 1975: Lowenthal and Weiss, 1976; Fuchs, 1977; Sales, 1977; Rubin, 1979; Schram, 1979). This may be simply a consequence of the end of the rigors of child rearing. However, another explanation of the fact that this period and the pre-child period of marriage show the highest levels of satisfaction is that these are also the period of lowest gender role differentiation. The greater similarity of roles (Simpson and England, 1981) may combine with the increased free time to yield increased well-being during these life-cycle stages.

Of course, there may also be negatives associated with the empty-nest phase. This is the period where health problems and the coming financial needs of retirement first appear as serious issues on many households' horizons. Further, with today's higher divorce rates, a lower percentage of first marriages reach this point intact, and of all marriages which do so, fewer continue intact through this period. Finally, there has long been a belief that American women, particularly full-time homemakers, experience a crisis of "role loss" when children leave the home (Bart, 1969). However, although many homemakers have defined themselves primarily in terms of this nurturing role (Rubin, 1979), and our culture depreciates women more than men as they age (Sontag, 1972; England et al., 1981), the evidence simply does not support the notion that most women experience more than a short transitional unhappiness when the nest empties. On the contrary, there is substantial evidence that many women experience relief, increased self-confidence, the exhilaration of freedom to pursue jobs or hobbies more fully, and enhanced enjoyment of sexuality (Neugarten, 1968, 1970, 1974; Neugarten and Datan, 1974; Lowenthal et al., 1975: 74; Rubin, 1979).

For men, the empty-nest coincides with a time when some realize that they will fall short of their early career aspirations (Vaillant, 1977), feel threatened by their wife's new employment interests and the associated decrease in her nurturant activities (Rubin, 1979), and feel a pull toward extramarital sexual affairs (Johnson, 1970). Yet, although these strains may exist, the evidence on increased marital satisfaction during the empty-nest period suggests that for men also, any increased difficulties are more than compensated for by the increased pleasures of the period.

A number of changes in demographic and related behavior between the 1950s and 1980s have affected the way individuals experience the empty-nest period. The increased divorce rate means that fewer couples have their original marriage intact when their children leave home. For men, this means that many have gone through an empty-nest stage at the time of divorce, often followed by remarriage and a reconstituted household, which may include newly conceived children and/or children by the new wife's previous marriage. This newly reconstituted household will then itself undergo an empty-nest phase. For women, who usually have custody of their children and have a somewhat lower probability of remarriage than men, this means either entering the empty-nest phase without a husband or finding a new husband who is willing to live with and help support the children.

The recent rise in female employment also affects the way women and men experience the empty-nest phase. This occurs primarily because fewer women now remain out of the labor force through their children's teenage years, so that the trauma of the full-time homemaker losing the organizing principle of her day occurs even less often than it did in the 1950s.

Finally, declining mortality has increased the expected duration of life after the children leave home. However, as this period has lengthened at the older end, another recent trend has been operating to shorten it from the younger end. This is the tendency toward later age at marriage, and delayed childbearing within marriage. If this is not entirely offset by the trend toward smaller family size, couples may typically enter the empty-nest stage at a later age in the future.

B. Retirement and Mortality

The proportion of men who retire prior to age 65 has increased greatly in the postwar period. Thus, between 1950 and 1980, the labor force participation rate of males over the age of 65 declined from 42 to 19% (Flanagan et al., 1984: 134). For men aged 55 to 65, the decline was from 89 to 73%. Yet, at the same time, the labor force participation of women in this age group increased from 25 to 40% (Soldo, 1980: 20). We are thus witnessing a convergence, in which male and female employment rates come to resemble one another during the empty-nest phase, and both sexes retire by age 65 or younger.

The increase in early retirement came about largely because of the existence and increased generosity of the Social Security program. However, growth in national income and wealth has also contributed to this trend via the increased holding of non-Social Security wealth. Among the aged, this is largely due to the value of their home equity; such equity accounts for fully 75% of the wealth of the aged (Merrill, 1984). Despite an income decline of one-third to one-half at the time of retirement (Soldo, 1980: 21), Social Security plus the flow of income from assets is sufficient for most couples to retire at or before age 65. Today, the income of the population aged 65 and over breaks down as follows: 39% from Social Security, 7% from other publicly funded pensions, 7% from private pensions, 23% from earnings, 18% from income on assets, and 4% from public assistance. By comparison with the early 1960s, these income shares show increases in Social Security, private pensions, and income from assets, and decreases in earned income and public assistance (Russell, 1982: 145).

Retirement is often accompanied by a decrease in the sex differentiation of couples' roles, although some male dominance and female specialization in household work certainly persists (Lowenthal et al., 1975; McGee and Wells, 1978). Neugarten (1968:140) concludes that as they age, "men seem to become more receptive to affiliative and nurturant promptings; women, more responsive toward and less guilty about aggressive and egocentric impulses." Retirement is often followed by a sense of emotional loss (rather like unemployment at younger ages, although less extreme (Havighurst et al., 1969). Yet individuals generally anticipate that the costs outweigh the benefits. Certainly many have chosen early retirement since Social Security regulations weakened the financial penalty for retirement at age 62 rather than 65.

The fact that early retirement has been affordable to so many is all the more remarkable when we consider that total years retired per person have increased as mortality among the elderly has declined. Among males, life expectancy at birth has increased from 46 years for those born in 1900, to 66 and 70, respectively, estimated for those born in 1950 and 1978. For women the comparable life expectancies were 48, 71, and 77 (Soldo, 1980: 16). The leading causes of death have shifted from communicable, infectious diseases to chronic diseases; heart disease, cancer, and stroke now account for two-thirds of all deaths (Soldo, 1980: 15).

One consequence of the fact that women outlive men is that women can expect to spend a period of widowhood. This period averages even longer than dictated by sex differences in mortality alone, since husbands are generally older than their wives, and women who are widowed are much less likely to remarry than widowers, who often marry younger women (Soldo, 1980: 25). In 1978, only 46% of women, but 78% of men over 65 had a present, living spouse. For those 75 years and older, the contrast is even greater; 68% of men but 22% of women were living with a spouse (Soldo, 1980: 25). Women are more apt than men to live in institutions such as nursing homes, since men are usually survived by their wives who take care of them if they have an illness before death. Nonetheless, only 9% of the elderly over 75 were institutionalized in 1976 (Soldo, 1980: 26).

Although well-being of various sorts may decline in old age, the trend in the status of the elderly presents quite a positive view. In fact, Preston (1984) shows that the last 25 years have seen a dramatic improvement in the economic status of the elderly. For example, the percentage of the elderly living below the government poverty line has declined dramatically, particularly since 1970 (Russell, 1982: 145). In 1970, even after considerable improvements in the economic status of the elderly, the incidence of poverty in this age group still was double the national average. Yet by 1982 it had fallen below the national average. This improvement relative to average incomes of the rest of the population is even more dramatic if in-kind benefits (mainly Medicare for the elderly) are included in the calculation. Furthermore, although the elderly have higher suicide rates than those in the preretirement ages, these rates have declined since 1960, while those for younger age groups increased.

These increases in well-being among the elderly have received a strong impetus from the expansion of Social Security, Medicare, and, to a lesser extent, private pensions. Yet demographic factors may place the funding of these programs in some jeopardy over the next 50 years. We consider these issues below.

IV. THE CONSEQUENCES OF DEMOGRAPHIC CHANGE

A. Financing Social Security and Private Pensions

The 1970s were a period of great ferment in the discussion and implementation of public policy toward the provision of retirement income. The most widely discussed issue was the possible future insolvency of the Social Security system, but issues of private pensions and Medicare also raised concerns.

Social Security payments to retirees and their survivors (OASI) have, since 1950, been financed on a pay-as-you-go basis, with a tax on the earnings of all employed workers funding payments to current retirees. Thus, each generation pays for the retirement of the previous one. In the mid-1970s, questions arose concerning the future solvency of the system. (For a review of the history of Social Security policy and debates see Harpham, 1984.) The prospect of insolvency can be traced to several sources. First, payment levels in real dollars and as a proportion of full wage replacement increased dramatically in the 1950s and 1960s. Since 1972, payments have been tied to the Consumer Price Index, yielding automatic cost-of-living increases. A technical error in the 1972 amendments, not corrected until 1977, led to double indexing for those who retired during that 5-year period (Harpham, 1984:18). The squeeze of the 1970s and early 1980s occurred because high unemployment and the lack of wage growth limited revenues, while high inflation and declines in mortality among the elderly increased obligated payments. This threat to solvency was dealt with primarily by increasing the Social Security tax rate on current workers, and raising the ceiling above which earnings are free from this tax. Since the crisis was largely due to a recessionary economy (affecting revenues negatively) combined with high inflation (affecting committed payments positively), it could well reoccur in the future. However, a more dramatic crisis threatens the solvency of the system; its roots are in the demographic trends of baby boom and bust.

Since Social Security has evolved into a system in which each generation supports the retirement of the previous one, the relative size of consecutive cohorts is crucial to determining how burdensome Social Security taxes will be for the currently employed. To begin with, the more than century-long fertility decline, combined with decreasing mortality among the elderly, has produced an ever increasing ratio of elderly to working age adults. This ratio cannot level off until both fertility and mortality cease declining. And although the rate of decline in both fertility and mortality may slow, both are likely to continue to decline throughout the century.

However, the even greater problem for Social Security solvency is the added effect of the baby boom cohort's retirement, which will begin about 2010. Since fertility rose so greatly and then declined so precipitously between 1946 and 1965, the baby boom and baby bust cohorts are more dramatically different in size than would have been the case had fertility continued its slow decline throughout the century without the baby boom. Thus a "crunch" of crisis proportions will hit the Social Security system about 2010, and continue for several decades.

Assuming that something like the current system will remain in place, there are only a limited number of options for keeping it solvent. Since the 1977 amendments, Social Security has been committed to holding constant both the ratio of benefits to wages in the period prior to retirement, and the purchasing power of one's benefit level after retirement. Using a simulation model which explicitly accounts for the relationship between demographic and economic variables, Auerbach and Kotlikoff (1984:259) estimate that the payroll tax must be raised to about 25% of earnings to hold wage replacement levels and the inflation adjustment provisions in place. But to raise the tax on one cohort while keeping the benefit and inflation formulas constant is to lower the rate of return on collected taxes for that cohort (Russell, 1982: Chapter 6). Yet trustees of the Social Security program estimate that even if taxes are raised as often as necessary to keep benefit and inflation formulas in place, positive (albeit declining) rates of return to the social security tax will be experienced by cohorts entering the labor force through the year 2000 (Russell, 1982: 157–159). Alternatively, if only currently scheduled tax changes occur, Auerbach and Kotlikoff (1984) estimate that earnings replacement rates will have to be cut by 30 to 40%. Other possible changes include measures to encourage employment, such as raising the age at which retirement benefits first become available, taxing benefits for those with earnings above a certain level, or making Social Security a means-tested program to provide income only for those elderly with low incomes in the absence of the payments. All of these options will undoubtedly be debated in the years before the baby boom cohort retires.

On the positive side, Auerbach and Kotlikoff (1984) list four factors which may ameliorate the fiscal "crunch" : (1) Despite increased social security tax rates, per capita economic welfare may rise as a consequence of the decrease in the number of economically dependent children in the economy. (2) For the same reason, the economy's ability to absorb the needed increases in social security taxes may be greater than in previous times. That is, if per capita expenditures on programs for children are held constant, aggregate expenditures for these programs can be reduced with no reduction in per capita welfare. In fact, Bouvier (1980: 30–31) points out that the dependency ratio (the ratio of children and elderly to the working age population) will probably be no higher in 2020 than it is in 1980 under assumptions of either 1.7 or 2.0 births per woman. (3) As employed cohorts become smaller, making labor relatively scarce, the increased captial/labor ratio in the economy may lead to higher real wages, which would sustain a higher level of taxation (although they also dictate higher payment levels via the formula). (4) Smaller family sizes may permit households to accumulate greater private savings before retirement, if macroeconomic conditions do not deteriorate.

Problems parallel to those of the Social Security system also exist within the publicly funded Medicare and Medicaid programs. The federal Medicare program was created in 1965 to help the aged pay for medical expenses. This program involves hospital insurance, supported by a payroll tax on current workers, and supplementary medical insurance, financed by general federal tax revenues and premiums paid by enrollees. Both parts are subject to various deductible and copayment provisions. By the late 1970s about 95% of the elderly were covered by the two sides of the program (Russell, 1982: 132–133). However, Medicare will not pay the cost of nursing home care. Thus, the aged in need of such care must wait until their incomes and savings are sufficiently low to qualify for (means-tested) Medicaid. (This program, like AFDC, is funded partly by the federal government and partly by the states, with administrative rules set by the states.) Thus, in 1978, Medicaid paid about 40% of the nursing home expenses of the elderly (Fisher, 1980). Through Medicare and Medicaid combined, the federal and state governments paid for about 60% of the medical expenses of the aged in the late 1970s (Fisher, 1980). However, with recent attempts to cut federal expenditures, these shares may begin to decline (Russell, 1982). Taken together, federal and state expenditures on Medicare and Medicaid went from 6% of the gross national product in 1965 to 9.4% in 1980 (Russell, 1982: 134).

The impact of demographic change on the financing of medical care for the elderly is similar to its impact on financing Social Security. This similarity results from the fact that medical care is also primarily financed on a pay-as-you-go basis, in which taxes on current workers pay for the medical care of the currently retired. Thus, the relative size of the employed and retired cohorts is once again a key issue in determining the difficulty of financing the system. As with Social Security, both declining fertility and mortality dictate that each successive cohort is smaller than the last, with the most precipitous decline occurring between the baby boom cohort and the one following it. There is an analog to the inflation adjustment in the Social Security system that makes the system of financing medical care perhaps even more of a time bomb than Social Security. Medicare does not provide a specified amount of cash to the elderly for use in buying medical care.

Rather, it provides whatever medical care is needed, subject to various deductible and copayment provisions. Thus, since the cost of medical care has risen much more rapidly than the cost of living in general, the per capita cost of the program has mushroomed. The resulting policy debate has focused on constraining the amount doctors and hospitals are permitted to charge for particular services or diagnoses, increasing the share of fees for service or insurance the elderly must pay themselves, or moving to a national health insurance system. The political strength of the American Medical Association has prevented the European brand of socialized medicine from being seriously considered.

Private pensions are another source of retirement income. Among 45 to 54 year olds employed in 1979, 72% of men and 48% of women were covered by such a pension (Russell, 1982:146, note 31). Pension coverage is concentrated among unionized and government workers, and professional and managerial employees. In general, high-wage workers also benefit from more generous pension programs. The Employee Retirement and Income Security Act (ERISA) of 1974 was passed to regulate private pensions. Its principal provisions were designed to liberalize vesting rules, establish requirements for how fully pension plans must be funded (what proportion of obligated funds must be on hand), and create a governmentally chartered body to insure workers against pension plan bankruptcy. Pensions and their vesting provisions are now an important feature of the implicit (and partially explicit) contracts between employer and employee discussed in Chapter 6. ERISA seems not to have increased or decreased the proportion of the labor force covered by pensions, but it has increased the proportion who are vested (Rogers, 1980). ("Vested" means that one has rights to some proportion of one's pension regardless of whether one continues to work for that employer.)

Vesting provisions have been shown to be a significant determinant of employee turnover rates, and the fact that ERISA forced less stringent vesting rules may have slightly increased employee turnover in the aggregate (Wolf and Levy, 1984). However, this is not the primary reason for public concern over private pensions. Rather, concern arises because some large pension plans in declining industries may be seriously underfunded. This can occur because, despite government regulation, employers have considerable leeway in determining the extent to which their system is funded. They often use this discretion to shift contributions to the retirement plan across years in a way that maximizes their tax advantage, and to minimize contributions when the firm is in hard times. If there is considerable underfunding of private pension plans in declining industries, ERISA may lead to a considerable payment burden being shifted to the federal treasury. Thus, Social

Security, Medicare, and ERISA-induced payments may be in head-to-head competition for funding within future federal budgets.

Social Security, with its universal coverage and its compromise between an insurance and a needs-based program, has been the most popular program of the welfare state. This popularity is hardly surprising, since currently retired individuals have experienced a higher return on their collected taxes than is likely to ever occur again. Further, until quite recently, the taxation levels required to provide this cohort-specific windfall were relatively moderate. As demographic and economic forces make financing Social Security, medical programs, and even private pensions more difficult, this consensus may break down, and the conflicting interest of competing age groups may define the cleavages in the ensuing debate. Gender may also become salient, since females constituted 60% of those over 65 in 1980, and this sex imbalance is expected to remain constant or increase in the years ahead (Russell, 1982: 130). [This is a relatively recent development; until 1940, men were in the majority among the elderly (Russell, 1982: 130), presumably because of more deaths among women in childbirth.] For example, when President Reagan proposed reducing the minimum benefit under Social Security, a benefit going primarily to women who had few years of employment experience and do not have access to survivors' benefits of a husband, the women's movement was as active as elderly groups in opposing the cut.

B. The Baby Boom Generation

As the oldest of those born in the baby boom approach their fortieth year, it is interesting to ask how this generation is faring economically in comparison with the smaller cohort preceding it. In general, the economic fate of the baby boom cohort seems to have been affected more strongly by the macroeconomic and structural conditions of the periods during which they spent each portion of their life cycle than by their cohort size (Russell, 1982). In short, period effects have predominated over cohort effects.

Despite their great numbers, the baby boom cohorts enjoyed unprecedented advantages as children. School expenditures per pupil rose during the postwar period in which they were educated. Their average educational attainment is the highest of any cohort to date. Indeed, it is higher than the cohort following them (Preston, 1984).

There has been much speculation about the economic disadvantage of membership in an unusually large cohort. This follows in a straightforward fashion from the logic of supply and demand. For example, as a large cohort enters the labor force, too many inexperienced workers may be chasing too few jobs. Youth unemployment rates were very high in the 1960s and 1970s when the baby boom cohort entered the labor market, but the evidence is inconclusive on whether these rates can be attributed to cohort size (Russell, 1982). As for wages, males in the baby boom cohort did suffer some losses due to their cohort size, but there is a debate over whether these pure "cohort effects" on wages were relatively shortlived (Welch, 1979; Berger, 1985). Welch points out that one would expect a depressing effect of cohort size on wages to be largest for jobs requiring higher levels of training and skill, since in these jobs the young, entering workers are poor substitutes for older workers with more experience, so the young wokers must absorb the entire wage loss associated with the excess supply. By comparison, young unskilled workers may be close substitutes for older unskilled workers, so that in unskilled jobs older workers will absorb some of the wage losses caused by the entry of a large cohort. Indeed, this is what happened in the early 1970s, as relative wages for younger workers declined, with the strongest declines occurring among college graduates (Welch, 1979).

Much of the economic fate of the baby boom cohort has been determined by period specific economic conditions which affected other workers in a similar manner. Thus, the baby boom cohort has been adversely affected by the economic stagnation of the 1970s and early 1980s. Because of this, real earnings of cohorts of adults that entered the labor force during the 1970s did not grow as the earnings of earlier cohorts had. Thus, the baby boom members have not had as steep wage trajectories as the cohorts before them. Yet this is not a cohort effect, as evidenced by the fact that since 1970 real earnings have been stagnant for every age group (Russell, 1982; Levy and Michel, 1985; and see Table 7.2, Chapter 7).

The skyrocketing price of houses during the 1970s is often pointed to as evidence of the disadvantages faced by the baby boom generation. In fact, however, the older members of the baby boom generation faced a more favorable climate for housing purchases than had prevailed earlier. However, those who failed to purchase a house prior to 1980 (mainly the younger baby-boomers) were seriously disadvantaged. Here again, period effects have been much more important than cohort size. The notion that the baby boom members have been disadvantaged vis-à-vis housing follows from the observation that housing prices rose considerably faster than other prices or average family income during the 1970s, when the early baby boomers were reaching their mid-20s. However, the actual financial burden of owning a home rose less than most other prices during the 1970s, but one needs to look at more than simple indexes to see this (Hendershott, 1980; Downs and Giliberto, 1981). The "real" cost of housing rose more slowly than is first apparent due to three factors—fixed-rate mortgages, the favorable tax treatment accorded homeowners, and the investment aspects of homeowning. In periods of strong inflation, such as the 1970s, there is a great advantage in fixed-rate mortgages which provide protection from escalating interest rates even as the fixed payment becomes easier to meet as incomes rise in line with inflation. Because owners can deduct mortgage interest and property taxes from their taxable income, the greater the marginal tax rate, the greater the tax advantages of ownership. Thus, as the rising nominal incomes of the 1970s combined with progressive income tax rates push wage earners into higher tax brackets, home ownership became increasingly attractive. Also, rising housing prices keep some from buying, but also induce others to buy, since home ownership becomes a good investment (a form of savings) as well as consumption. For these reasons, among others, home ownership rates increased throughout the 1970s (Russell, 1982: 115–119). However, the decline of real housing prices relative to other prices reversed abruptly in 1979 and 1980, when skyrocketing interests rates outstripped the various tax and investment advantages of homeownership, and the cost of homeownership began to rise faster than other prices. Thus, younger members of the baby boom generation may face worse housing prospects than older members. Yet Russell (1982) concludes that "any changes that occur are less likely to arise from the effect of these cohorts on the housing market than from the future course of prices and interest rates, and their interaction with the tax code." In short, period effects seem more decisive than cohort size for the economic well-being of those born during the baby boom.

One case where the effects of cohort size may be decisive is with regard to the economic fate of the baby boom members during their retirement. The size of these cohorts will so strain the Social Security and Medicare systems as to substantially lower the rate of return to the Social Security taxes they will have paid. Yet, if the baby bust generation bears the brunt of paying for the retirement of the baby boomers, its rates of return to Social Security taxes may be even lower. It is still too early to see which political compromises will emerge from the scramble to finance the retirement of the baby boomers. The fact that many of the decisions will be made within the arena of democratic politics, rather than within the private sector, suggests that the relatively large size of the baby boom voting block may be of some advantage.

V. SUMMARY

This chapter has sought to round out the discussion of household behavior by focusing on consumption, financial decision making, and the later life-cycle stages. We have considered the permanent-income hypothesis, an explanation of life-cycle behavior in which households engage in consumption consistent with their long-range income prospects, saving and borrowing across time periods so as to maintain a relatively constant standard of living. This notion complements our previous discussion of the implicit contract between husband and wife. This contract is intertemporal and involves consumption, saving, and standard-of-living decisions, as well as the earnings, division of labor, and fertility decisions discussed in earlier chapters. Taken together, these outcomes provide the basis on which each individual assesses the benefits and costs of the current partnership.

We have also examined the financial implications of childbearing early in marriage, the gains in marital satisfaction often accompanying the empty-nest phase, and the trend toward early retirement. Finally, we considered the consequences of demographic trends for the solvency of the Social Security system, and the fate of the baby boom and bust cohorts thus far in their life cycles.

Throughout this portion of the book, we have stressed a view of marriage or other cohabitational arrangements as long-term, implicit contracts, with pecuniary and nonpecuniary benefits and costs derived in part from relationship-specific investment. The other important relationship possessing these attributes is employment, the subject of the following portion of the book.

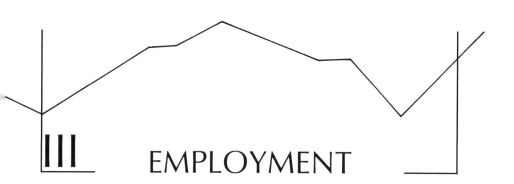

III EMPLOYMENT

Men, and an ever increasing proportion of women, spend much of their adult lives in paid employment. Many authors contrast employment with the household or family sector by referring to paid employment as "work" or the "market sector." In our view, however, behavior in this sector should not be differentiated too sharply from that of the household sector. In particular, both involve productive *work* carried out within an implicit contract framework, a contract arrived at after search within a *market*. Both spheres also involve a set of structural positions.

Thus, we emphasize the parallels between household and employment relationships. We do not dispute the fact that relationships within families involve more love, altruism, and personal commitment, and are of longer duration than relationships between employers and employees. Yet there is sufficient narrowly self-interested behavior in the search for and bargaining within household relationships, and sufficient relationship-specific investment and honoring of implicit contracts within the employment relationship, to create instructive parallels between the two spheres. These parallels make some of the same concepts useful in studying household and employment relationships. Thus, we continue to focus on search within markets, implicit contracts, the relationship between individual behavior and socioeconomic structures, and sex differentiation. Our discussion of employment also continues our focus on the reciprocal causal links between households and employment, particularly as they involve gender roles and their change.

This section has two objectives. First, in Chapter 6, we explore the properties of the employment relationship. Second, in Chapter 7, we examine differences between male and female employment experiences, and changes in these differences between the 1950s and the 1980s. Both chapters draw from sociology and economics to provide an integrated view of employment and gender.

THE EMPLOYMENT
RELATIONSHIP

6

I. INTRODUCTION

This chapter analyzes the relationship between employers and employees. We begin with the process of search, and then move on to consider several types of employment relationship parallel to those used to discuss marital matches in Chapter 3—spot markets, contingent-claims contracts, and implicit contracts. We argue that, among the three types of relationship, the view of employment as an implicit contract is the most accurate, and such contracts often involve internal labor markets. Following this, we turn to the contributions of sociology, focusing on how individuals are allocated to positions, and how rewards attach to these positions. Central ideas here are the notions of feedback from employment to household behavior, and the segmentation of labor markets and the economy. Throughout the chapter we focus alternatively on aspects of employment as viewed by both sociologists and economists, but we conclude by sketching a single integrated treatment incorporating features of each disciplinary perspective.

II. THE SEARCH FOR JOBS AND EMPLOYEES

A. The Supply Side of Search

Individuals search until an acceptable job is found. The reason there is a period of search is that finding a job involves gathering information about which employers are hiring at what wage rates in the job(s) for which one qualifies. Search is sometimes engaged in by those already holding jobs, to keep abreast of job opportunities and going wages. Thus, the potential for turnover is always present in the employment relationship, and is likely to be on the minds of both employee and employer. Stigler (1961) pioneered thinking on the central role played by the information-gathering of job search, and this view has provided an important modification to the neoclassical model of how labor markets function.

The information-gathering of search can be accomplished in several ways. According to one recent survey, the share of searchers using various methods was as follows: 16% using tips from friends and relatives, 78% going to an establishment where they hoped an opening existed, 24% going to state employment agencies, 6% going to private agencies, and 35% responding to newspaper advertisements (U.S. Department of Labor, 1983a). (Percentages do not add to 100 because some searchers used more than one method.)

Of course, finding and accepting a job often involves more than ascertaining the wage, making application, and showing up for work. Searchers may also consider nonpecuniary features of jobs as well as fringe benefits, mobility prospects, and the probable wage trajectory before agreeing to the employment relationship. Employment typically *is* a relationship that will endure for at least some time period. It is this intertemporality which helps to make search important and expensive, and job-taking a more than casual event. Just as one shops more carefully for a home than for a pound of hamburger, and just as the interest rates individuals are currently paying on their home mortgages reflect past market conditions as much as current conditions, so too with jobs. Individuals search for jobs because they know that the ensuing employment is likely to last some time, and their current employment situation reflects past as well as current market conditions.

The fact that most jobs are found only after at least some search explains the existence of what economists call "frictional" unemployment (Flanagan et al., 1984: 584–85; Okun, 1981). At any one time there will be some people searching for a job, even if there are enough jobs to go around in the economy. During the period of search, individuals are counted as unemployed (unless they are searching while holding another job). The length of time an individual will stay unemployed is related to his or her "reservation wage," the minimum wage that will be accepted. Of course "wage" must be understood to summarize all aspects of the job, not just take-home pay. Once this "wage" is understood to include fringe benefits, working conditions, opportunities for advancement, and so on, we see that the notion of a reservation wage is just the economist's shorthand for "acceptable job." Our discussion in Chapter 3 applied a similar notion to the search for a spouse or other cohabitational partner.

Searchers keep on looking until they are offered a job at or above their reservation wage. Of course, they set the level of this wage as high as they think they can find within a reasonable period of time—yet they are under some pressure to be realistic. The extent of this pressure depends upon the magnitude and duration of unemployment insurance and other sources of income while they are searching. It also depends upon family circumstances. If their search experience suggests they have been unrealistic about the wage level available to them, or if they are living on savings which are running low, individuals adjust their reservation wages downward (Lippman and McCall, 1976). On the other hand, the longer one plans to hold the next job, the higher it pays to set one's reservation wage. This is because the costs of search—including wages foregone while searching—are more apt to be paid back, and with interest, if the better job one is holding out for is of long duration.

B. The Demand Side of Search

With the national unemployment rate above 5%, as it has been since the early 1970s, one might expect that only workers have to search, and that employers can just sit back and choose. Indeed, the level of effort required on each side of the market does vary with the unemployment rate. However, even in a "buyer's market," selecting one applicant to hire requires the information-gathering we have called search. Employers screen prospective workers because labor is not homogenous. But, just like prospective employees, employers have imperfect information. They wish to predict which potential employees will be the most productive, stay with the employer long enough to repay the costs of hiring and training, have the lowest reservation wage, and be otherwise cooperative. Imperfect information on each of these scores leads employers to think of workers in terms of identifiable groups whose desirability can to some extent be predicted from group membership.

Using educational credentials to make these predictions is an example of a screening strategy that is probabilistic and, thus, "statistical." An employer requiring a high school or college diploma for entrance into a particular job may base this requirement on the observation that, on average, school dropouts make less productive workers. This is a statistical generalization that may be true "on average" but will always be in error for some individual cases. (We can all think of some high school dropouts who are more productive than some college graduates.) Yet, despite some of the individually incorrect decisions it generates, this screening device makes sense for some employers, since it is prohibitively expensive to develop a screening device capable of detecting the unusually productive high school dropout or the unusually unproductive college graduate. It is the lack of information about potential employees' future behavior, coupled with the costs of acquiring such information, that leads employers to categorize applicants according to group memberships that are almost costlessly observable, and to base hiring decisions on the "averages" they have observed for these groups. (For an early treatment of such "labor market signaling" see Spence, 1974.)

Such a statistically based screening process may use other easily discernible group memberships, for example sex or race, to categorize applicants. In this case the screening process is called "statistical discrimination" by most sociologists and economists (Lewin and England, 1982). The process is called "discrimination" because an ascriptive criterion (such as race or sex) is explicitly used to make the hiring decision. The process is "statistical" in the sense that decisions are based on approximately correct group productivity averages, rather than on dislike for group members or erroneous perceptions of average group productivity. The search costs that would be entailed in developing more direct productivity measures help explain the popularity of statistical discrimination. Nonetheless, the use of a worker's sex, race, religion, or national origin to determine that individual's treatment in any employment context was outlawed by Title VII of the Civil Rights Act of 1964.

III. SPOT MARKETS—THE ORTHODOX
ECONOMIC VIEW

The integrated view of employment which is the goal of this chapter draws on a new labor economics highlighting imperfect information, search, implicit contracts, and internal labor markets.Yet it is useful to first provide a brief primer of the orthodox neoclassical view of labor markets, since many of its elements remain in newer views. The orthodox view of "spot markets" can be summarized as follows: Prices equilibrate supply and demand in competitive markets where many independent actors have perfect information, such that labor is paid its marginal revenue product at all times. We explain the rudiments of this view below.

A. Supply, Demand, and Equilibration

In a competitive labor market where the wage rate adjusts freely, the price of labor (the wage rate received) and the quantity of labor employed are determined by the intersection of the supply and demand curves for labor. This is shown in Fig. 6.1. The supply curve (or schedule) shows how the wage rate determines the number of person-hours of labor that will be supplied to the market. This relationship between the wage available and the amount of labor supplied depends on individuals' reservation wage (the wage at which they would decide not to be employed at all) and (for any particular job) their opportunities in other jobs. The supply curve indicates what wage will be required to bring a given number of person-hours into employment. The demand curve depicts how many person-hours of labor employers are willing to employ at any given wage. This depends on the gain to them from employing one additional person-hour; if it is less than the wage rate, they will decide against it.

Thus one can think of the supply-demand diagram as a picture of two bivariate relationships, each drawn as a curve on the same two axes. There is one relationship between the wage and the quantity of labor people will supply, and another relationship between the wage and the quantity of labor employers will demand. Usually these two curves have the opposite slope; the higher the wage rate, the more labor workers will wish to supply[1] and the less labor employers will wish to employ. Given this, how many person-hours will actually be employed, and at what wage? The centerpiece of the model is that "market forces" created by all individuals seeking their best outcome will move the wage rate up or down the two curves toward that equilibrium point where the quantity of labor supplied equals the quantity of labor employers demand. Graphically, this is the point where the supply and demand curves intersect. (In Fig. 6.1 the equilibrium wage is W, and the quantity of labor employed is Q.) In a true "spot market" for labor, such as might be approximated by a hiring hall for unskilled laborers, where employers (say, building contractors) appear every day to hire as many as they need, the wage rate and the number employed adjust on a day-to-day basis so as to constantly "clear the market." A "cleared market" for labor is one in which everyone who desires to work at the prevailing wage is employed. Some goods, such as fresh produce or raw materials are typically traded in genuine spot markets. But as we shall see, labor markets are seldom spot markets. (For a lucid treatment of the neoclassical view of labor markets, see Flanagan et al., 1984: Chapter 2.)

An exogenous change in the supply of labor refers to a change in the quantity of labor that will be supplied at each wage. We call the change exogenous if it comes about for reasons other than a change in demand. Similarly, an exogenous change in demand is defined as a change that occurs for reasons other than a change in supply. Thus, exogenous changes in demand are depicted by a movement of the entire demand curve, whereas changes in the amount of labor demanded that come about because of an exogenous shift in supply are depicted by a movement up or down the demand curve. (The analogous proposition holds for supply changes.) These distinctions are reflected in economists' convention of using the terms "supply" or "demand" to refer to the position of the entire schedule or curves—not to a particular point on a curve. The X axis value of any point on the curves is called the "amount supplied" or "amount demanded." Thus, when economists say that "the demand for labor increased," they mean that the demand curve shifted outward such that the quantity of labor that employers will hire is now higher for any given wage than it was before. For example, the demand for labor in an industry will go up if the demand for the product sold by the industry goes up. This shift outward in the demand curve causes the market equilibrium point to move since the demand curve now crosses the (unchanged) supply curve at a higher point. The result is an increase in the number of people employed that is accomplished through an increase in the market wage rate. Similarly, and exogenous increase in supply is represented by an outward (rightward) shift of the supply curve. An example of such an exogenous increase in supply would be the entry of the large baby boom cohort into the labor market. This moves firms along their (unchanged) demand curves to a new intersection point at which the increase in the number of people employed is accomplished through a decrease in the wage rate.

This supply-demand model involves adjustments in the amount of any particular type of labor supplied or demanded. The adjustments are accomplished through the equilibrating mechanism of price. Later we will explain why the new labor economics posits that markets often clear by quantity rather than price changes, leading to more than merely frictional unemployment in the presence of wages that are "sticky downward" (i.e., do not fall).

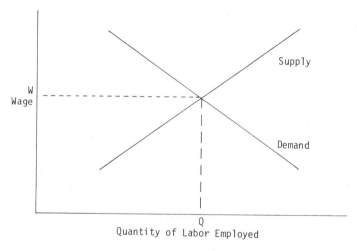

Figure 6.1. Supply-demand diagram. With these supply and demand schedules the equilibrium wage will be *W* and the quantity of labor employed in equilibrium will be *Q*.

B. Marginal Productivity and Labor Demand

Marginal productivity theory states that, at any point in time, a firm pays each employee only as much as the last (marginal) worker (of that type of labor) adds to the revenue of the firm. Competition in the labor (not product) market is seen as responsible for this.[2]

The mechanism of competition can be seen in common sense terms as follows: If a firm pays workers less than their marginal revenue product, the firm risks another firm bidding away their workers by offering an amount between what the first firm is paying and the marginal revenue product. A succession of such competitive moves will lead the prevailing wage back to the marginal revenue product. Similarly, if a firm pays more than the marginal revenue product of labor, their profits will be lower than those of competing firms and they will either go out of business or represent an increasingly small share of the market if they persist in this practice. An implication of this reasoning is that, in equilibrium, the demand curve for any type of labor will be the same as the marginal revenue product curve.

As pointed out by Granovetter (1981), sociologists often misunderstand the contention that labor is paid its marginal revenue product as an exclusively supply-side proposition. The contention does not merely mean that individuals are paid according to their human capital. The development of human capital theory by Schultz (1961, 1963), Mincer (1958, 1974), and Becker (1964) was originally seen as an antidote to treating the determination of wages by marginal revenue product as an entirely demand-side issue (Hicks, 1966). In this early demand-side view, labor was seen as homogeneous, with productivity determined by capital investment and the technical relations of production.

Economists still see the demand side as important to the operation of labor markets. The tilt of the labor demand curve indicates the (own-wage) elasticity of labor demand, and it can be measured at either the firm or industry level. The classic determinants of this elasticity are known as the Hicks-Marshall laws. Two of these laws are particularly important for our purpose. They state that this elasticity or wage/employment trade-off is higher when (1) the price elasticity of demand for the product being produced is high, and (2) when labor costs are a large share of the total costs of production (Flanagan et al., 1984: 88). (See also Hamermesh and Grant, 1979; Hicks, 1966: 241–247; Marshall, 1923: 518–538.) The first law draws attention to the firm or industry's position in the market for the good or service it produces. A high price elasticity of demand for its product means that the firm or industry's attempt to raise prices leads to a large decrease in the quantity it is able to sell. Thus, if forced to raise wages, such firms are especially likely to employ less labor. The second law implies that the labor demand is more elastic in labor-intensive than in capital-intensive firms or industries. Later, we will use these laws to interpret some of the findings of the new structuralist research in sociology, research aimed at measuring the effects of firm or industry characteristics on workers' wages.

The human capital of workers also helps determine their productivity, and thus the demand for their labor. That is, human capital investment improves productivity, so that employers are willing to pay a higher wage for workers with more human capital. The most common forms of job-relevant human capital investment are schooling and on-the-job training. Schooling costs money in direct out-of-pocket expenses for tuition and books, and it has an opportunity cost of the earnings foregone while one is attending school. Thus, present consumption must be foregone to make the invest-ment. As with any other investment, the rate of return is one determinant of the amount invested. Thus, while the decision to invest in human capital is typically viewed as a supply-side or household matter, the fact that the wage is higher for those with more education results in part from a demand-side decision based on the higher (predicted) productivity of such workers. Yet the process by which workers with varying amounts of human capital are matched to jobs with varying potential productivities, and the question of whether actual productivity is an additive or interactive function of charac-teristics of workers and characteristics of their jobs, has not been adequately addressed, even by the new labor economics (Granovetter, 1981).

As early as 1964, Becker emphasized firm-specific training that is re-ceived on the job. He posited that the costs of this specific human capital are shared by employers and employees. Employees "pay" their share through lower wages during the training period. Thus, even this early view of the human capital investment decision did not assume it to be made entirely on the supply side. As we shall see, the seeds of the new notion of implicit contracts were already in this notion, since firm-specific training creates incentives for both employers and employees to make employment a long-term relationship, rather than "spot" phenomena in which markets are cleared by price movements in every short period. In the spot market view, wages for experienced workers decline every time demand for product declines. This is because firms are seen as profit maximizers *in every short period.*

C. The Erosion of Discrimination in Competitive Markets

One implication of the orthodox view of labor markets is that any form of discrimination should erode in competitive markets. Discriminating against minorities or women because of "tastes" (Becker, 1957) or erroneous perceptions of their productivity amounts to setting the demand curve for their labor below the marginal revenue product curve. Employers who will not hire women or minorities in certain jobs force them either to offer their labor to other employers at a lower wage or to find themselves unemployed. Employers who will hire women and minorities in all jobs reap the benefits of the discriminators' acts in lowered labor costs. Since those who will hire women and minorities have a cost advantage, those who discriminate in hiring will eventually lose market share or go out of business. As this happens (or as the discriminators stop discriminating to prevent this), the market wage for women and minorities should rise to become commensurate with their marginal revenue product. Because it saves on search costs, statistical discrimination by employers (discussed above) may "tax" those indulging in it less than other forms of discrimination, thus slowing its demise. This is one way in which search theory has modified the neoclassical view. As we shall explain below, the sociological notion of feedback effects between employment and other institutions also helps explain the persistence of discrimination, even in the face of market forces tending to erode it.

IV. THE LONG-TERM EMPLOYMENT RELATIONSHIP

Spot markets, or something close to them, may occasionally be found in the allocation and pricing of very unskilled labor. However, in most types of jobs one can see the joint benefits to employers and employees of some kind of long-term contract. This is because the employment relationship is expected to last for some time, because search and transaction (hiring and training) costs are high, because individuals wish to insure themselves against adverse future outcomes, and because, unlike inanimate goods, human employers and employees can change their behavior for the worse as the relationship proceeds. For these reasons, some sort of contract between employer and employee may be beneficial to each side, and it behooves employers to give attention to the social-psychology of motivating performance over time. The ensuing understandings may be explicit or implicit, detailed or general. We begin the discussion with explicit contracts that condition the claims of either side to the occurrence of very specific contingencies.

A. Contingent-Claims Contracts

Explicit contracts have two features: a statement of the conditions under which either party has what obligations, and a means of enforcing these provisions. If these two features were easily arranged, many jobs might involve explicit contracts covering every possible contingency. Such contracts are called "perfect contingent-claims contracts." They might include statements about future wage increases, promotion chances, pensions, and layoff protection due employees. Employers would wish such contractual promises to be contingent upon both the employee's performance and the economic conditions confronting the firm. For example, if the firm experienced an unexpected increase in the cost of raw materials, or a decline in the demand for their product, employers would want these facts to condition whether they had to give raises or could decrease the pay of workers. Employers would also want a promise from employees to stay with the firm until the investment in on-the-job training had been paid off or to compensate the employer for the cost of the training. Employees, in turn, would wish any such agreement to be contingent on the offers available to the employee in other firms. It is clear that such contracts would have to cover many contingencies indeed.

While explicit contracts exist in unionized jobs and some others, we seldom see contracts as detailed as those described above. Such detailed contracts are impractical because of their excessive "transaction costs" (Williamson et al., 1975; Wachter and Williamson, 1978), including: the time it takes to bargain over the contract, the costs of obtaining information about whether the contingencies of the contract have been met (e.g., whether the employee's performance has been adequate or whether the firm has faced sufficient adversity in product markets to justify no wage increase), and the costs of enforcement of the contract, perhaps including lawyer's fees in case of a contract breach. These costs are quite high in comparison with the benefits of such contracts. As a consequence of these costs, perfect contingent-claims contracts are almost as rare in employment as they are in marriage.

B. Implicit Contracts

Yet something like a contract seems likely to arise in at least some jobs. After all, employers pay for on-the-job training in the form of out-of-pocket costs and in the productivity foregone while an experienced worker teaches the new worker. Employees also absorb some of the costs of training by accepting lower wages during this period. Such firm-specific training in the early stages of the employment relationship leads to a situation of "bilateral monopoly" between employer and employee. Because of the skills learned, the worker is more productive to the employer than workers that might be newly hired. Because part of the training is often not transferable, the worker is now more productive to this employer than to any other employer. Thus both the employer and the employee are better off within the relationship than were they to quit it. The difference between the gains from the relationship and what each could obtain outside the relationship is the "surplus" (sometimes called an "economic rent") that is divided through bargaining. The bargaining over this surplus is not affected by the usual competitive market processes because there is no alternative purchaser of the labor for whom it has the same value and no alternative worker with the same value for the employer. Both features result from the firm-specific nature of the training, which is a kind of relationship-specific human capital analogous to that which occurs in the early period of marriage. Thus each side has a sort of monopoly power over the other, although this does not imply that each side has equal power. As in our game-theoretic discussion of marital bargaining, the alternatives of either party outside the relationship will affect their bargaining within the bilateral monopoly of the employment relationship.[3]

If perfect contingent-claims contracts are rare, and spot markets are unsuitable for jobs involving much firm-specific human capital, then what arrangement results from the bilateral monopoly in such jobs? According to the new labor economics, the real-world outcome is often "implicit contracts," which may or may not be combined with some explicit contractual agreement. An implicit contract refers to a situation where both employees and employers can to some degree count on the performance of the other by observing what they have done in the past.

An example of how implicit contracts work can be seen in the way they provide for a modicum of wage and employment security. First, employers seldom lower nominal wages even though it is legal to do so. (However, workers' real buying power sometimes decreases when raises fail to keep pace with inflation.) Workers observe that nominal wages are "sticky downward," and assume that this will hold for the future as well. Workers also make inferences about the wage trajectories, promotions, and pensions they can anticipate by observing what the employer has done in the past. Employees also observe the conditions under which workers have previously been terminated or temporarily laid off. Okun (1981) notes that when employers lay off workers in response to poor business conditions, this is less likely to violate trust in an implicit contract than if they lower wages. This is because employees do not directly witness "business conditions." If the wage were lowered, employees might suspect that the employer was simply trying to increase profits under the guise of a claimed business downturn. Indeed, the employee's inability to observe business conditions might lead employers to attempt such deceits. In contrast to employers' continual short-term incentives to reduce wages, the employer has no incentive to lay off workers except under product demand declines. Thus, layoffs, in combination with seniority-based recalls, are more consistent with the maintenance of trust within an implicit contract than are wage decreases. This is what Okun means when he says that labor markets often "clear" by quantity rather than price adjustments. Okun's reasoning hinges on the availability and costs of different types of information. This illustrates one way in which implicit contract theory draws upon the central innovation of search theory, the recognition that information is imperfect and costly.

Common to these examples of implicit contracts is that the employee observes preferential treatment for experienced over inexperienced employees in wages, promotion, protection from layoffs, callbacks from layoff, and pensions. *We take this preferential treatment of experienced workers to be the operational definition of implicit contracts in employment relationships.* Workers' observations of this preferential treatment often lead them to perform well enough not to be terminated early on, and to stay in the job during the early years even if they could find jobs offering a higher current wage. The concentration of payoffs in the later years also increases the likelihood that those who self-select themselves into jobs with implicit contracts are those with a propensity to remain in one job a long time. Thus, some economists have departed from the spot market view that workers are paid their marginal revenue product in every period. They have concluded that wage appreciation with experience and the concentration of other benefits in the later years are explained in part by employers' desire to provide such incentives rather than entirely because of increasing productivity with experience (Lazear, 1979; Lazear and Moore, 1984; Medoff and Abraham, 1980, 1981).

Implicit contracts have no explicit mechanisms of enforcement. So what protects the employee from the employer reneging on the terms of the "agreement?" If the employer lowers wages, lays off experienced workers first because they are more expensive, or decimates a pension plan, there is little the experienced employee can do about it. Indeed, such events do occur, particularly during recession and in firms whose competitive position is eroding. Every employer may have a short-term incentive to renege on such contracts since, if they are sufficiently "back-loaded," the employer may be paying employees greatly in excess of their marginal revenue product toward the end of their career. However, there is a powerful long-term incentive that makes observance of such understandings the rule rather than the exception in the industrial relations of certain parts of the economy. This incentive stems from the fact that the firm's reputation as an employer strongly affects the quality of workers it is able to attract, the turnover rate among its trained workers, and the enthusiasm with which workers perform their tasks. The reputation of the employer with one cohort of workers is determined by the trajectory of earnings and benefits the previous cohort is receiving. Thus, employers who can afford long-term planning have an incentive to engage in what Okun (1981) has whimsically called the "invisible handshake."

Okun (1981) uses the notion of implicit contracts to help explain the elevated unemployment and stagflation of the 1970s. His view is that exogenous shocks (such as the OPEC price increases) gave the first impetus to an acceleration of inflation, even as the economy weakened during the 1974–1975 recession. Then, because a significant portion of the economy was characterized by implicit and explicit (union) contracts, the adjustments that were made entailed layoffs more than lowered wages. With the deterioration of the competitive position of the United States in the face of foreign competition, fewer workers than usual were called back from layoff. Workers' slowness to adjust their expectations downward was a rational generalization from past experience with callbacks, a response to relatively high income replacement rates under unemployment insurance and trade adjustment assistance, as well as a commentary on how high their wages were in contrast to those in more marginal industries. The existence of a sector of the labor force with such contract features implies that wages can fail to decline even in the face of widespread unemployment.

The notion of implicit contracts as incentive systems operating through their reputation effects also helps to explain another "lumpy" feature of social change—why plants may shut down and move rather than negotiate lowered wages when their position in product markets deteriorates. In some jobs and industries, the system of industrial relations has relied on reputation effects of long-term contracts to the extent that employers think it more viable to completely sever the relationship than to make the incremental wage reductions that spot market theory would predict. If a firm's position in its product market gets bad enough that the employer no longer finds the reputational benefits of honoring the contract to outweigh the costs of maintaining seniority rights, the contract will be broken. Once it is to be broken, it may be more profitable to start over again in a new locality with cheaper (usually nonunion) labor.

How does implicit contract theory change the orthodox view that wages are determined by marginal revenue product? Recall that in the orthodox view, it is competition (the presence of many buyers and sellers of each skill-type of labor) that causes wages to correspond to marginal revenue products in each period. Implicit contract theorists have pointed out that after firm-specific training, there are a very limited number of potential buyers and sellers of labor with this specific set of skills. This lack of competition means that the wage in these posttraining periods can no longer be determined competitively. Also, it would be a violation of the implicit contract and would adversely affect a firm's reputation if they made downward adjustments in the wage when a decline in demand for the firm's product lowered the marginal revenue product of labor. Thus, to the extent that there is a competitive market and an equilibrium wage in jobs with implicit contracts, it is a market for long-term contracts and an expected lifetime wage. The package one "contracts" for includes compensation and increasing protection from unemployment over the life cycle. Yet, the orthodox assumption about the relationship between wages and marginal revenue product has not been dropped completely. It has been changed from a view of spot markets in which labor is paid its marginal revenue product through recontracting in each short period to a view that labor is paid its marginal revenue product over the life cycle, but not in each period. This suggests that implicit contracts pay labor less than its marginal revenue product in the early years and more than its marginal revenue product in the later years. Yet, other strands of the new labor economics question even this relationship between compensation and marginal revenue product. These views of motivational structures in internal labor markets are discussed next.

C. Internal Labor Markets

Arising out of the work of institutionalist economists such as Dunlop (1958), studies of internal labor markets (Doeringer and Piore, 1971) were for a long time largely ignored by the neoclassical mainstream. Recently, this has changed. One hypothesis receiving attention is that of "rank-order tournaments" (Lazear and Rosen, 1981; Carmichael, 1983). The notion is that employers set up "contests" in which rewards are based on rank-order performance rather than some metric measure of productivity. The fact that many workers see themselves as in the running of the "contest" is hypothesized to act as an incentive for performance. Thus, a tournament where the prize greatly exceeds the marginal revenue product of the winner may be a rational personnel policy for profit maximizing firms, even though it departs from paying each worker his or her marginal revenue product, either in each period or over the life cycle. [For a related model proposed by a sociologist, see Rosenbaum (1979, 1984).] Casual observation of the huge salary increment when an individual becomes "the boss" suggests the widespread use of such devices. These new compensation models such as rank-order tournaments may substantially reorient the study of the employment relationship by economists. This is because, for the first time, mainstream economists are acknowledging the importance of compensation schemes directed at the social psychology of worker attachment and effort. In doing so, they will come to see the firm more structurally, as a collection of slots to which differential rewards are attached. Both aspects of this reorientation move economists closer to the contemporary sociological view of employment to which we now turn.

V. SOCIOLOGICAL VIEWS OF EMPLOYMENT

Taking all of society as their subject, sociologists entertain hypotheses about causal links moving in either direction between households and employment. In particular, sociological views of employment involve reciprocal links between individuals' characteristics, their structural position (defined in terms of job characteristics), and the rewards attaching to these positions. This sociological view differs from economists' tendency to see tastes and human capital decisions made in the household as exogenous to the demand-side behavior of employers. (See Burstein, 1979: note 5; Schultz, 1981: 151–152; Leijonhufvud, 1981: Chapter 9. Note that institutional economists do not necessarily view household behavior as exogenous; see Gordon, 1972: 45–46; Piore, 1979.) This sociological insight puts economists' answers to the question of how individuals are allocated into jobs into a broader framework.

A. The Allocation of Individuals to Positions

How are individuals allocated to structural positions? Here we define structural positions in terms of the characteristics of the occupations, industries, or firms in which a particular job occurs. Sociological answers to this question typically involve one central theme: structural positions influence the persons in them by reinforcing behavior that is useful for survival in that position, but counterproductive for mobility to another position. These effects often spill over onto the children of those holding the position as well. It follows that a major determinant of one's structural position is the sort of position one has held previously, and the sort of position one's parents held. A few of the many strands of research supporting this view are reviewed below.

The tendency of men and women to end up in positions similar to those of their parents is the central implication of a long line of sociological research. Such research includes ethnographic studies of class cultures (e.g., Gans, 1962), survey research on class differences in socialization patterns (Kohn, 1969; Kohn et al., 1983: Chapter 1; Kerckhoff, 1972), quantitative studies of social mobility and status attainment (e.g., Blau and Duncan, 1967; Featherman and Hauser, 1978; Treiman and Terrell, 1975), and evidence that schools aid class reproduction by encouraging the outlooks most appropriate to the type of jobs held by the parents of their students (Bowles and Gintis, 1976). To economists (and some sociologists, e.g., Banfield, 1970) these findings might be interpreted as evidence of class differences in taste and investment that are exogenous to employment experience. In contrast to this, most sociologists interpret the correlation between parental position and offspring's position as partially due to effects of parents' work situation on the homelife they create. Recent discussions of the similarities between human capital theory and status attainment research notwithstanding (e.g., Horan, 1978), the two traditions differ sharply in their assumption about the exogeneity or endogeneity of household behavior to employment experience.

The contention that the structural position of adults shapes their own behavior so as to make the person more like the position receives its most sophisticated test in the recent work of Kohn et al. (1983). The possibility of selection bias has always threatened attempts to use the correlation between characteristics of positions and their incumbents as evidence that "the role molds the person." Kohn et al. have demonstrated the endogeneity of a number of traits by using longitudinal data in a way that greatly reduces the threat of selection bias by using individuals as their own controls. That is, along with other variables, the dependent variable at a previous time point is controlled in assessing the effect of one's job on subsequent psychological functioning. The analysis shows that holding a job with considerable self-direction and substantive complexity promotes a self-directed (as opposed to conformist) orientation, and a flexible intellectual outlook. The psychological characteristics are then shown, in turn, to affect one's future chance of achieving an occupational position involving autonomy and complexity. This research implies that individuals develop the psychological styles required to survive in the structural position they hold. In broad strokes, this is also a theme of Kanter's (1977) "Men and Women of the Corporation"—that behavioral differences between groups are a product of the jobs they have been allowed to enter, rather than being exogenous to actual work experience.

How is this sociological view different from economic models that see individuals rationally exercising their preferences as they invest in themselves and search for jobs? To some extent, we are provided with an explanation of individual behavior molded by jobs and only partially under conscious control. Yet this behavior can also be regarded as a rational response to the contingencies of reinforcement within a particular role. Individual characteristics necessary for day to day physical or psychological survival within a particular position may make it difficult to move from that position. This makes it risky to cultivate the characteristics that would permit mobility, since if the attempt fails, one may be worse off than before. (For exactly this explanation of survival strategies and the consequent difficulties of escaping from poverty, see Stack, 1974.)

Social networks of employment information are one nonpsychological resource provided by jobs. Mobility is partially defined and limited by the fact that one's position provides best access to networks of people in similar positions. Given the extensive use of informal networks in job finding (Granovetter, 1973, 1974; Lin et al., 1981), it is clear that even economists' notion of "search" is somewhat endogenous to the position one currently holds or previously held.

The endogeneity of supply-side behavior contributes to the explanation of race, sex, and ethnic differences in job placement as well. At the simplest level the argument is that members of any particular group will have a tendency to remain in the position they previously held. Controversy over the explanations of racial, sexual, and ethnic differences in job position often hinges on attempts to disentangle discrimination by employers from differences in the supply-side qualifications or preferences brought to the labor market. The larger picture is that group differences and discriminatory treatment of ascriptive groups in the labor market are reciprocally reinforcing. Feedback between households and labor markets often creates new forces for discrimination even before old discrimination has been eroded by competitive market forces.

Consider, for example, the practice of sex discrimination in the 1950s. How will such discrimination affect behavior in the household? If women are discriminated against in labor markets, fewer females will aspire to or train for male jobs (knowing that they are unlikely to get them), more couples will specialize with the wife doing household work and the husband doing paid work, more educational and geographical investments will be made in male careers, and traditional socialization will seem more rational to parents. These developments will reinforce employers' tastes for discrimination, and allow correct statistical calculations that fewer women than men are suited for male-dominated jobs. New discrimination may thus be created before the market forces we discussed earlier have had time to erode the discrimination begun in the earlier period. These feedback effects operate at cross-purposes with market mechanisms eroding discrimination.

We have thus far presented sociological research as if it could only explain lack of mobility, but rarely explain change in a group's structural position. The sociological view is certainly not that things never change, but rather that since household and employment institutions contain so many self-reinforcing elements, they often resist change until the pressures are great enough to force a substantial change. Thus change is often slow to come and then sporadic rather than continuous and fluid as the spot market model would predict. As discussed above, the economic theory of implicit contracts shares with the sociological view the implication that adjustments to change are often slow to come, but considerable (as in plant shutdowns) when they finally occur.

To take one example, let us compare trends in women's status in the

1960s with the trends of the 1970s and 1980s. Although many women entered the labor force in the 1960s, most other features of their status remained relatively constant: the level of occupational sex segregation, the sex gap in pay, and husbands' and wives' relative contribution to housework. Since the early 1970s a number of interrelated changes have come at a heightened pace: sex discrimination clauses in EEO laws were given more administrative teeth (Burstein, 1979), young women started choosing male-dominated college majors in large numbers (Beller, 1984; Jacobs, in press), the divorce rate increased dramatically (Cherlin, 1981), the women's movement became organized and visible, women began to vote differently from men (Rossi, 1984), and the first female vice-presidential candidate was nominated by one of the two major political parties. While the changes were slow in coming, the pace quickened when a whole set of institutions began to move together. We expect that changes in systems of allocation of persons to positions generally have this sporadic character.

B. Positions and Rewards

The "new structuralism" in sociology has moved concern away from questions of how the characteristics of individuals affect their allocation to positions, and toward an examination of those characteristics of job slots which determine their rewards. The thrust of such research has been to show that certain structural locations (defined in terms of occupational, industrial, or firm characteristics) affect the rewards and rates of return received by those in the positions.

One line of research had its genesis in notions of economic segmentation originated by institutionalist economists. While these developments were largely ignored by mainstream economists, sociologists have provided the major empirical documentation for the asserted structural effects. Their findings suggest that higher wages, fringe benefits, and rates of return to human capital typically accompany jobs located in firms with high capital intensity, large organizational size, oligopoly in product markets, unionization, and high profit levels (Beck et al., 1978; Hodson, 1978, 1983, 1984; Horan et al., 1980; Tolbert et al., 1980; Kalleberg et al., 1981; Hodson and Kaufman, 1982; Lord and Falk, 1982; Parcel and Mueller, 1983). These effects are still seen after adjusting for the human capital (education and experience) of the individuals holding the positions. The higher earnings that come with positions in these firms or industries seem not to be offset by either higher risks of unemployment (Schervish, 1983) or low fringe benefits (Lord and Falk, 1982). Baron and Bielby (1980, 1984; see also Baron, 1984) have shown that those organizations with environmental dominance (measured by such things as size and share of product market) and an internally complex structure offer workers better mobility prospects up career ladders. Still other strands of structuralist research have divided jobs according to "class," (Wright and Perrone, 1977) or sex composition (England and McLaughlin, 1979; England et al., 1982; England, 1984b), showing that jobs involving control over labor and those that are predominantly male have higher earnings and opportunities for raises or promotions. In each of these bodies of structuralist research, it appears that with certain advantaged positions, total compensation across the life cycle is greater. This new structuralist research reflects an emerging emphasis among sociologists on the study of how rewards attach to positions, not merely to the individual characteristics that select people into positions. This is a reorientation that is also occurring among the new labor economists (Malcolmson, 1984), albeit more slowly.

VI. SUMMARY: AN INTEGRATED VIEW

What are the consequential features of the employment relationship? In this section, we sketch an integrated view drawing on sociology and economics, while summarizing highlights of the chapter. We focus on three questions about employment: first, which individuals come to occupy which job positions; second, how do characteristics of jobs determine the compensation they offer; and third, why does change in these matters often proceed in a sluggish and then sporadic rather than continuous and fluid manner?

Economists have offered human capital and search theories to explain the allocation of individuals to job positions. Both refer to investment made largely on the supply-side of labor markets, often in the household. Those who invest more (or have more invested in them by others) gain better jobs, on average. Search theory modifies human capital theory by pointing out the costliness of information to both prospective employees and employers. These costs imply that sorting of individuals into positions will not be as perfect a match of human capital to positional requirements as would obtain if information were free. Search theory also helps explain why employers engage in statistical discrimination, using costlessly observed ascribed characteristics to predict job-relevant characteristics in deciding whom to hire.

Even with the modifications of search theory, human capital theory is misleading if investments are seen as exogenous. Rather, "investment" must be understood in the broader context of reciprocal links between employment and households. This broader view is supplied by the sociological insight that positions mold individuals in such a way as to discourage mobility to different positions by these individuals or their offspring. Thus, imperfect initial sorting of individuals into positions may have long-term effects. This view also implies that the investments made in individuals' human capital (broadly construed) are not merely a matter of "free choice," but depend critically on positionally determined tastes and resources of their parents and the positions they land in during their own early lives. This has long been the sociological view, and parts of it are now acknowledged by economists studying the household (Becker, 1981: Chapters 6 and 7).

Thus, both search costs and feedback effects from employment experiences onto household investment decision lead ascriptive characteristics (such as race, sex, and social class background) to have effects on the jobs individuals attain. These effects operate in part through their effects on human capital investment (broadly construed) and in part through discrimination.

A second issue concerns those structural characteristics of positions that determine the rewards they offer. Among the rewards considered are pay, pay trajectories over time, promotion chances in internal labor markets, and probabilities of unemployment. The view that positions intervene between individual characteristics and rewards, and that the rewards attach to the positions, is increasingly common in sociology and economics. It should be no surprise that the human capital requirements of positions are correlated with their reward levels. What has required more explanation is why other characteristics of occupations, industries, and organizations contribute to reward levels. The research explicitly addressing these questions has been the "new structuralism" in sociology. Below, we suggest two fronts on which the findings of this research can be integrated with reasoning from economics.

First, we see an affinity between findings of the new structuralists and work on implicit contracts. Sociologists typically find that advantageous structural positions show higher rates of return to experience through seniority wage increases or promotion in internal labor markets. Thus, these jobs entail preferred treatment for experienced over inexperienced workers. Honoring an unwritten contract to give preferential treatment to experienced workers is the operational definition of implicit contracts in the employment relationship. Implicit contract theorists appear to assume that all jobs are characterized by such contracts. In fact, however, jobs vary greatly in the extent to which they have these contract features. We suggest that it is precisely the kinds of jobs sociologists have found to be structurally advantageous that have the strongest (implicit or explicit) contract features.

Capital intensive production processes lead to implicit contracts because such jobs typically involve significant firm-specific human capital investment by employers. This investment creates the incentives for employers to award increasing benefits with experience so as not to lose their investment through turnover. Firms and industries characterized by large organizational size, oligopolistic pricing, and high profit rates are more likely to be able to afford the long-term view associated with such contracts. Across all firms and industries, such contracts are more likely in the managerial and supervisory positions that offer more on-the-job training that structuralists operationalizing "class" have found to have higher rates of return to experience. Contracts are also more likely in predominantly male than female jobs as a form of statistical wage discrimination against women because of the greater intermittence of female employment. In sum, the structural positions that predict high rewards to experience are those in which employers have the greatest incentive to organize internal labor markets and honor implicit contracts for their reputational effects in lowering turnover, attracting good workers, and generating high morale.

If implicit contracts explain the steeper reward *trajectories* in structurally advantageous jobs, what explains the higher *average* compensation in such jobs (net of the human capital of job holders)? Many factors are at work here, but we focus on two ways that the economics of the demand-side illuminate findings by sociologists. A key economic insight is the trade-off between employment and wage rates. This is indicated by the downward slope of the labor demand curve of Fig. 6.1. This means that, other things being equal, employees who bargain for a higher wage will find that fewer positions are available. A determinant of employees' bargaining position is the "price elasticity of labor demand," the percentage by which the quantity of labor demand falls when wages increase by 1%. Where a small increase in wage rates leads the employer to significantly decrease employment, workers requesting such an increase may put jobs in jeopardy. Where an increase in wage rates leads to very little decrease in the quantity of labor employers demand, workers are in a stronger position to press for pay increases. This is true in both unionized and nonunionized situations, although it may take unions to provide the organizational resources necessary for effective bargaining. Thus, whatever determines the elasticity of labor demand will also affect employees' bargaining power. Since the Hicks-Marshall laws are precisely about the determinants of this elasticity, they are instructive here.

One of the Hicks-Marshall laws discussed above states that labor demand curves are more elastic when the price elasticity of demand for the product is high (i.e., when a percentage increase in price will create a relatively large percentage decrease in the quantity sold). The price elasicity of the product made by each firm is greater than the price elasticity for the entire industry that makes this same product. This is because buyers can more easily substitute products of a competing firm than they can substitute an entirely different product in response to a price increase. This implies that when a firm is a monopolist in its product market, the demand curve for the product is less elastic since it *is* the curve for the entire industry. Accordingly, the labor demand curve is less elastic, and the opportunities for bargaining over this "rent" are relatively good for workers. This conclusion does not necessarily follow for oligopolists (Scherer, 1980), although there is a tendency of oligopolists to behave like monopolists. Thus, the less elastic labor demand curves, not just the simple fact of a larger pie of revenue, may explain the relatively high wages in oligopolistic industries.[4]

The other Hicks-Marshall law discussed in this chapter states that labor demand curves are more elastic when labor is a higher proportion of the total costs of production. Since labor's proportion of costs will be lower where production is capital intensive, this helps explain why employee bargaining is more successful in capital intensive industries. In addition, some of the effect of capital intensity on wages may be because of the implicit bargaining power gained by workers when they work with expensive machinery that they could sabotage. More "sociological" reasons for structural effects such as this (Hodson and Kaufman, 1982) are important accompaniments to the economic effects dictated by the Hicks-Marshall laws.

Finally, we suggest that both sociological and economic views need to be integrated to explain why change is both sluggish and sporadic, rather than continuous and fluid. This is true in both of the areas we have discussed: the allocation of persons to positions, and the allocation of rewards to positions. The adjustments dictated by market forces do occur, but seldom as quickly or as fluidly as would be predicted by the orthodox spot market model.

Why have discrimination and differentials by sex and race not eroded steadily? Market forces operate to erode discrimination by giving the advantage of cheaper labor to those who do not engage in hiring discrimination. But working at cross-purposes with these market forces are feedback effects between employment and household sectors. Discrimination affects household decisions, often begetting new differentials and discrimination before the original discrimination has eroded. These self-reinforcing elements of the "system" of ascription have been emphasized by sociologists; they explain why change is slow in starting, but may proceed rapidly once it has begun on many fronts. Trends in sex differentials in employment will be examined further in Chapter 7.

The persistence of "structural effects" on wages are another case in which the sluggish and sporadic nature of change in the face of market forces requires explanation. For example, why didn't nominal wages fall in "core" industries and firms experiencing a serious erosion of their product market competitive position during the 1970s? Why, rather than the smooth marginal wage adjustments predicted by the spot-market view, do we see no reactions in wages, sometimes followed by the more drastic adjustments of unemployment, plant shutdowns, and plant relocations? Implicit contracts provide an explanation. They do not allow a lowering of benefits to the workers that firms have invested in. Unemployment with seniority-based callbacks is less likely to violate the implicit contract than lowering wages. When employers finally decide it *is* in their long-term interest to violate the contracts, the changes are likely to be drastic, involving starting over completely with a new (cheaper) work force.

NOTES

[1]Sometimes labor supply curves are backward-bending (i.e., take on a negative slope) above a certain wage. This is because a higher income may lead one to work less (purchase more leisure) despite the greater reward for each additional hour worked. Economists call the former the "income effect" and the latter the (own-wage) "price effect." It is an empirical question as to which predominates.

[2]In monopolistic (and oligopolistic) product markets, workers are paid their marginal revenue product which may differ from the value of their marginal product. In competitive markets, marginal revenue product equals the marginal product times the given market price that the product brings. By using the term "marginal revenue product" throughout our discussion, our statements do not require the assumption that product markets are competitive; orthodox theory predicts they will hold in competitive, oligopolistic, or monopolistic product markets as long as labor markets are competitive.

[3]Either party has the power to terminate the employment relationship in favor of another employer or another employee. However, the owners of physical capital have another option as well. They own capital that they could liquidate and directly consume if necessary. Employees generally do not have such an option—unless they possess large savings or qualify for a generous government transfer program in the absence of working. Thus employers generally have more bargaining power than employees. This conclusion, like conclusions about marital power, is troublesome for economists if interpreted to entail making interpersonal utility comparisons.

[4]See Freeman and Medoff (1984: 52, and note 15 on p. 266) for conflicting evidence on the effects of oligopoly and wages.

7

GENDER, JOBS, AND WAGES

I. INTRODUCTION

In this chapter we employ the framework presented in Chapter 6 to examine patterns and determinants of gender inequality in paid employment. There are three key dimensions along which to gauge women's relative status in the world of employment—whether they are employed outside the home, what jobs they hold, and how much they are paid. While these three dimensions of difference between male and female roles are related, they have not shown the same rate of change. Rather, there has been dramatic change in the proportion of women's lives spent in paid employment since 1950, substantial changes in which jobs women hold only since 1970, and change in the sex gap in pay only since about 1980. We treat each of these topics in turn.

II. LABOR FORCE PARTICIPATION

A. Trends for Women

Between 1950 and 1980, female labor force participation increased from 34 to 52% (U.S. Department of Labor, 1983b: 11). It continues to trend strongly upward. (Women's labor force participation rate is the share of women over 16 years old who are employed or are unemployed and looking for work. Homemakers, students, retired persons, and others not looking for work are "out of the labor force.") Particularly dramatic increases in labor force participation have occurred among women with young children. Table 7.1 shows that from 1950 to 1980 the labor force participation of married women whose youngest children were between 6 and 17 increased from 28 to 62%, an increase of 121%. Even more dramatically, the rate for women with children under 6 rose from 12 to 45%, a 275% increase!

Table 7.1. Percentage of Married Women in the Labor Force 1950–1980[a]

Year	All married women	With no child under 18	Children 6–17 only	Youngest child under 6
1950	24	30	28	12
1960	33	35	39	19
1970	41	42	49	30
1980	50	46	62	45

[a]Source: 1950: Employment and Training Report of The President (U.S. Department of Labor, 1979: 295); 1960–1980: U.S. Department of Labor (1982: 6). Data pertain to those married women who were living with their husbands.

What are the causes of this increase in women's employment? One explanation is the economic necessity associated with the increasing number of female-headed households. However, although increasing divorce rates and later age at marriage do account for some of the overall rise in female employment, the bulk of the increase has come from married women with children.

What, then, accounts for the changed behavior of married mothers? Some argue that families' economic need has increased because of an alleged failure of male earnings to keep pace with inflation. This view is largely incorrect. Median (inflation-adjusted) male income increased almost continuously from 1950 to 1970, and was roughly constant during the 1970s (see Table 7.2). This does not refute the claim that many wives work because of family economic need; in every decade, women whose husbands had lower incomes were more apt to be employed. However, it does show that there has not been a *reduction* in average male incomes that could account for the dramatic *rise* in wives' employment since the 1950s.

A more convincing explanation of the increased employment of married women comes from combining observations by Oppenheimer, a sociologist and demographer, and economists Butz and Ward. These explanations rely upon a basic mechanism discussed in the previous chapter—the forces of supply and demand operating through price changes.

Oppenheimer (1970) points out that during the postwar period, jobs that for decades had been sex-typed as female showed greater labor demand growth than traditionally male jobs. This growth resulted from the maturation of the economy that produced declining employment shares in agriculture and manufacturing, and increasing employment shares in service industries (e.g., health, insurance, retail sales), and service occupations (e.g., waitresses, sales clerks, nurses, secretaries). Since service jobs were already predominantly female, employers sought women to fill the growing number of positions. The social acceptability to employers, employees, and consum-

Table 7.2. Median Personal Income of Men and Women, 1950–1982, in Constant 1982 Dollars[a]

Year	All persons with income		Year-round full-time workers	
	Male	Female	Male	Female
1950	10,304	3,821	NA[b]	NA
1951	10,968	3,882	NA	NA
1952	11,290	4,170	NA	NA
1953	11,624	4,208	NA	NA
1954	11,467	4,167	NA	NA
1955	12,104	4,037	15,289	9,860
1956	12,791	4,080	15,864	10,048
1957	12,609	4,116	16,195	10,312
1958	12,495	3,926	16,520	10,354
1959	13,237	4,050	17,356	10,617
1960	13,299	4,111	17,712	10,741
1961	13,517	4,128	18,271	10,781
1962	13,951	4,283	18,592	11,032
1963	14,221	4,326	19,138	11,211
1964	14,460	4,509	19,554	11,546
1965	15,367	4,653	20,185	11,675
1966	15,781	4,873	20,687	11,974
1967	16,054	5,207	21,072	12,136
1968	16,591	5,602	21,680	12,674
1969	16,927	5,613	22,823	13,368
1970	16,580	5,561	22,830	13,523
1971	16,452	5,739	22,954	13,587
1972	17,189	5,997	24,314	13,966
1973	17,498	6,073	24,909	14,092
1974	16,543	6,033	23,805	14,042
1975	15,877	6,071	23,169	13,843
1976	15,983	6,063	23,499	14,094
1977	16,124	6,277	24,004	14,039
1978	16,179	6,019	23,764	14,264
1979	15,664	5,787	23,244	14,004
1980	14,678	5,763	22,459	13,578
1981	14,299	5,793	21,961	13,221
1982	13,950	5,887	21,655	13,663

[a]Source: U.S. Bureau of Census, 1984: 123–25. These figure include sources of income other than earnings from employment. However, they are so dominated by wages and salaries that figures on median earnings are similar and show basically the same trends.

[b]NA indicates figure is not available.

ers of women filling these traditional niches combined to bring increasing numbers of women into paid employment. Thus, Oppenheimer credits the increase in female employment to an increase in labor demand within jobs already labeled female.

However, this explanation requires an element of economic analysis to be convincing. After all, the simple existence of more "help wanted" ads in women's jobs would not necessarily bring women into employment. As discussed in Chapter 6, when economists talk about an increase in demand, they mean a rightward shift in the demand curve. With the supply curve unchanged, this leads to a new market equilibrium, where more workers are brought into the market because a higher wage rate is offered. There is evidence that even though women's wages did not rise relative to men's, women's absolute inflation-adjusted wages did go up in the 1950s and 1960s (Butz and Ward, 1977, 1979a,b; Smith and Ward, 1985; see also Table 7.2). As a consequence, the opportunity-cost of working exclusively in the home increased. That is, even if the value women and their families placed on work done in the home stayed constant, the upward shift in the wage rate available to women increased the benefits foregone by staying home.

The wage increases for female were not confined to the service sector, although they occurred there as well. Rather, they were reflective of the general increase in productivity and profitability of the American economy. This upward wage shift is bound to have pulled more women into paid employment (Butz and Ward, 1977, 1979a,b; Smith and Ward, 1985). As described in Chapter 4, rising female wages also contributed to declining fertility.

No doubt other, less easily measurable factors, also worked to increase female employment. In the language of neoclassical analysis, the female labor supply curve may also have been shifting outward since the 1950s. This is particularly likely during the 1970s, when women's wages, adjusted for inflation, ceased to rise (see Table 7.1), yet their employment kept on climbing. Possible causes of this shift, including changing sex-role socialization, later age at marriage, lowered fertility, high divorce rates, and rising monthly payments for houses were discussed in Chapters 3 and 4. High male unemployment rates since 1970 may also have contributed to the trend. Yet these explanations apply best to the post-1970 period, whereas female employment rates have been increasing since 1950. For this pre-1970 period, the best explanation remains the expansion of traditionally female service jobs, and the increase in women's wages that pulled more of them into the labor force.

B. Gender Differentials

As women have increased their labor force participation, men have decreased theirs (see Fig. 7.1). Most of this decrease involves men's earlier retirement. The smaller decline among younger men comes from an in-

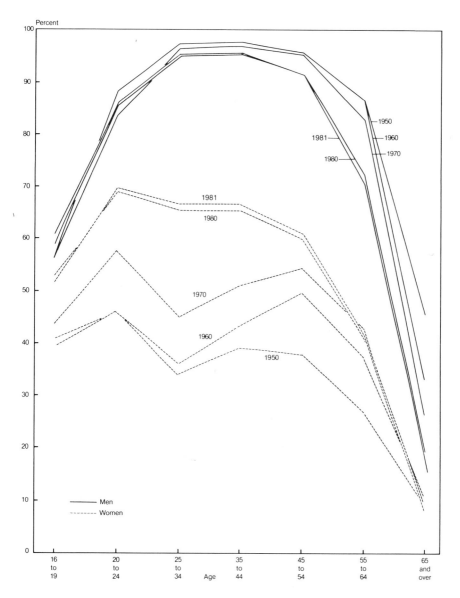

Figure 7.1. Percentage of men and women in the civilian labor force, by age, 1950–1981. From U. S. Department of Labor, 1983b.

crease in discouraged workers, especially blacks who are unemployed but have given up seeking employment (Freeman and Wise, 1982). (Close examination of Fig. 7.1 shows that like men, women also retired earlier in 1980 than 1970. However, among women, rising labor force participation at younger ages has more than compensated for this trend.)

As for unemployment, women generally show higher rates than men, but the male and female rates move closer together during recessions, when women's rates increase less than men's (Waite, 1981: 25). This is largely due to the jobs occupied by women.

Women generally work in lower paying occupations (Treiman and Hartmann, 1981) and industries (Beck et al., 1980; Hodson and England, in press) which provide relatively low levels of firm-specific training (England et al., 1982; Lloyd and Niemi, 1979; Corcoran and Duncan, 1979). As discussed in the previous chapter, these jobs have few implicit contract features. Because they are low paying and have relatively flat pay trajectories, women have less incentive than men to avoid turnover, which is typically associated with a period of unemployment. Thus, the structural placement of women within the economy partially explains the supply-side behavior (women leaving and reentering the market more than men) often used to explain sex differentials in unemployment. While women's specialization in child rearing is no doubt a factor in generating their structural placement in the economy, it is not entirely so. This is demonstrated by the effect of women's wages on both fertility and time spent out of the labor force after a birth (Butz and Ward, 1977, 1979a,b; McLaughlin, 1982; Shapiro and Mott, 1979). Thus, the sort of feedback effects between household and employment behavior discussed in the previous chapter are relevant in explaining sex differentials in unemployment as well.

The effect of the business cycle on layoffs in any particular job category is partially determined by the sensitivity of productivity in that job to declines in product demand. For example, when demand for autos falls, the marginal revenue product of secretaries falls less than that of workers on the assembly line. Consequently, the cyclical nature of the sex gap in unemployment arises in part from women's employment in white-collar occupations.

A final explanation for the greater increase in men's unemployment during recessions is the fact that fewer women than men are employed in production jobs in capital-intensive, unionized manufacturing industries. Such jobs, being characterized by well-developed contracts, use layoffs with seniority-based recalls rather than permanent terminations or age reductions as a response to recessions (Schervish, 1983; Farkas and England, in press). Thus, during the recession of 1982, male unemployment rose so high that it actually exceeded female unemployment for the first time since 1950 (Nilsen, 1984). Since then, it has returned to below the female rate.

III. JOB SEGREGATION BY SEX

While the proportion of women in the labor force has increased continuously since 1950, declines in job segregation have been slower to occur.
Occupational segregation by sex actually increased slightly during the
1950s and decreased only minimally during the 1960s (England, 1981). It is
only the 1970s that have seen a significant decline in segregation, a decline
that is greatest among younger cohorts and in white-collar rather than
blue-collar occupations (Beller, 1984). Prior to explaining this desegregation, it is useful to examine the forces acting to maintain segregation. After
all, occupations are still quite segregated by sex, even among the youngest
cohorts where the greatest change has occurred. In accounting for segregation, we will consider the factors of sex role socialization and human capital
accumulation on the supply side. On the demand side, we will consider the
role of employer discrimination and organizational characteristics such as
structured mobility ladders.

A. Socialization and Sex Role Norms

Children anticipate sex-typical jobs by a very early age (Looft, 1971;
Nemerowicz, 1979; Marini and Brinton, 1984). Nemerowicz's sample of
middle-class children in 2nd, 4th, and 6th grade showed 54% of the girls
planning to be teachers, nurses, housekeepers, secretaries, or waitresses.
These job categories accounted for only 1% of the boy's aspirations. In
contrast, 57% of the boys saw themselves as firefighters, policemen, car
mechanics, doing construction or repair, or in a sports-related job. These
categories accounted for only 4% of the girls' projections. The socialization
of children is sometimes discussed as though the only important issues
concern the quantity and quality of cognitively and emotionally enriching
inputs provided by parents. However, as we discussed in Chapter 4, there is
also an issue of the extent to which socialization differs according to the
child's sex. Girls are taught to emphasize social skills, verbal skills, physical
attractiveness, and domestic responsibility. Boys learn to emphasize technical skills, authoritativeness, and physical prowess. This socialization is by no
means complete, but it does create a strong tendency toward traits, tastes,
and expectations appropriate to sex-typical jobs.

Cognitive learning and reinforcement are two mechanisms of such
socialization (Stockard and Johnson, 1980; Marini and Brinton, 1984).
Cognitive learning theory (Kohlberg, 1966) posits that children learn to
distinguish males and females, and thereafter they infer from the sex
segregation in jobs and roles among adults that this is "the way things are"
and "the way things should be." By contrast, reinforcement theory focuses
on socialization that proceeds from reward and punishment rather from

simple observation. Parents and others reward girls for traditionally female traits and job aspirations, while rewarding boys for typically male traits and aspirations. In Chapter 4 we argued that cognitive learning is the more pervasive of these two forms of childhood socialization. This implies that the links between such socialization and job segregation involve the two-way causation we have called feedback. That is, segregation in jobs among adults provides the data for children's learning how roles "should" be, and this helps determine their job plans as adults. However, such socialization is less effective for females than for males because the roles to which females are socialized have fewer rewards attached to them. A consequence of these conflicting inducements for girls is that more girls than boys aspire to sex-atypical jobs and roles (Nemerowicz, 1979; Maccoby and Jacklin, 1974; Marini and Brinton, 1984).

Yet childhood sex role socialization is sufficiently effective to be strongly reflected in occupational distributions (England, 1984a). Women fill most nurturant occupations such as teaching, social work, child care, and counseling. Couples' assumption that domestic work is women's work makes it difficult for women with families to work in elite male occupations demanding extensive overtime, travel, or geographical mobility. (However, women's domestic responsibilities cannot explain their absence from most other male-dominated jobs.) The notion that males should hold authority is seen in the lack of women in positions of authority over workers or clients, especially where these are male. The greater emphasis on developing the quantitative, mechanical, and physical abilities of boys increases the over-representation of men in jobs with these requirements.

Sex role socialization has helped perpetuate job segregation. Yet the reduction in segregation among younger working-age cohorts during the 1970s cannot be explained by changing childhood socialization. For the cohorts entering the labor market during the 1970s were reared in the 1950s, a time of traditional sex role socialization. Thus, changes in adult practices provide the most likely explanation of changing segregation in the 1970s.

B. Human Capital and Job Segregation

Some economists look to human capital theory to explain job segregation by sex. In this view, human capital appreciates due to investment of time and money by parents, through schooling, and through job training and experience. One's job-relevant human capital can also depreciate through obsolescence or nonuse (for example, while a women is using other skills at home). Thus, differences between groups' earnings may reflect differences in their human capital investment profiles.

Research in this area has focused primarily on investment in years of schooling and years of employment experience. Since men and women in the labor force both have a median of 12.7 years of schooling (U.S. Department of Labor, 1983b), differences in average amount of schooling does not explain why women hold different jobs than men. Men hold more bachelor's and graduate degrees than women, but more males than females are high school dropouts, so that average educational attainment is the same within each group. This has been true for decades, as Table 7.3 shows. In fact, in the early 1950s women averaged over a 'year *more* schooling than men (U.S. Department of Labor, 1983b).

However, men and women differ in average employment experience. For example, a 1974 national sample showed employed white males averaging 20 years of experience while employed white females averaged 12 years (England, 1984b). Thus, it is conceivable that the underrepresentation of women within some male jobs results from demands for years of continuous employment before one enters these jobs. Yet, several studies have shown that women with more continuous experience are no more apt than other women to be employed in predominantly male occupations (England, 1982; Daymont and Statham, 1983; Corcoran et al., 1984). If even women with extensive job experience are usually in traditionally female jobs, intermittent employment or insufficient experience cannot be the principal causes of women's underrepresentation in male jobs, although it may explain the absence of women from a few jobs at the top of promotion ladders. Furthermore, extensive sex segregation exists in entry level positions, where males and females are both just starting out (Green, 1983; Greenberger and Steinberg, 1983).

More sophisticated applications of human capital theory emphasize life-time plans, wage depreciation while women are at home, and wage

Table 7.3. Median Years of Schooling Completed by Men and Women in the Labor Force, for Selected Years[a]

	Median years of schooling completed	
Year	Men	Women
1940	8.6	11.0
1952	10.6	12.0
1962	12.1	12.3
1970	12.4	12.5
1975	12.6	12.6
1981	12.7	12.7

[a]Source: U.S. Department of Labor, 1983b: 109.

appreciation while on the job. Thus Polachek (1979, 1981, in press) proposed a supply-side explanation for sex segregation that emphasizes the depreciation of human capital while one is a homemaker. Wage depreciation occurs if a woman has a lower real wage upon returning to paid employment than she had when she quit her job to take up full-time homemaking. Two hypothetical jobs with different levels of such depreciation are depicted in Fig. 7.2. (In examining this figure it is important to distinguish wage depreciation from the wages one foregoes by being out of the labor force.) Polachek argues that certain occupations entail greater risks

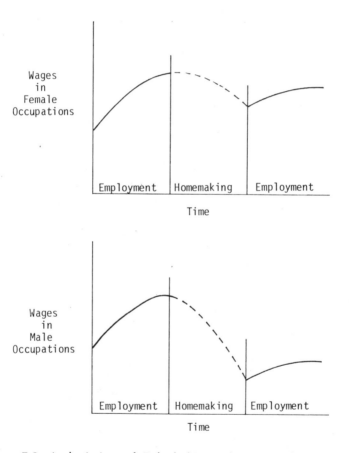

Figure 7.2. A depiction of Polachek's explanation of occupational sex segregation in terms of different depreciation rates for female and male occupations. A broken line indicates the hypothetical wage if one reentered the labor force at that point in time. From England, 1984b.

of depreciation than do others, and that women who plan intermittent employment will maximize lifetime earnings by choosing occupations with low depreciation penalties. (For example, real estate agents may suffer relatively little wage depreciation while out of the labor force, even though their earnings foregone during this period may be quite high.) Since most men plan continuous employment, they do not have this incentive to choose occupations with low depreciation rates. Thus, Polacheck argues that sex differences in plans for employment continuity lead to sex differences in the job choices that maximize men's and women's lifetime earnings. In this view, men's and women's pecuniarily rational choices will lead jobs with low depreciation rates to be predominantly female, whereas jobs with high depreciation rates will tend to be male.

Polacheck's hypothesis regarding the lesser depreciation of female jobs has not been supported by empirical evidence. Using cross-sectional data for 1967 and 1976, England (1981, 1984, in press) has shown that, contrary to the implication of Polacheck's theory, rates of wage depreciation suffered by women while out of the labor force are not higher in jobs containing high percentages of males than in predominantly female jobs. These cross-sectional findings have been replicated using the longitudinal features of the Panel Study of Income Dynamics (Corcoran et al., 1984). These results show that the depreciation penalty—the amount by which a woman's wage declines between the time she leaves and returns to employment—is no lower in female- than in male-dominated jobs. Thus, women gain no pecuniary advantage from choosing female jobs.

Another application of human capital theory focuses on rates of appreciation rather than depreciation (Zellner, 1975). Economists typically assume that, other things being equal, jobs with steep wage appreciation have lower starting wages. (This trade-off is shown in Fig. 7.3.) The lower starting wages are a price employees pay for the training they receive, training that will lead to strong wage appreciation later. Zellner hypothesized that if when choosing a job one faces a trade-off between starting salary and wage appreciation, women who plan limited years of employment will choose jobs with high starting wages and low rates of appreciation. This is because they may not be employed long enough for the benefits of appreciation to offset lower starting wages. In the terms of Chapter 6, the hypothesis is that women may choose jobs with weak implicit contract provisions because reaping the benefits of these provisions requires longer tenure than they anticipate.

As with Polacheck's theory, Zellner's hypothesis suggests that since men and women differ in the number of years they plan to be employed, the job choices that will maximize their lifetime earnings also differ, and this leads to segregation. However, in this case, data should show that predominantly female jobs have higher starting wages but lower wage appreciation than male jobs. Yet this is not the case; in fact, male jobs offer women higher

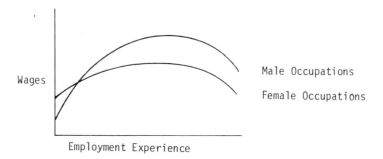

Figure 7.3. A depiction of Zellner's explanation of occupational sex segregation in terms of different starting wages and appreciation rates for female and male occupations. From England, 1984b.

starting wages than do female jobs (England, 1984b; Greenberger and Steinberg, 1983).[1]

In brief, female occupations offer lower earnings than male occupations at every educational level and life-cycle stage. Female occupations offer women neither higher starting wages nor lower wage depreciation than male occupations. Thus, women pay a price in lifetime earnings for their employment in female jobs. We conclude that, to the extent that the supply-side choices of women explain segregation, these are motivated by sex role norms, since there is no pecuniary gain to women from the choice of female over male jobs. Men, on the other hand, have both sex role socialization and pecuniary motives directing them toward the choice of traditionally male jobs.

The specific hypotheses offered by human capital theorists to explain segregation have not been well supported. But are there any ways in which issues of human capital accumulation, broadly construed, are relevant to segregation? We think there are two. First, explanations of the effect of sex role socialization on job segregation can be translated into the language of human capital. Sex role socialization refers to the fact that males and females are encouraged to develop different forms of human capital—the forms appropriate for the segregated occupations that each gender has traditionally populated. These differences can be seen in the skills and traits learned at home and in the courses of study selected by males and females in secondary and higher education.

Yet sex differences in courses of study and occupational choices have diminished within recent cohorts (Beller, 1984; Jacobs, in press). The theory of human capital with its emphasis on lifetime planning can help explain these changes. These changes, which began in the 1970s, can hardly be a consequence of childhood socialization, since women reared during the 1950s and 1960s received quite traditional socialization. Rather, it is the increase in the continuity of employment these young women now anticipate that helps explain why they have been making less traditional choices of college major and of occupation. Counter to Polachek's contention, we have argued that the financial price to women of choosing the female occupations their socialization suggested has always been high. But it has been raised even higher by women's shift toward lifetime employment and the correlated uncertainty about whether one's marriage will end in divorce. Thus, the most recent cohort of female entrants to employment has greater pecuniary motivation than any previous cohort to defy the dictates of their socialization and choose a male occupation yielding higher lifetime earnings. Of course, an important factor in their ability to make nontraditional choices has been the decline in discrimination in the 1970s.

C. Discrimination in Hiring, Placement, and Promotion

Discrimination by employers has historically been an important factor in job segregation by sex. Why do employers discriminate in allocating men and women to jobs? The major theories emphasize tastes, error, statistical generalization, and group monopoly as determinants of discrimination. (For reviews see Lewin and England, 1982 and Blau, 1984.)

Becker (1957) coined the term "taste discrimination" to refer to a preference for not hiring members of a particular group. He pointed out that since tastes provide nonpecuniary satisfaction, employers will be willing to pay a price to indulge them. When some employers refuse to hire women, they must accept lower wages in order to find jobs. Employers who *will* hire women consequently gain from lowered labor costs. Discriminators pay a price in the sense that they must compete against nondiscriminators who have lowered labor costs. Consequently, market forces should discourage the practice of such discrimination. This economic theory can be applied to the case of occupational sex segregation, with the proviso that the taste involved is a preference for seeing women in traditionally female jobs and males in traditionally male jobs. These tastes may be determined by sex role socialization regarding which jobs are appropriate to men and women. Indeed, Becker presented his theory as describing the economic consequences of tastes; determinants of tastes, he felt, must be explained by sociologists or psychologists (Becker, 1957: 1).

Continuing with the types of discrimination, "error discrimination" occurs where employers do not have discriminatory tastes, but they erroneously underestimate the potential productivities of women in men's jobs and therefore hesitate to hire women in these jobs. (The same may apply to the occasional male seeking entrance to women's jobs.) Once again, one would expect market forces to erode such discrimination, since employers not making the error will be able to hire cheaper labor.

A more subtle notion is the concept of statistical sex discrimination, discussed in Chapter 6 in connection with the information costs of search. This occurs when hiring decisions are based on differences between male and female averages on predictors of productivity. For example, if employers correctly observe that, on average, women have less mechanical knowledge than men, they may decide not to hire any women in positions requiring mechanical knowledge, screening out even those atypical women with extensive mechanical skills. Or, because women have slightly higher turnover rates than men, employers may resist hiring women in jobs where they must provide expensive training, thus screening out even those women who would have stayed for decades. (For a discussion of sex differences in turnover rates, see England, 1984.) Since men and women have overlapping distributions for virtually all characteristics of interest to employers, the use of sex group means guarantees that some individual mistakes will be made. Yet such statistical discrimination may still be economically efficient for employers in the absence of less costly means of inferring the future productivity of potential hires.

A "monopoly" model of discrimination (Arrow, 1971; Krueger, 1963) has been applied to sex-based job segregation by Madden (1973, 1975). An example of the monopoly form of discrimination can be seen in South Africa where all whites—employers and employees—collude to exclude blacks from many positions. (An example in a product rather than labor market is OPEC, with its collusive pricing policies.) Applied to sex discrimination, such collusion might involve men—as husbands, employers, legislators, and co-workers—honoring a gentleman's agreement to keep women out of certain jobs. Under such a "cartel," men as a group will make pecuniary gains at the expense of women as a group. Employers may participate in the cartel with male employees to discourage men from joining with women in unionization or some other unified workers' drive for higher wages. On the other hand, individual employers have some incentive not to honor the group monopoly, since they can gain cheaper labor if they stop discriminating. (For a similar model proposed by a sociologist to explain ethnic segregation, see Bonacich, 1972, 1976.)

It is difficult to estimate how much of the observed sex segregation of jobs has its proximate cause in employer discrimination, and how much in supply-side factors. This is because we seldom have data containing information on the qualifications of applicants and employees, their preferences for job placement and promotion, and the resulting occupational distribution. However, one way to investigate the question of whether discrimination is operating is to ask managers their opinion of the appropriateness of men and women for various jobs. Such studies often unearth discriminatory attitudes and actions. For example, Hakel and Dunnette (1970) asked managers to rank a number of applicants' characteristics on a scale from unfavorable to favorable. The average manager saw female gender as favorable for clerical applicants but saw male gender as favorable for managers, management trainees, and engineers. Summers et al. (1976: 41–42) report on managers who used sex as a screening criterion for staffing production jobs. Levinson (1975) documented discrimination by having interviewers of each sex respond to job advertisements by telephone. He found that 28% of the females inquiring about traditionally male jobs and 44% of the males asking about typically female jobs were told that persons of their sex would not like or be good at the job.

A major research project on discrimination was begun in 1972 at the School of Business Administration at the University of North Carolina (Rosen, 1982). As part of this project, Rosen and Jerdee (1978) report the results of a national survey of 884 male managers and administrators across 66 establishments. Participants anonymously completed a questionnaire requesting a comparison of men and women on numerous traits relevant for managerial effectiveness. For each trait, participants could choose from a five-point scale with "men much more than women" at one end and "women much more than men" at the other. Averaged across all respondents, men received higher scores than women on understanding the "big picture" of the organization, approaching problems rationally, getting people to work together, understanding financial matters, sizing up situations accurately, administrative capability, leadership potential, setting long-range goals and working toward them, wanting to get ahead, standing up under fire, keeping cool in emergencies, independence, self-sufficiency, and aggressiveness. Characteristics attributed to women more than men included clerical aptitude, being good at detail work, enjoyment of routine tasks, crying easily, sensitivity to criticism, timidity, jealousy, excessive emotionality regarding their jobs, absenteeism, likelihood of quitting, and putting family matters ahead of their job.

Other surveys in Rosen and Jerdee's project showed that managers are more likely to recommend a man than an identically described woman for a prestigious training conference, and are more apt to terminate a female than a male engineer for absence from work (Rosen and Jerdee, 1974b). These findings were obtained by presenting the surveyed managers with hypothetical situations and asking for their decision. Differences in their treatment of men and women were ascertained by giving one-half the respondents a particular situation to respond to, while the other one-half received the identical situation with the gender of the employee's name changed.

In yet another phase of the project (Rosen and Jerdee, 1974a), 235 male undergraduate business students were asked to assume the role of a consultant involved in hiring decisions. The students were given hypothetical job descriptions and information regarding an applicant for each position. Each student was given one hypothetical applicant for each of two positions, one managerially demanding, and one routine. Some students reviewed an application with a male name while others reviewed the identical application with a female name attached to it. Overall, females were selected significantly less often than males (59 versus 71%), but the sex difference in selection was greatest in the demanding position, where 65% of the males but only 46% of the females were selected.

These research findings suggest discrimination on the basis of some combination of tastes, error, statistical generalization, and male monopoly. Most striking is that these findings were obtained after 1972—many years after sex discrimination in employment became illegal. This evidence does not refute the notion that discrimination has declined in the last decade, but it does suggest that at least some discrimination persists.

Given this evidence of discrimination, what arguments are offered by those who believe that very little sex discrimination in hiring, placement, or promotion persists in the economy? As discussed in Chapter 6, some economists base such arguments on the theoretical notion that discrimination should erode in competitive markets, even without government intervention (e.g., Lindsay, 1980). As described previously, they reason that employers who will not hire women in certain jobs force women who desire these jobs to offer their labor to other employers at a lower wage. The employers who will hire women in "men's jobs" gain lower labor costs as unintended benefits of the discriminator's acts. Since nondiscriminators will have a cost advantage, economists expect discriminators to lose market share, go out of business, or change their ways.

We agree that market forces work in the direction of eroding discrimination, but think that discrimination often brings countervailing forces into existence, so that it may not disappear without government intervention. Economists have failed to recognize feedback effects between households and labor markets, effects that create discrimination anew before it has completely disappeared. As pointed out in Chapter 6, if women are discriminated against in the job market, fewer will aspire to or train for male jobs, more couples will employ a specialized division of labor, and traditional socialization will seem more rational to parents. These developments will reinforce stereotypical notions about women and allow correct statistical calculation that fewer women than men are suited for male-dominated jobs. Given the empirical evidence of managers' discriminatory attitudes and behavior, and the theoretical argument regarding feedback from discrimination, we conclude that discrimination has been an important, though declining, force in occupational segregation.

D. Structured Mobility Ladders

One organizational feature—structured mobility ladders—deserves special mention for its role in perpetuating job segregation by sex (Roos and Reskin, 1984: 250–251). Jobs may be categorized according to the extent to which they are attached to mobility ladders. This distinction corresponds loosely to that between jobs involving few versus many implicit contract features (see Chapter 6), since implicit contracts often provide wage increases with experience through provision of opportunities to ascend mobility ladders. Once segregation has occurred at jobs that are ports of entry to firms, whether from discrimination or sex role socialization, it will be perpetuated via the differential training and associated mobility opportunities leading upward from these jobs. Thus, the existence of structured mobility ladders, or internal labor markets, carries much of the segregation in entry level jobs into the future without a need for further discrimination. Typically, one remains on either a short "female ladder" or a longer "male ladder" with implicit contract features (Kanter, 1977; Grinker et al., 1970).

IV. THE SEX GAP IN EARNINGS

Between 1950 and 1980 the overall sex gap in earnings remained remarkably constant. As shown in Table 7.4, among full-time, year-round workers, women's median earnings fluctuated around 60% of that of men for decades. However, since 1980 the sex gap in pay has finally declined, with the earnings of women employed full-time year-round moving from

Table 7.4. Pay of Women Employed Full-Time, Year-Round as a Percentage of Pay of Men for Selected Years[a]

Year	Women's earnings as a percentage of men's
1956	63.3
1960	60.7
1964	59.1
1968	58.5
1972	57.4
1976	60.0
1980	60.5
1983	64.3

[a]Source: Adapted from Smith and Ward, 1984: 23.

60% of male earnings to 64% between 1980 and 1983 (Smith and Ward, 1984). The shifts have been even greater among younger workers. Between 1980 and 1983, this ratio moved from 78 to 86% among those aged 20–24, and from 69 to 73% among those aged 25–34 (Smith and Ward, 1984).[2]

A. Segregation and the Sex Gap in Pay

A large portion of the male-female earnings gap results from the concentration of women in lower-paying jobs rather than from differential compensation to men and women holding the same jobs. Thus, when male and female earnings are compared within occupational categories, the income difference is much smaller than that for the labor force as a whole (Fuchs, 1974: 23–26; Malkiel and Malkiel, 1973: 693–705). In addition, other things being equal, men tend to be represented more heavily than women within relatively capital-intensive and unionized (and thus higher paying) industries (Hodson and England, in press).

Analysts repeatedly find that the finer the job classification they employ, the lower the earnings differential between men and women holding that job. At the same time, the finer the job classification, the more sex segregation of jobs is revealed (Bielby and Baron, 1984). In this way ever greater shares of the sex gap in earnings are attributed to job segregation. Thus, sex role socialization, discrimination in hiring, placement and promotion, and structured mobility ladders—as explanations of sex segregation—also help explain the sex gap in pay. This also suggests that the substantial declines in segregation that began after 1970 bode well for women's relative earnings. In addition, two other factors directly affect the sex gap in pay—human capital, and the type of wage discrimination at issue in "comparable worth." We discuss each of these in turn.

B. The Supply Side: Human Capital and Family Responsibilities

If human capital is measured by years of schooling, then since men and women average equal levels, this cannot explain the sex gap in pay. However, years of work experience do appear to provide part of the explanation for the earnings gap. Mincer and Polachek (1974; see also Polachek, 1975) argue that roughly one-half the gap can be explained by differences in the amount of time men and women are employed rather than working at home as homemakers. A replication by Sandell and Shapiro (1978) concludes that sex differences in years of experience can explain about one-quarter of the earnings gap. Finally, in the most exhaustive analysis to date, Corcoran and Duncan (1979) decompose sex differences in wages into portions attributable to sex differences in years out of the labor force since completing school, years of work experience prior to one's current job, years with the present employer (broken into those years which did and did not involve training), the proportion of working years that were full-time, absences from work due to illness of self or others, limits placed on job hours or location, and plans to stop work for nontraining reasons. All these variables explained 44% of the earnings gap between white men and women. Thus we conclude that somewhere between one-quarter and one-half of the sex gap in pay have their proximate source in sex differentials in job experience.

Corcoran and Duncan (1979) found the most important factor to be years with one's current employer, especially the years during which the employer is providing training. To the extent that employers discriminate in not providing as much training to women as men, some of the pay gap explained by this factor may reflect demand-side discrimination rather than supply-side choices. Here again, we see evidence that women are less often in jobs with well developed implicit contract features.

Are trends in sex differences in job experience consistent with trends in the sex gap in pay? Until recently, the data had not been assembled to answer this question. One might think that as women's employment increases, this would necessarily tend to close the sex gap in experience. But, in fact, the upward surge in female employment affects aggregate averages of women's years of experience in two conflicting ways. On the one hand, the fact that fewer women are leaving the labor force (at all or) for long periods to rear children increases the average experience of women in the labor force. On the other hand, the continued entrance of new female workers with little experience depresses the number of years of experience of the average employed female. Smith and Ward (1984) have recently assembled data estimating the average experience of employed men and women for each year between 1920 and 1980. It appears that the experience of employed women relative to men failed to increase over this period due to the continued entrance of new women with little experience. Thus there is no anomaly between the lack of change in relative experience and the lack of reduction in the sex gap in pay. Since 1980, however, women's relative experience has increased, and this may well be a factor in the declining sex gap in pay (Smith and Ward, 1984). (O'Neill, 1985 reaches a similar conclusion.) However, this does not mean that experience completely "explains" the sex gap in pay. As we have seen, experience explains no more than one-half of the pay gap between employed men and women at any particular point in time.

What of the other one-half of the sex gap not explained by experience? As already noted, a portion of this is explained by the segregation of women in low-paying jobs even when they do have substantial experience, with this segregation arising from both sex role socialization and discrimination. In addition, once segregation has occurred, some of the pay gap results from a form of demand-side pay discrimination, to which we now turn.

C. The Demand Side: Unequal Pay for Jobs of Comparable Worth

In an earlier section we discussed discrimination in hiring, placement, and promotion as demand-side phenomena affecting sex segregation and thus pay. A second type of sex discrimination occurs when men and women are paid unequally for equal work in the same job. Yet, across the economy as a whole, men and women rarely hold the same jobs, so this sort of discrimination is not a major source of sex differentials in pay. A third and distinct type of discrimination is identified by the issue of unequal pay for jobs of comparable worth. This occurs when the gender of those holding jobs affects the wages employers are willing to pay. It is this third type of discrimination that is at issue in the current debate over "comparable worth." (See England and Norris, in press, for a discussion of theoretical and legal issues involved in "comparable worth.")

Studies using a "policy-capturing" approach provide evidence that this type of discrimination is operating in the United States' economy. Such research seeks to assess whether the pay of jobs is determined in part by the sex of the individuals performing the work. To estimate whether, and to what extent, such discrimination is operating, one must first determine what factors are determining the wage levels of various jobs. These factors may be thought of as the (explicitly or implicitly) operating policies that are determining wages. Of course, many of these policies involve responses to market forces. Once operative policies are identified, it is possible to estimate whether jobs populated by women pay less than predicted on the basis of these factors.

This approach is best operationalized via multiple regression analysis. Comparable-worth discrimination is said to occur when one finds an effect of the sex composition of jobs on their pay level that remains even when other job characteristics shown to be determinants of pay levels are entered as control variables. Jobs rather than individuals are generally taken as the unit of analysis. In this case the dependent variable is the average, median, or starting pay in the job, and separate regressions are run to predict male and female wages. All job characteristics thought to be significant determinants of wages are entered as independent control variables. The sex composition of jobs (measured either as percentage male or percentage female) is entered as the independent variable whose net coefficient measures the extent of discrimination. If women choose or are confined to jobs that would be low paying quite apart from their sex label, these differentials in wages will not be included in the measure of wage discrimination; regression analysis will partial out such differentials. Thus, a policy-capturing approach does not treat every instance of a lower paying job filled by females as sex discrimination. Nor, for that matter, does this approach rest on normative judgments by the researchers as to what characteristics of jobs *should* determine their compensation or constitute "true worth." Rather, the approach seeks to determine what policies are actually operative in the labor market. Thus, the focus is on employers' revealed standards of pay worth (including responses to market forces), and the test is whether the sex make-up of jobs appears to be one of these.

Two studies have used this research strategy with detailed 1970 Census occupational categories as the unit of analysis. England *et al.* (1982) regressed median earnings (male and female separately) for full-time year-round workers on the characteristics of these occupations. The characteristics serving as control variables were measures of the skill demands of each job as described by the "Dictionary of Occupational Titles." The variables included the general educational requirements of the job; specific vocational preparation; requirements for cognitive skills of intelligence, verbal aptitude, numerical aptitude, and complexity of the task with data; perceptual skills of clerical, color, form, and spatial perception; manual skills of finger dexterity, manual dexterity, motor coordination, eye-hand-foot coordination, physical strength, and the complexity of the task with things; and social skills of speaking persuading, supervising, instructing, negotiating, and mentoring. The inclusion of these variables captures employers' wage setting policies fairly well; 75% of the variance was explained for each sex.

After controlling for these skill characteristics, England *et al.* (1982) found that each 1% female in an occupation has a net depression effect on annual earnings of $30 for males and $17 for females. Thus, the difference between the median annual earnings of two occupations alike in their skill requirements but one of which is 90% female and the other of which is 90% male would be $1360 for women and $2400 for men. Both men and women suffer wage losses from holding "female" jobs. However, since women are more concentrated in such jobs, this net effect of sex composition lowers women's earnings relative to men's for reasons quite apart from the skill requirements of their occupations. This is the sort of pay inequity at issue in debates over comparable worth. England *et al.* (1982) estimate that it accounted for 32% of the sex gap in earnings among full-time, year-round workers in 1970. A similar study by Treiman and Hartmann (1981: 28–30) used a more limited set of skill measures from the more recent fourth edition of the "Dictionary of Occupational Title," and arrived at virtually the same estimate of the net effect of the sex make-up of jobs on their pay levels.

Other studies have examined the issue of comparable worth within firms rather than economy-wide. Such studies typically use job elevation to determine skill and training levels and other job requirements. In this procedure, points are assigned to each job. Studies of this type typically find that predominantly female jobs pay about 20% less than male jobs scoring the same number of job evaluation points. This is illustrated by Table 7.5, which shows the pay levels and points of a number of predominantly male and female jobs at issue in a comparable-worth suit against the State of Washington.

Some economists reject the existence of comparable-worth discrimination by invoking crowding in female occupations, rather than pay discrimination, to explain the low wages of female jobs (Lindsay, 1980). Bergmann's (1974) crowding thesis holds that the low wages in women's jobs result from the exclusion of women from male jobs.[3] In her view, this exclusion of women from male jobs may result from either discrimination or household sex role socialization. In either case, the consequence is an increase in the supply of labor to female jobs, an outward shift in the labor supply curve. According to the laws of supply and demand, discussed in the

Table 7.5. Selected Results of the Washington State Comparable-Worth Survey[a]

Job title	Job evaluation points	Average annual salary, 1983–1984	
		Male dominated	Female dominated
Warehouse worker	97	17,030	
Delivery truck driver	97	19,367	
Laundry worker	105		12,276
Telephone operator	118		11,770
Data entry operator	125		13,051
Intermediate clerk typist	129		12,161
Civil engineering tech	133	18,796	
Library technician	152		13,963
Licensed practical nurse	173		14,069
Auto mechanic	175	22,236	
Maintenance carpenter	197	22,870	
Secretary	197		14,857
Chemist	277	25,625	
Civil engineer	287	25,115	
Senior computer systems analyst	324	24,019	
Registered nurse	348		20,954
Librarian	353		21,969

[a]Source: Remick, 1984.

previous chapter, this leads to more individuals being employed, but at a lower wage rate. By contrast, comparable-worth discrimination shifts the labor demand curve for female jobs inward, leading to lower employment at lower wages. That is, if this sort of wage discrimination is operating, it means that for any given quantity of labor, and any given contribution of that labor to marginal revenue product, employers are not willing to pay as high a wage if the job contains many females. These contrasting hypotheses about why female jobs have low pay are illustrated in Fig. 7.4 and 7.5.

Both crowding and comparable-worth discrimination lead to lower wages in female occupations than in male occupations with identical marginal revenue product curves. Crowding and comparable-worth discrimination could operate simultaneously; they are not incompatible. Thus, a portion of the sex gap in earnings attributed to comparable discrimination may in fact be due to crowding. Although this is difficult to test empirically, given the difficulty of observing the placement of supply curves, we think it doubtful that most women's occupations are more crowded than men's.

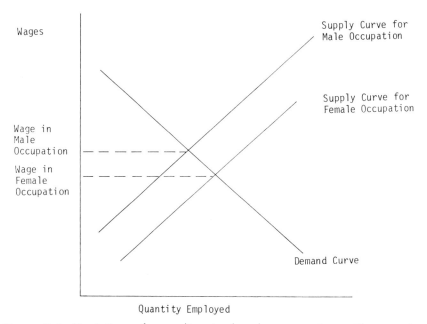

Figure 7.4. Depiction of crowding in female occupations. The supply curve to female occupations is shifted outward in comparison to the supply curve facing male occupations. The two occupations have identical demand curves. From England and Norris, in press.

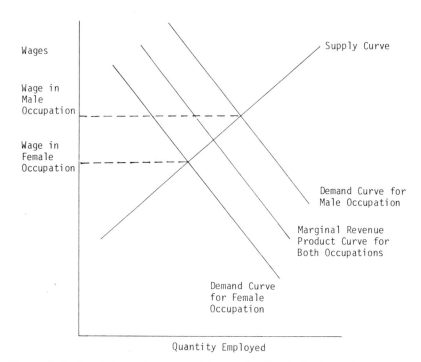

Figure 7.5. Depiction of comparable-worth discrimination. Two occupations face identical supply curves and have identical marginal
revenue product curves. Yet the demand curve for labor in the
female occupation is farther toward the origin than the demand
curve for the male occupation. From England and Norris, in
press.

Thus we doubt that crowding is the major explanation for the low wages so
typical of female jobs. This is partly because occupational sex segregation
applies to men's as well as to women's jobs. Indeed, there is evidence of
discrimination against men trying to enter female occupations as well as
women trying to enter male jobs (Levinson, 1975). In addition, it is doubtful
that patterns of self-selection crowd female jobs more than male jobs since,
as previously discussed, males are socialized to avoid traditionally female
roles more than females are trained to avoid male roles (Maccoby and
Jacklin, 1974: 328). Stevenson (1975) takes the fact that women are concentrated into fewer detailed Census occupational categories than men to
indicate greater crowding in female than male jobs, but this does not
necessarily follow, since job categories differ greatly in size. A further
argument against the contention that women's jobs are more crowded than

men's comes from evidence that the traditionally female jobs of the service sector have experienced unusually large increases in labor demand in this century (Oppenheimer, 1970). In light of these considerations, it is our judgment that significant net coefficients on occupational sex composition in earnings functions reflect wage discrimination against female occupation rather than crowding.

As we have discussed, all models of discrimination have an anomalous status within neoclassical economics. This is because market forces should lead to the erosion of discrimination within competitive labor markets (Arrow, 1972: 90–92, 99; Lindsay, 1980: 23–25; England and Lewin, 1982). In the case of comparable-worth discrimination, the erosion would occur as follows: If female occupations are underpaid, women will be pecuniarly motivated to move into male occupations. If they do move, this will integrate male occupations while creating a temporary "shortage" of labor in female occupations. This inward shift in the supply curve to female occupations would then lead to movement up the (constant) demand curve to a higher equilibrium wage in the female jobs. Of course, this cannot occur if employers discriminate against women seeking to enter higher paying male jobs, but as we have discussed, the neoclassical model predicts the erosion of this form of discrimination as well. Also, if women can be hired at lower wages in female occupations than men will accept in male occupations, employers have an incentive to attempt to substitute female occupations for male occupations, and eventually this should cause a shortage of labor and rising wages in these newly female occupations.

Yet, these dynamic implications of the neoclassical model do not require rejection of the thesis of comparable-worth discrimination (as Lindsay, 1980, has claimed) any more than they require rejection of the models of hiring discrimination that are now at least ambivalently accepted by economists (Arrow, 1972; Becker, 1957; Lloyd and Niemi, 1979; Phelps, 1972). Even committed neoclassicals often concede that hiring discrimination can persist for an extended period of time, although they believe that it will disappear in the long run. As we argued for hiring discrimination, feedback effects between the employment and household aspects of sexism may be one reason why the long run is so long. The feedback effects between households and employment that we have emphasized throughout this book may serve to perpetuate the wage discrimination at issue in comparable worth, as it does other types of discrimination.

A related economic argument against the doctrine of comparable worth (Hildebrand, 1980) asserts that firms must pay market wages to compete effectively in their product markets, and that it is "the market" rather than discrimination that dictates a lower wage in female than in male jobs. Our point is that this market wage may reflect comparable-worth discrimination.

Recall that what economists mean by the "market wage" is the wage defined by the point where the supply and demand curves cross. We have defined comparable-worth discrimination as the case where the sex composition of jobs affects where employers place the demand curve for labor. If discrimination affects the placement of many firms' demand curves, it affects the "market wage" by definition. If one's definition of the market wage includes the neoclassical assumption that demand curves are entirely determined by marginal revenue product at a point in time, one is assuming that the market forces of competition already have forced the erosion of discrimination. Thus employing this neoclassical assumption to argue that market wages rather than discrimination dictate lower wages in female jobs is tautological, since it assumes the very lack of discrimination it purports to show. In contrast to such circular reasoning, the policy-capturing approach discussed above empirically investigates the existence of comparable-worth discrimination. This is done by assessing whether sex composition has a net effect on jobs' pay when other relevant determinants of their pay have been statistically controlled.

V. SEX DISCRIMINATION AND THE LAW

The most significant federal laws regulating sex discrimination in employment are the Equal Pay Act of 1963, Title VII of the Civil Rights Act of 1964, and Executive Order 11246, issued in 1965, which mandated Affirmative Action by federal contractors and grantees. The Equal Pay Act of 1963 required that men and women performing the same work must be paid equally unless the difference in pay is explained by merit, a piece rate, seniority, or some factor other than sex. Although the Equal Pay Act has led to litigation correcting many inequities, it contains no provision outlawing the discriminatory segregation of men and women in distinct jobs, nor does it require employers to pay men and women equal wages when their jobs entail different tasks but comparable skills, qualifications, and working conditions. However, Title VII has been used for these purposes, as we explain below.

Title VII of the Civil Rights Act states that:

> . . . It shall be an unlawful employment practice for an employer (1) to fail or refuse to hire or to discharge any individual or otherwise to discriminate against any individual with respect to his compensation, terms, conditions, or privileges of employment, because of such or individual's race, color, religion, sex, or national origin; or
> (2) to limit, segregate, or classify his employees or applicants for employment in any way which would deprive or tend to deprive any individual of employment opportunities or otherwise adversely affect his status as an employee, because of such individual's race, color, religion, sex, or national origin . . . .

This act was motivated by concern over racial discrimination in housing, employment, and public accommodations. When it was passed in 1964, blacks could not patronize many restaurants, hotels, and stores in the South. (The long survival of such practices is yet another argument against the ability of unaided market forces to erode discrimination, unless "the long run" is defined as over 100 years.) During the Congressional debate over the bill, a Southern Congressman seeking to defeat it introduced an amendment also prohibiting sex discrimination. To his surprise, both the amendment and the bill passed, and their consequences have been far-reaching.

After passage of the bill, President Johnson created the Equal Employment Commission (EEOC) to aid enforcement of the law by receiving complaints and mediating out-of-court settlements. Since the passage of amendments to Title VII in 1972, the EEOC has also had the authority to bring discrimination suits and provide legal counsel for plaintiffs alleging discrimination. Persons desiring legal redress for violation of Title VII must file a complaint with the EEOC before taking other legal action. However, if they are not satisfied with the results of the EEOC's deliberations and mediation, and if the EEOC does not decide to take the case to court, they may hire a private attorney and pursue the case in the courts independently of the EEOC.

Court cases alleging discrimination are of two principal types: individual and class-action suits. In an individual suit, one person, the plaintiff, alleges that a defendant employer violated the law by engaging in discrimination. In a class-action suit, the plaintiffs are an entire group of individuals (not all of whom must be named) who are alleged to have suffered from similar discriminatory actions by a particular employer. Thus a "class" can be all women denied promotion, all blacks terminated, etc. Court decisions on thousands of Title VII cases have by now clarified what plaintiffs must prove to win a case, as well as the elements of a successful defense. Standards of proof are similar whether the alleged discrimination occurred in hiring, placement, promotion, termination, or pay—all of which are covered by the very general language of Title VII. The standards of proof also differ little according to whether discrimination by race, color, sex, religion, or national origin is alleged. For plaintiffs, there are three principal methods of proof: showing intent, differential treatment, and disparate impact. Below, we discuss each of these as they apply to sex discrimination. (For a primer explaining EEO statutes, administrative regulations, and court cases, see Levin-Epstein, 1984.)

Directly showing intent is seldom attempted by plaintiffs, since the "smoking gun" is rarely available. Such evidence would include written policy to exclude women from certain positions, or a statement by the manager responsible for a particular personnel decision admitting that it was influenced by the sex of the employee or applicant.

Differential treatment occurs when men and women with the same qualifications are treated differently. In class action suits, this is typically demonstrated via statistical analysis of personnel actions. Examples include the finding that, after adjusting for qualifications, a higher proportion of male than female job applicants are hired, or promoted, or that males are paid more than females in the same job. (This last form of discrimination is also prohibited by the Equal Pay Act.)

The third method of proving discrimination was validated by the (1971) decision of the U.S. Supreme Court in Griggs v. Duke Power Company. In this case the court ruled that where an employer uses a screening device which is nondiscriminatory on its face (e.g., test scores, educational credentials, or height, weight, or experience requirements), but the device has an adverse and disparate impact on a group protected from discrimination, the plaintiffs will have made a "prima facie" case of discrimination. This would occur, for example, if more women than men fail a physical test for firefighters. However, establishing such a prima facie case of discrimination does not settle the issue. Rather, it means that the burden of proof now shifts to the defendant, who must prove that the screening device is indeed job-related. That is, the employer must show that this device does indeed screen out individuals who would perform the job less well. It is only if the prima facie case has been made *and* the defendant *cannot* show that the selection device is job-related that the plaintiffs win the case. The disparate impact doctrine is often employed in class-action suits.

Title VII has been widely employed in attempts to prove sex discrimination with regard to hiring, promotion, or equal pay for equal work (this latter also being covered by the Equal Pay Act). Because of the general language of Title VII, plaintiffs have more recently attempted to litigate comparable-worth discrimination under this statute.

These attempts gained some legal status with the 1981 U.S. Supreme Court decision in County of Washington, Oregon v. Gunther. In this case an employer (the county) decided to violate its own written calculation of the relative worth of a female compared to a male job in setting wages. The Supreme Court construed this decision as intentional discrimination. Following this ruling, in 1983 a federal district court found the State of Washington guilty of sex discrimination in a comparable-worth case. The state had commissioned a consulting firm to evaluate civil service jobs. They found that the state systematically paid predominantly female jobs at a lower rate than male jobs with similar job requirements. (For examples of the findings, review Table 7.5.) The state did not dispute these findings, but for years did nothing to correct the situation. As of 1985 the case was being appealed by the State of Washington, and may reach the Supreme Court. In each of these court cases evidence of intent to discriminate by sex was found by the court in the discrepancy between the employer's own job evaluations and pay levels. However, the courts have not explicitly stated that one must prove *intent* in order to prove comparable-worth discrimination under Title VII.

There are two major unresolved issues in the legal status of comparable worth. One is whether the courts will find employers guilty when they have not performed their own study evaluating the worth of jobs prior to the case, but rather an evaluation study of the jobs is presented by experts for the plaintiff. In the major cases won by plaintiffs in federal courts through 1984 (International Union of Electrical Workers v. Westinghouse, 1980; Gunther v. County of Washington, Oregon, 1981; and American Federation of State, County, and Municipal Employees v. State of Washington, 1983), the employers commissioned the job evaluation studies prior to the filing of the case, yet failed to abide by its conclusions when they set wages. A policy-capturing study of wage policies that found a net effect of sex composition on wages might be similarly construed as evidence of comparable-worth discrimination using either the differential treatment or disparate impact doctrines. However, no court has yet taken this action. If such studies are not permitted to bear a portion of the plaintiff's burden of proof, the long-term ramifications of the Washington and Gunther cases may prove to be minor. This is because many employers have not undertaken formal job evaluations, and there is now an incentive for them to avoid evaluations. On the other hand, if "policy-capturing" studies undertaken specifically for litigation are permitted as evidence, judges will have to decide which job characterisitcs can be used as control variables in the equations predicting jobs' wages. Defendants and plaintiffs will have different interests in the specificity of the control variables allowed in policy-capturing analyses, and judges will have to arbitrate these differences.

A second issue in the legal status of comparable worth involves the situation where employers claim that they are merely offering the prevailing market wage for a particular job. For example, consider an employer paying secretaries less than janitors. The employer may argue that although the differential cannot be justified in terms of skill or marginal product, it is necessary because of prevailing market wages in the two fields. That is, forcing the employer to pay secretaries more than do other employers would put him at a competitive disadvantage in pricing goods and, hence, lower his profit. The counterargument is that if comparable-worth discrimination is prevalent, the market wage reflects this discrimination; but if the law were not interpreted to make "market wage" a defense for *any* employer, no one employer would be at a competitive disadvantage with respect to the others by being forced to correct this discrimination in setting wages in women's jobs. No case hinging on this issue has as yet reached the Supreme Court, although some district courts and at least one appellate court (Spaulding v. University of Washington, 1984) have allowed the "market wage" argument as a defense. Should the Supreme Court concur, the courts will be ineffective in eradicating much of comparable-worth discrimination.

Although it is too soon to discern the effect of Title VII on comparable-worth discrimination, there is substantial evidence that the statute has decreased other forms of sex discrimination such as the failure to admit women to high-paying "male" jobs (Burstein, in press; Beller, 1979, 1982a,b).

It also appears that Executive Order 11246 has improved women's job status. This is the order that mandated Affirmative Action, the requirement that government contractors and other employers receiving federal aid set goals and timetables and make a "good faith effort" to bring the proportion of minorities and women in various job categories up to a level consistent with estimates of their availability in a qualified labor pool. [As one can imagine, employers and the enforcing agency, the Department of Labor's Office of Federal Contract Compliance Programs (OFCCP), often disagree over the proper data to use for these "availability estimates," and over what constitutes a "good faith effort" to meet them.] A recent study (U.S. Department of Labor, 1984) suggests that Affirmative Action has helped women. It shows that establishments covered by the Order (that is, those who do business with or receive aid from the federal government) showed a greater shift of women into nontraditional jobs between 1974 and 1980 than establishments not covered by the Order. Also, establishments chosen for a review by the OFCCP showed more such movement in women's opportunities than establishments covered by the Order but not reviewed.

Smith and Ward (1984) argue that neither Title VII nor Affirmative Action have had a substantial effect on the sex gap in pay. They base their argument on the fact that the sex gap in pay has declined only since 1980, a period during which federal funds for antidiscrimination enforcement were cut back substantially. However, we think this view is misleading. It may well have taken until 1980 for the effects of the enforcement escalation that occurred after 1972 to be fully effective. This is consistent with the fact that segregation started declining during the 1970s (Beller, 1984).

VI. SUMMARY

In this chapter we have surveyed gender differences in employment experiences as well as trends in these differences. We noted dramatic increases in female employment rates, along with modest changes in female occupational segregation and only very recent change in the sex gap in earnings. We have focused as much on explaining the remaining gender differentials as on explaining postwar changes.

The most powerful explanations of pre-1970s increases in female labor force participation are the increases in the wage rates available to females, and rising labor demand in occupations already sex-typed as female. A more eclectic set of explanations was suggested for the continued upward trend in female employment past the mid-1970s.

We conclude that job segregation by sex has persisted because of sex role socialization affecting job choices; discrimination in hiring, placement, and promotion; and structured mobility ladders that perpetuate much of the segregation that occurs in entry-level jobs. The extent of such segregation decreased little until the 1970s. We attribute these declines in segregation to declines in discrimination, as well as to nontraditional job choices by recent cohorts of young women.

The sex gap in pay did not begin to erode until about 1980. Yet, even in 1983, females employed full-time year-round earned only 64% of male earnings. We attribute this pay gap to job segregation, to differences in average years of job experience of men and women, and to comparable-worth discrimination. The latter occurs when employers set wages lower in female than in male jobs involving different tasks but making a comparable contribution to the firm's product. We attribute the very recent erosion of the pay differential to increases in women's experience relative to men's, to declines in discrimination, and to the trends toward job desegregation that occurred in the 1970s and 1980s.

The argument throughout the chapter has drawn on sociology and economics, and on supply- and demand-side explanations of gender differences. We have stressed throughout that one cannot reduce explanations of job segregation and pay differences by sex to simplistic one-factor stories attributing everything either to "supply-side household decisions" or to "demand-side structure and discrimination." Rather, both types of effects are operative, with feedback effects cycling back and forth between them. These feedback effects have often operated to preserve sex differentials, even where market forces tend to erode them. Yet once substantial change begins, it may also be magnified via these same feedbacks.

NOTES

[1]The evidence is mixed on whether female jobs show lower wage appreciation than do male jobs. England (1984) found that the wage appreciation in dollars per year was lower in female jobs, but wage appreciation expressed as a percentage change was not. If female jobs do offer flatter wage trajectories, this is just one more disadvantage of female occupations, and a reason it is not *pecuniarily* rational for either women or men to choose them. However, if two individuals had an equal taste

for a female occupation, the disadvantage of choosing the female occupation would be greater for the person planning continuous employment. Thus, the kernel of truth in Polachek's view may be that men have, on average, more of a pecuniary motive than women to avoid female occupations. Females are also penalized for choosing female jobs; the penalty is just less for them.

[2]Blau and Beller (1984) show that when adjustments are made for changes over time in the composition of "full-time year-round" workers by weeks worked per year (which do vary somewhat even within this group), the reduction in the adjusted sex gap in pay is seen to have begun its decline several years prior to 1980. O'Neill (1985:Table 3) considers data sources that adjust for hours worked (which vary from 35 to over 40 hours per week within those classified as full-time) and concludes that the convergence began about 1979 in age groups under 45.

[3]Bergmann believes that much of the pay gap between male and female jobs can be explained by crowding arising in part from previous discrimination in hiring, placement, and promotion. Yet, despite the fact that she does not see these wage gaps as arising from what we call "comparable-worth discrimination," she has advocated policies requiring employers to adjust the wages of female jobs upward (Bergmann, in press; Bergmann and Gray, 1984). She views these policies as a practical and relatively quick way to move women's wages to what they would have been in the absence of sex discrimination in the allocation of individuals to positions.

IV THE FUTURE

8

FUTURE TRENDS
IN HOUSEHOLDS,
EMPLOYMENT, AND GENDER

I. INTRODUCTION

The preceding chapters present a way of viewing households and employment, and the gender differentiation in each. We have also described the dramatic changes that have occurred in these arrangements between the 1950s and 1980s. In seeking to explain both stable patterns and change, we have created a conceptual framework that draws selectively from economics, sociology, and demography. This has emphasized individual choice, social structure (defined by the distribution of "slots," or other socioeconomic aggregates), and the implicit contracts that characterize long-term relationships such as marriage and employment. In this chapter we take a brief look ahead, trying to see what the coming decades will bring in each of these areas.

Following usual demographic practice, we will extrapolate current trends in cases where they seem to be long-term in nature, rather than short-term aberrations. We will also employ a variation on this approach based on measured effects between variables; if some variable, Y, has been shown (in cross-section or time series data) to be positively affected by a second variable, X, and X is trending upward in the long-term, we will predict increases in Y as well. Or, more conservatively, we may use such correlational information to discuss the likely determinants of a particular phenomenon, stopping short of predicting the actual direction of change. Finally, we will make some predictions based on tensions, conflicts, or dissatisfactions inherent in present arrangements. These may lead to change if the power of currently unsatisfied individuals is somehow increased. Social, economic, and demographic projections are notoriously difficult to make. (For example, no one foresaw the baby boom.) Accordingly, the projections offered here should be taken as little more than a catalog of the trends inherent in the current state of affairs. They should not be taken as our view of the changes we consider desirable; often, what we predict and what we would prefer diverge sharply.

In concluding this chapter, we also present our view of the future of the study of households, employment, and gender. We stress the need for continuing efforts to achieve the various integrations we have begun in this book—relating sociology, economics, and demography; seeing the parallels and reciprocal links between gender differentiation in households and in employment; and seeing the role of individual choice, structural regularities, and contracts in these arrangements. Thus we conclude by outlining some issues that must be addressed if the development of an integrated view is to continue.

II. HOUSEHOLDS

What will the American household be like in the decades ahead? We begin by considering the issues raised in Chapter 3—markets for partners, the nature of marriage or cohabitation as an informal contract, marital power, divorce, and the blended families that result from remarriage.

We argued that the search for partners functions as a "market" (although not a spot market) in which one's level of desirability influences the partner one can attract, and in which the (material and psychic) costs of search limit how long one holds out for a preferred partner. We believe that this description will continue to characterize the search for intimate partners. What is likely to change are the criteria that heterosexual males and females use to define desirability. Changes in these standards will follow changes in the structural placement of men and women within the role division of marriage. Thus, to the extent that women's employment and earnings continue to increase, they may come to weigh men's earning power less heavily, and place greater importance on emotional or sensual attributes. Men may pay greater attention to a woman's earning power, leading them to weigh youth, beauty, and traditionally feminine emotional qualities less heavily. By this reasoning, as well as by a simple extrapolation of recent trends, we predict that the ages of men and women at first marriage will continue to converge. As these changes occur, the positive correlations between partners' traits that are the hallmark of assortative mating will increase. Applying this to earnings suggests increased inequality in the distribution of family incomes as the tendency for high-earning women and men to marry one another increases.

Cohabitation and marriage will remain informal, implicit contracts. In the early 1970s, many journalists predicted a move to explicit marriage contracts as women sought strengthened rights. Yet little movement toward formal (or contingent-claims) contracts has occurred. If formal and legal understandings become more important within cohabitation and marriage, it will likely result from increasing governmental intervention, brought about by political pressure. Groups will seek new laws involving marital rape, child support payments, child custody for fathers or lesbian mothers, and divorce property settlements. In these ways, there may be a push toward more formal, state-enforced marital contracts. Yet individual couples will not move toward formal contingent-claims contracts for the same reasons they have not in the past. The costs of negotiation and enforcement are prohibitive, and the effort put into such negotiation at the beginning of the relationship detracts from investment in the "public good" of the relationship. In fact, the informal nature of contracts between partners will become clearer as cohabitation continues to increase as a stage prior to marriage. The initial relationship-specific investments of learning to live with a partner are now often made during this period of cohabitation.

We expect that the marital power of women will continue to increase, but that the average power of men and women in marriages will not equalize until child rearing is fully shared, a move that has begun only in "vanguard" groups, and there only modestly. We argued that women's disadvantage in marital power occurs because their marital role involves greater relationship-specific investment than does men's role as earner. Earnings are readily transferable to another relationship, while the gains from learning the emotional nuances and raising the children of a particular man are less transferable. If this role asymmetry is the proximate source of women's power disadvantage, it follows that as women's employment and earnings continue to increase relative to men's, so too will their marital power.

However, we have thus far seen little tendency for women's increased employment to affect the amount of child rearing men do. Rather, women remain the primary caretakers of their children, and this care is supplemented by care purchased in the market or provided by female relatives. If this continues, equality of men and women is unlikely to occur for several reasons. First, it seems unlikely that women's earnings will fully converge to men's if they continue to bear this major responsibility, and we have seen that earnings affect marital power. Second, even if women's earnings became equal to men's, their caretaking role would lead them to desire, and be thought most appropriate for, custody of the children in case of divorce. Their custody of children would disadvantage them in the market for second marriages, and in their marital power within those second marriages. Finally, Chodorow's (1978) argument that psychological proclivities toward dominance in males are fostered by having a primary caretaker of the opposite gender suggests that men will continue to push for more power in marriage if they are reared primarily by women. Thus, while we believe that women's marital power will trend upward, whether it comes to equal men's depends on whether a change in men's household responsibilities accompanies the (already strong) upward trend in women's employment. This, in turn, depends on whether women use some of their newly gained marital power to push for this change in men's roles, rather than using it only to increase their control over decision making in traditionally male areas (such as automobile purchases).

The divorce rate will likely continue to increase, although possibly at a much slower rate than heretofore. We argued that the factors pushing the divorce rate upward were not an increased dissatisfaction with marriage (which seems to be more satisfying than ever), but rather an increase in the economic viability of household splitting. This change occurred because of economic growth that drove men's wages up and increased women's wages and probability of employment. Thus, both women and men are more apt to choose divorce because ex-wives and their children are now more able to survive economically without the husband's earnings (although such female-headed households still have a very difficult time). At the same time, an increased cultural importance has been given to "self-fulfillment," and this has been accompanied by increased acceptance of actions placing self-interest above familial responsibility.

What does this suggest about the future trajectory of divorce? Insofar as increases in divorce come with increased economic prosperity, our prediction hinges largely on a prediction about national trends in income. It is extremely difficult to predict the direction of our national economy after postwar years of growth, the stagflation of the 1970's, several recessions of the 1970s and 1980s, and a recent reemergence of growth in the mid-1980s. Theorizing about the aggregate performance of the economy involves debates about the advantages and disadvantages of an aging "postindustrial" economy within the present world economic system. Such issues are beyond the scope of this book (but see Norton, forthcoming). Thus, as for a number of phenomena whose trend depends on the trend of economic growth and wages, we will have to content ourselves with a contingent statement. Economic stagnation will likely lead to a lesser rate of increase in the divorce rate, whereas continued economic growth will lead to a slightly higher rate of increase. Another factor that could slow the rate of increase in divorce would be if men increased their participation in childrearing. Such a move would undoubtedly strengthen their attachment to children, and thus increase the costs to men of divorce (whether through the psychic cost of increasing distance from the children or the dollar cost of supporting them alone if custody is gained). The current trend toward state and federal legislation tightening enforcement of court-awarded child support will increase the cost of (or lessen the gain from) divorce for men. However, enforcement costs are so great that payments are likely to remain sporadic.

Increasing employment, relative wages, and belief in the importance of self-fulfillment suggest that women's decisions to divorce will continue unabated.

We expect that fertility rates will continue their century-long decline, or at least remain at currently low levels. (Of course, the total number of births will continue to increase as the baby boom cohorts pass through the childbearing years, but these echo effects will become smaller with each succeeding generation.) Unlike Easterlin, we do not believe that the smaller birth cohorts of the baby bust will show increased fertility because of the economic gains from small cohort size. Rather, female employment in the early years is now so well established that any wage advantages from being a small cohort will redound to women as well as men. Increases in women's wages have been shown to lower fertility, and to do so more strongly at higher rates of female employment. Thus, we believe the question is not whether childbearing per woman will increase, but how much more it will decline. From a societal perspective, the replacement level seems a "natural" place for the fertility decline to stop. But fertility decisions, while greatly affected by aggregate conditions, are not made by couples because of their effects on those aggregates; so there is nothing magical about zero population growth as a stopping point. We doubt that more than a minority of couples will decide against raising a family at all, since the benefits of children for emotional intimacy and a sense of immortality are apt to be as salient in the future as today. The important questions are how large this minority will be (fueled in part by fears about the probability of divorce), and the extent to which childbearing couples will opt for two versus one child. If female employment during the child rearing years becomes almost universal (as it is, for example, in the Soviet Union), and day care for children is institutionalized as "normal," trends in women's wages will no longer have an opportunity-cost "price" effect on fertility, since there will be no trade-off between women's wages and having children. If this point is reached, then a positive time-series relationship between affluence and fertility rates may emerge. At such a point, the rate of economic growth may become decisive for fertility trends. Instead of increases in men's and women's wages having conflicting effects, they might both become positively related to fertility. This could bring fertility back above its present level, but we doubt that this will actually occur.

Investments in the cognitive human capital of children have been rising throughout this century. Yet this trend may have reversed around 1970 since fewer fathers are now supporting their children (owing to out-of-wedlock births and divorces), the quality of public school teachers has declined, and per capita expenditures on public programs for children (for example, AFDC) have failed to keep pace with inflation. There are several reasons why this trend may continue. First, if, as we expect, divorce rates remain high, women continue to retain custody of their children, and men continue to be negligent in child support payments, then a large number of children will be raised within female-headed households. Even if women's earnings increase relative to men's, they are unlikely to equal men's for decades. Even then, it is likely to be disadvantageous (in terms of inputs of both time and money) to be reared in a household with one rather than two parents. Second, despite increasing awareness of the need to improve the quality of teachers and standards in public education, actually doing so will be both difficult and costly. With current sentiments for fiscal austerity, and the continued ability of the elderly to compete in the political arena for scarce public funds, increased expenditures for schools and other children's programs appear unlikely. (Offsetting this is the fact that decreased fertility implies fewer children to support in public education, so per capita expenditures could increase even as total expenditures on children's education do not.) Further, if the public schools continue to deteriorate we may cross a threshold past which most upper middle class parents put their children in private schools rather than rallying behind efforts to improve public schools. This, in combination with a reduced proportion of adult households containing children, would further reduce political support for public school expenditures. Thus, aggregate decreases in investment in children's cognitive human capital seem a real possibility despite public concern that our national future hinges on "high-tech," knowledge-intensive industries.

In concert with decreased per capita investment in children's human capital, such investments may also become less equally distributed. This follows from the dependence of such investment on the level of family income, and the likelihood that continued assortative mating in concert with an improvement in women's relative earnings will lead to increased inequality in family income. Further, the continued trend toward divorce divides children into those in one-earner (usually female-headed) families and those in two-earner families. Finally, the trend toward increased use of private schools by the upper middle class, combined with further deterioration of the public schools, might increase inequality in the level of educational services received by various class groups. In time, this could decrease the national rate of intergenerational occupational mobility. We make this prediction cautiously, since the level of intergenerational mobility has been relatively constant throughout the century. Yet existing trends do point toward greater inequality in family incomes and, hence, inequalities of opportunity for children.

It is difficult to predict the future of the division of labor in household work. As female employment continues to increase, and fertility remains low, time spent in housework will continue to decline. Yet how it will be apportioned between the sexes is less clear. Thus far there have been only slight increases in males' housework, despite substantial increases in female employment. However, younger men do perform slightly more housework than older men. If this is a cohort rather than age effect, it may indicate greater changes to come. Since many household tasks are considered onerous by both men and women, men will likely increase their contribution only if women use some of their new-found marital power as leverage on this front.

Since a major form of socialization occurs simply by children observing adult behavior, changes in adults' sexual division of labor in the household and employment will be the major determinant of sex role change for children. It is clear that children will be exposed to an increasing number of females in traditionally male employment roles. The extent to which they will observe more males in traditionally female household and employment roles seems more uncertain from current trends.

Aggregate levels of consumption and savings will be affected by the level of economic growth and the changing demographic composition of the population. As we said earlier, future trends in economic growth and wages are difficult to predict. The mix of goods and services consumed will be affected by the age structure. Thus, as the baby boom ages, demand will shift toward products purchased by middle aged and older adults and away from those for children and younger adults. As the baby boom cohort moves out of the childbearing ages into middle age and the empty nest, stages in the life cycle where savings rates are higher, aggregate saving should increase. The empty-nest period will likely continue to be a relatively satisfying life-cycle stage. However, we expect the age of onset of this period to rise as more couples marry late and delay their childbearing.

Mortality will continue to decline for both men and women, although possibly at a slower rate than during the 1960s and 1970s. Furthermore, as male and female experiences become more similar, the sex gap in mortality may decline, although this may take decades to become visible. Decreased mortality should increase the period of retirement, and more similar male and female mortality rates should increase the years of retirement that couples spend together. However, other forces may operate to shorten the period of retirement. For example, recent amendments to the Age Discrimination Act raise the minimum mandatory retirement age from 65 to 70. Concern with the solvency of the Social Security system at the time the baby boomers retire has already led to proposals to increase the minimum age at which benefits can be collected. Unless these developments are offset by higher savings from economic growth, workers may be retiring later. Or, at the least, the downward trend in the retirement age may cease.

For the most part, the fate of those born during the baby boom has been influenced by economic conditions of the periods during which they experienced each life-cycle stage rather than by the size of the cohort. Thus, the baby boom cohort received many years of schooling but has seen little real wage growth during the period of relative economic stagnation since 1970. Yet, when this cohort reaches retirement age, they are bound to suffer for their large numbers. Even the baby boomers' political clout will probably be insufficient to avoid changes in Social Security that will either (1) lower the level of benefits below those received by previous retirees, or (2) lower the rates of return in payments they receive on their Social Security taxes. Of course, if Social Security payments are kept at present real levels, the pay-as-you-go funding mechanism will force the baby bust cohort members to share the cost of the baby boomers' retirement.

III. EMPLOYMENT

The employment relationship is best understood by combining economic ideas on labor markets, search, and implicit contracts with sociological ideas on structural roles and the way in which individuals' behavior and rewards are endogenous to the roles they play within the economy.

In Chapter 6 we analyzed the search process linking employees to employers and specific jobs. This process, in which individuals weigh the benefits and costs of taking a new job, changed relatively little over time. One might expect that, in keeping with a general trend toward rationalization, employers will seek to develop increasingly sensitive screening devices to predict which applicants will be the most productive and cooperative. Yet the difficulties and costs of making such predictions, as well as political considerations internal to the firm, suggest that rough proxies (e.g., educational credentials) rather than sensitive instruments will continue to be used. The use of "statistical discrimination" by race and sex will likely continue to decline, but not disappear entirely, legal requirements notwithstanding. This will occur so long as sex and race groups differ in job-relevant average characteristics.

The labor market involves implicit contracts of extended duration between employee and employer. Thus it is neither a spot market where arrangements are recontracted constantly, nor a market for contingent-claims contracts where each side to the bargain is completely locked into a long series of legal provisions. We believe that the market for employment relationships will continue to operate somewhere between the ideal types of spot and contingent-claims markets. Jobs will not move toward being contingent-claims contracts because the transactions costs of negotiating and enforcing such contracts remain large. However, the years ahead may see some movement of the average job along the continuum between spot markets and well developed implicit contracts that offer extensive rewards for seniority. The question is in which direction the movement will likely occur. The distinctions between primary and secondary jobs, core and peripheral industries, and male and female occupations are related to this continuum, with a greater development of contract over spot features in the former category of each pair. Thus, we might approach the question by asking how many jobs of each of these types are apt to exist in the future economy. If we look at the changing industrial composition of jobs, the growth of the service sector and the competitive difficulties encountered by durable goods manufacturing suggest that fewer jobs will be in "core" industries with their implicit contracts flowing from high capital investment, unionization, and other features. At the same time the relative gains (in wages and the steepness of wage trajectories) of working in the core are declining as those industries decline. Further, there appears to be a trend toward declining rates of unionization. Taken together, these developments suggest a decline in the seniority-rewarding features of American jobs, and a move toward spot markets.

Yet other developments oppose this trend. The rise of new industries could increase the rate of capital investment, providing incentives for complementary investment in employment stability. Further, the increasingly continuous employment of women may persuade employers to turn some predominantly female occupations into jobs with greater rewards for seniority. It is also possible that as women's employment becomes more continuous, women will be more eager to unionize than they have been in the past. Overall, it is difficult to predict whether movement will occur toward the spot market end of the continuum, or toward implicit contract features in more jobs. What seems clear is that the bilateral monopoly feature of implicit contracts, as well as the generally greater power of employers, will continue to be features of the employment relationship.

We expect that female labor force participation and wage rates will continue to rise if the economy shows growth. Continued increases in divorce and decreases in fertility will also foster rises in female employment. We argued that earlier increases in female employment were largely the result of increased labor demand in the predominantly female occupations, accompanied by increases in the female wage rate that raised the opportunity-cost of being a homemaker. To the extent that these developments continue, we can surely expect continued female employment rate increases.

We also expect that future cohorts of women will continue to make wage gains relative to men. There are two basic sources of these gains. First, differences in labor force experience have always explained some portion (between one-quarter and one-half) of the sex gap in pay. But until recently, the gap between the average experience of employed men and women had not decreased, since the propensity of women to stay employed longer was being offset by the continued entrance of women with little experience. This bottleneck cleared around 1980, and women's relative experience is now increasing, thus increasing women's relative wages. Second, thanks to reduced hiring discrimination and less traditional job choices by women, they have moved increasingly into predominantly male jobs, which (other things equal) have always paid better. This is directly raising the wages of those women entering the "male jobs," and it may also indirectly produce upward pressure on the wages of traditionally female jobs. These declines in segregation will likely continue and become self-reinforcing since they provide employers with evidence that women perform well in jobs nontraditional for them, and they also provide less sex-differentiated cognitive inputs to children's socialization. However, one factor mitigates against continued decreases in the sex segregation of jobs. This is the decrease in resources for enforcement of discrimination laws brought about by the Reagan Administration, and the longer-term effects of their appointment of less activist judges. While these developments are likely to slow the pace of women's relative pay gains, we do not expect them to be as decisive as they might have been a decade earlier, prior to the firm establishment of a trend toward occupational desegregation. However, these events could slow the pace of desegregation where it is less well established—for example, in predominantly male blue-collar jobs. This would have serious implications for the relative wages of working class women.

Thus, we expect that increased female employment experience and women's entrance into traditionally male jobs will raise female relative wages. We are less certain that the underpayment of predominantly female jobs relative to their educational and skill requirements will cease. That is, we believe the future of "comparable worth" to be quite uncertain. Barring new legislation, the usefulness of Title VII in combating this form of discrimination hinges on two legal issues—whether the plaintiff can win when the employer has not already undertaken a job evaluation, and whether the "market wage" argument is a viable defense for an employer paying lower wages in female jobs than is commensurate with their job requirements. If the courts permit this defense, Title VII will become irrelevant to many comparable-worth cases in the private sector. Of course, some limited increase in the relative pay of female occupations will occur as female labor shifts to male occupations. Trends in the relative wages of predominantly female occupations may also depend on whether workers in these occupations unionize, or whether the political movement to raise the pay of female jobs in the public sector has a spillover effect in private sector wages. Here, the future is quite uncertain.

IV. GENDER

The different roles, positions, and outcomes of men and women have been central to our discussion of households and employment. Within this chapter we have documented numerous changes in gender roles occurring since 1950. Without repeating all of these, we wish to emphasize a generalization they suggest: in the postwar period, women's roles have changed more dramatically than men's. Below we elaborate on this point in such a way as to also predict the future course of change in men's roles within the household and employment.

Women's roles have changed so as to allocate less time to childbearing and housework, to spend more years in paid employment, and, among young cohorts, to be more likely to enter male occupations characterized by higher pay. In a more psychological vein, we see women becoming more androgynous. They are blending new orientations toward such "traditionally male" arenas as career achievement, negotiation, and assertiveness with their "traditionally female" orientations of nurturance and concern with the socioemotional dynamics of relationships. At the same time there has been much less (although some) change in the amount of time men spend on child care, their degree of emotional attachment to their children, their participation in housework, and their participation in traditionally female occupations. Although the proportion of males in the labor force has decreased, this has resulted from longer years of schooling, discouraged workers, and earlier retirement, not from men spending time out of the labor force as homemakers. Thus, we conclude that gender role change has been asymmetric, with greater movement of women into traditionally male spheres than vice versa.

This asymmetry of gender role change is not surprising, given the structural conditions and resulting individual incentives generating the changes. Many of the changes we have discussed (e.g., increased women's employment, decreased fertility, rising divorce) are mutually reinforcing, so that it is difficult and perhaps not fruitful to attempt to disentangle the causal order among them. But if one searches for a truly exogenous factor that was influential in starting some of these changes, yet does not seem to be explained by them, it would have to be economic growth and the disproportionate growth in labor demand in traditionally female jobs, along with their upward effects on women's wages. This propelled women's employment upward, and this in turn has been a major factor in reducing fertility, reducing the time women spend in household labor, increasing women's marital power, increasing the likelihood of divorce, and increasing women's employment experience and thus earnings. These changes have been mutually reinforcing. Thus it appears that the gender role transformation accelerated because macrostructural conditions increased the incentives women (and their husbands) had to decide on employment for the woman; that is, they raised the opportunity-cost of women remaining exclusively in household work.

Sex role change did not, in the main, result from women rising up to protest their subordination to men in the household and in employment, although such protests have indeed occurred throughout history. Indeed, it seems that women have strengthened their relative position vis-à-vis men not through deliberate attempts to change the contours of relationships between men and women (although this has been a side effect), but rather through efforts to improve the absolute position of themselves and their families. In short, claims regarding equity have not animated the changes, but have come to seem more natural because of them. Thus, we speculate that the organized women's movement, litigation directed at sex discrimination, and other appeals for equity between men and women are a by-product of decisions not originally directed at the male/female relational system. Nonetheless, once started, these appeals for equity have affected the relations between men and women. Yet the effects have been on the relative amount of time and energy women give to traditionally female roles, not on the fact of their specializing in these roles more than men do. Thus, the extent of traditional role performance by women has changed, but the dimensions of role specialization between men and women have not.

Under these conditions, there has been little to motivate men to adopt traditionally female roles, either from their own self-interest, or from a household utility perspective based on an efficient division of labor. Within a culture that has not only devalued female activities, but especially devalued men who are like females, a major alteration in pecuniary or nonpecuniary rewards is required to induce men to make these changes. Yet just as rising wages have made the opportunity-cost of time spent in child care greater for women, so too has this effect operated for men during the 1950s and 1960s. Thus, even had men been inclined to consider homemaking, their rising wages would have mitigated against a complementary change of men into home roles. Since there are still few couples where the woman has the higher wage, the notion of placing more of women's hours into overtime employment, and substituting male for female household labor, has not yet become an economic proposition. Similarly, the relative pay disadvantage of female occupations has changed little, so men have had little incentive to enter them.

What is surprising, however, is that employed women have not begun to insist on male role change as a means of easing their role overload. For example, the fact that husbands of employed women do little more housework than husbands of homemakers raises the question as to why employed women do not use their increased marital power to bargain for this change.

We are not sure of the answer to this, but we believe that if male participation is to increase within this sphere, it will come via women's explicit bargaining, backed up by a disinclination to form or stay in relationships with men whose domestic contributions are negligible.

Changes in men's participation in child care will come, if they do emerge, through the same mechanism of women's urging, backed by the power they gain from paid employment. One might argue that the intimate bonds that go with being the primary care taker of a child are inherently rewarding (more than housework or many paid jobs), and that this would propel men into the role. But men's socialization has not given them this view, and it may require experience of the role itself to develop this taste. Such experience may only come at women's urging, or out of changed efficiency considerations in cases where women have higher earnings than their husbands. If this experience, and the resulting shift in tastes, occurs, men may become more active in seeking custody after divorce. Thus, whether men will play a more active role in child rearing, and develop firmer attachment to children hinges in part on whether women achieve full equality in earnings or marital power.

Since we are arguing that changes in male roles will come largely through increases in women's power and at women's urging, we need to examine what gives women the motivation to engage in such urging. As we noted, one element in such motivation results from the role overload that many women are experiencing as they try to juggle paid employment with almost full responsibility for housework and child rearing. There is evidence that increasing numbers of women see this overload as a tension in current arrangements. Further, women have long had an incentive to encourage greater male participation in the emotional work of relationships. This is indicated by surveys showing women's dissatisfaction with the level of empathy and emotional intimacy in their relationships with men. The motivation has always been there to change this, but women had less power to urge the change, and equally important, their financial dependence on male earnings encouraged them to select men for their earning prowess rather than their relational skills.

Finally, women may have a motivation to encourage male participation in the instrumental and emotional work of the household so as to counter the trend toward diminishing the (traditionally female) sphere of home and family life and the values of this sphere. The value placed on the nurturance and personal connection of the household sphere resides more with women than with men, though somewhat with both sexes. Some of the backlash to the women's movement comes from the correct perception that this sphere is shrinking as women give less attention to it, and men do little to make up what has been lost. There are, of course, only two ways the trend can be reversed—either a movement of females back into these roles, or increased participation of men in these roles, thereby bringing men closer to women's level of participation. Thus, women face a dilemma. They like the rewards of their new participation in employment, but they also have more of a taste for seeing the traditionally female nurturant functions of the household performed than men do. Although there is a deep cultural aversion to males taking on traditionally female roles, women may begin to urge this, using their new power to shore up their old sphere by enlisting male participation. It is still too early to tell how common a response this will be.

Male participation in traditionally female occupations will have to increase if females continue to move into male occupations, and if the growth in labor demand in male occupations is no larger than the overall growth in the labor force. Both conditions are likely. This will further reduce the wage gap between men and women.

Thus, gender role change has been asymmetric, with women's roles changing more than men's, the relative amount of effort going into traditionally female roles decreasing, and men's roles changing as little as possible. A continuation of this scenario would increase women's power and resources relative to men's, but not permit full equality. The important question is how much men's roles will change to include child rearing, housework, emotional work, and, for some, paid work in what have been predominantly female occupations. To date, this change has been minor, and we do not see men making these changes unless women use their new found bargaining power to force the issue.

V. AN INTEGRATED VIEW

In discussing the behavior of households, employment, and gender, we have worked toward an integrated view, drawing from sociology and economics, as well as both of these disciplines' contributions to demography. Here we review how the perspectives of the two disciplines can be integrated.

Concepts central to economics include the notion of individual striving for maximum well-being, with the associated processes of estimating the benefits and costs (including opportunity costs) of alternative activities, and investing in both people and relationships (in particular, those pertaining to marriage and employment). At a market rather than individual level, key concepts involve supply and demand—the relationship between the price and quantity of a good or service offered or bought. Moderating the old view that these forces lead to (nearly instantaneous) equilibration of markets are the new economic notions of search and implicit contracts. Search theory argues that information about one's market options is both costly and imperfect. Implicit contracts are important because both cohabitation and employment involve investments that must be undertaken early in the relationship (for example, the on-the-job training of jobs or marriages), but yield many of their benefits far into the future. This means that both parties have an incentive to keep the relationship intact longer than it would be in a spot market, and these incentives often lead to informal agreements. Since these "contracts" are neither spot market relationships nor fully contingent-claims contracts, they do not fully reflect either current or past market conditions. One result is sluggishness of adjustment, and "lumpiness" of social change in employment and household relationships.

The sociological theory most similar to the economic view is exchange theory, and we have drawn on research within this tradition. Exchange theorists accept most of the assumption of economists, with the exception of economists' assumption that one cannot use interpersonal utility comparisons to conclude that some people are getting more of what they want than others. Relaxing this assumption, we have sought to explain why the role of homemaker yields less power than the breadwinning role because the latter gives one resources that are more liquid across relationships.

There is a long sociological tradition of studying the values shared within a society or one of its subgroups, and internalized by individuals through socialization within the household or other institutions. Economists seeking a sociological contribution to their understanding of household and employment behavior often point to these values (or "tastes," to use their preferred term) as the exogenous input to their models that help explain intergroup or intertemporal differences in behavior or rewards. We believe that tastes are one appropriate link between sociology and economics. However, we also believe that the "social forces" producing these tastes are not external (i.e. exogenous) to the behavior economists analyze. Rather, these social forces include characteristics of the position individuals hold—whether in households or employment. The position one holds requires and rewards certain behavior—and this has long-term effects on individual tastes and behavior. That is, individuals tend to acquire values and behavior patterns consistent with the employment and household roles they have held and those usually filled by people with their ascriptive characteristics. Thus, in recent decades sociologists have moved the study of values and individual behavior into a more structural context, and this view must be represented in any attempt to integrate sociology and economics.

Structural notions have also been central to recent sociological studies of the effect of job characteristics on earnings, net of individual characteristics. These findings can be integrated with search and contract theories as follows: Jobs vary in the extent to which they offer implicit contracts, and those jobs with high wages at every point in the life cycle are the same ones that have the best developed contract features rewarding seniority with wage increases, employment security, and pension plans. The anomaly posed for spot market economics is how such uncompensated differentials between jobs can persist. "Market imperfections" such as the lack of perfect information on both sides of the market, attendant costs of job mobility, and the presence of discrimination against women and minorities (itself perpetuated by feedback effects) go a long way toward explaining the persistence of these differentials.

We close by highlighting one feature of the integrated view which may be particularly important for future research. This is the reciprocal linkage between households and employment. It has rarely been possible to see one sector as the clear "prime mover" explaining a change in sex differentiation within the other sector. In the exceptional cases where this does occur (for example, the effect of economic expansion and rising wage rates, drawing women out of the household and into the labor force), the exogenous variable typically had nothing to do with sex differentiation, or the relative status of men versus women.

Aspects of the relative position of men and women in households and employment invariably affect each other. This seems obvious, but we have been surprised at how often both economists and sociologists have attempted to view one sector as the decisive exogenous determinant for the sex differentiation of the other. Thus, some economists have seen women's household role (which they believe to be determined by "exogenous" social or biological forces) as explaining the intermittent employment and low pay of women within the labor force. Another "life cycle" view also begins the causal arrow within the household, seeing early life decisions about both employment and household behavior as the determinants of adult roles within both sectors. Some sociological work emphasizing socialization agreed with this view that social forces are exogenous to employment outcomes. In contrast, we have argued that these social forces are not exogenous to the institutions of employment. For example, observations of adult employment roles is a major form of childhood socialization, leading to tastes for particular forms of achievement and assessments of what achievement is possible. Other economists and sociologists have reversed the causal arrow, pointing to discrimination against women in labor markets as affecting the division of labor at home and the way women behave on the job. The comprehensive view must see that the effects run both ways, but that such reciprocal links do not completely rule out change. Indeed, change in either sector will be the precursor of change in the other. It is time to abandon the search for the "exogenous" prime mover, and analyze the joint dynamics of households and employment as gender roles change.

BIBLIOGRAPHY

Adams, Bert N.
  1979   "Mate selection in the United States: A theoretical summarization." *In*
          Burr et al. (eds.), *Contemporary Theories About the Family*, Vol. I, pp.
          259–267. New York: The Free Press.
Arnold, F., Bulatao, R., Buripakdi, C., Chung, B., Fawcett, J., Iritani, T., Lee, S., and
Wu T.
  1975   *The Value of Children: A Cross-National Study*, Vol. 1: *Introduction
          and Comparative Analysis*. Honolulu: East-West Institute.
Arrow, Kenneth
  1971   *Essays in the Theory of Risk Bearing*. Chicago: Markham.
  1972   "Models of job discrimination" and "Some mathematical models of
          race in the labor market." *In* A. Pascal (ed.), *Racial Discrimination in
          Economic Life*. Lexington, MA: Lexington, Heath.
  1974   "Limited knowledge and economic analysis." *American Economic
          Review* **64,** 1–10.
Auerbach, Alan J. and Kotlikoff, Laurence J.
  1984   "Social security and the economics of the demographic transition." *In*
          H. J. Aaron and G. Burtless (eds.), *Retirement and Economic Behavior*,
          pp. 255–278. Washington, D.C.: The Brookings Institution.
Bahr, S. J.
  1972   "A methodological study of conjugal power: a replication and exten-
          sion of Blood and Wolfe." Unpublished doctoral dissertation, Wash-
          ington State University.
  1974   "Effects on power and division of labor in the family." *In* L. W.
          Hoffman and F. I. Nye (eds.), *Working Mothers*. San Francisco:
          Jossey-Bass.
Balswick, Jack O. and Peek, Charles W.
  1971   "The inexpressive male: A tragedy of American society." *The Family
          Coordinator* **20,** 363–368.
Banfield, Edward C.
  1970   *The Unheavenly City*. Boston: Little, Brown and Company.
Baron, James N.
  1984   "Organizational perspectives on stratification." *Annual Review of
          Sociology* **10,** 37–69.

Baron, James N. and Bielby, William T.
    1980   "Bringing the firm back in: stratification, segmentation, and the
            organization of work." *American Sociological Review* **45**, 737–755.
    1984   "The organization of work in a segmented economy." *American
            Sociological Review* **49**, 454–473.
Barro, Robert J.
    1984   *Macroeconomics*. New York: John Wiley and Sons.
Bart, Pauline
    1969   "Why women's status changes in middle age: The turns of the social
            ferris wheel." *Sociological Symposium* **3**, 1–18.
Barton, Allen H.
    1968   "Bringing society back in: Survey research and macro methodology."
            American Behavioral Scientist **12**, 1–9.
    1970   "Commentary and debate: Allen Barton comments on Hauser's con-
            text and consex." *American Journal of Sociology* **76**, 514–517.
Bean, F., Curtis, R., and Macrum, J.
    1977   "Familism and marital satisfaction among Mexican Americans: The
            effects of family size, wife's labor force participation, and conjugal
            power." *Journal of Marriage and the Family* **39**, 759–767.
Beck, E. M., Horan, P. M., and Tolbert, C. M. II
    1978   "Stratification in a dual economy." *American Sociological Review* **43**,
            704–720.
    1980   "Social stratification in industrial society: Further evidence for a
            structural alternative." *American Sociological Review* **45**, 712–719.
Becker, Gary S.
    1957   *The Economics of Discrimination*, 1st ed. (2nd ed., 1971). Chicago:
            University of Chicago Press.
    1964   *Human Capital*, 1st ed. (2nd ed., 1975). New York: National Bureau
            of Economic Research.
    1981   *A Treatise on the Family*. Cambridge, MA: Harvard University Press.
Becker, Gary S. and Gregg Lewis, H.
    1973   "On the interaction between the quantity and quality of children."
            Journal of Political Economy **81**, S279–S288.
Becker, Gary S., Landes, Elisabeth M., and Michael, Robert T.
    1977   "An economic analysis of marital instability." *Journal of Political
            Economy* **85**, 1141–1187.
Beer, William R.
    1983   *Househusbands: Men and Housework in American Families*. New
            York: Praeger.
Beller, Andrea H.
    1979   "The impact of equal employment opportunity laws on the male/
            female earnings differential." In C. Lloyd et al. (eds.), *Women in the
            Labor Market*, pp. 304–330. New York: Columbia University Press.
    1982a   "The impact of equal opportunity policy on sex differentials in
            earnings and occupations." *American Economic Review, Papers and
            Proceedings*, pp. 171–175.
    1982b   "Occupational segregation by sex: Determinants and changes." *Jour-
            nal of Human Resources* **17**, 371–392.
    1984   "Trends in occupational segregatin by sex and race, 1960–1981." *In
            B. F. Reskin (ed.), Sex Segregation in the Workplace: Trends, Explana-*

  tions, Remedies, pp. 11–26. Washington, D.C.: National Academy Press.

Ben-Porath, Yoram
  1973   "Economic analysis of fertility in Israel: Point and counterpoint." *Journal of Political Economy* **81,** S202–S233.
  1982   "Economics and the family—match or mismatch? A review of Becker's A Treatise on the Family." *Journal of Economic Literature* **20,** 52–64.

Berger, Mark C.
  1985   "The effect of cohort size on earnings growth: A reexamination of the evidence." *Journal of Political Economy* **93,** 561–573.

Bergmann, Barbara
  1974   "Occupational segregation, wages and profits when employers discriminate by race or sex." *Eastern Economic Journal* **1,** 103–110.
  Forth- *The Economic Emergence of American Women.* New York: Basic.
  coming

Bergmann, Barbara and Gray, Mary W.
  1984   "Economic models as a means of calculating legal compensation claims." *In* H. Remick (ed.), *Comparable Worth and Wage Discrimination: Technical Possibilities and Political Realities,* pp. 155–172. Philadelphia: Temple University Press.

Berk, Sarah Fenstermaker
  1980   *Women and Household Labor.* Beverly Hills: Sage Publications.

Berk, Sarah Fenstermaker and Berk, Richard A.
  1979   *Labor and Leisure at Home: Content and Organization of the Household Day.* Beverly Hills: Sage Publications.
  1983   "Supply-side sociology of the family: The challenge of the new home economics." *Annual Review of Sociology* **9,** 375–395.

Bielby, William T. and Baron, James N.
  1984   "A woman's place is with other women: Sex segregation within organizations." *In* Barbara F. Reskin (ed.), *Sex Segregation in the Workplace: Trends, Explanations, Remedies,* pp. 27–55. Washington, D.C.: National Academy Press.

Blake, Judith
  1981   "Family size and the quality of children." *Demography* **18,** 421–442.

Blalock, Hubert M.
  1984   "Contextual-effects models: Theoretical and methodological issues." *Annual Review of Sociology* **10,** 353–372.

Blau, Francine
  1984   "Occupational segregation and labor market discrimination." *In* Barbara F. Reskin (ed.), *Sex Segregation in the Workplace: Trends, Explanations, Remedies,* pp. 117–143. Washington, D.C.: National Academy Press.

Blau, Francine D. and Beller, Andrea H.
  1984   "Trends in earnings differentials by sex and race: 1971–1981." Presented at the Annual Meetings of the American Economics Association, Dallas, TX.

Blau, P. M. and Duncan, O.D.
  1967   *The American Occupational Structure.* New York: Wiley.

Blood, R. O., Jr.
    1963   "Rejoinder to 'Measurement and bases of family power.'" *Journal of Marriage and the Family* **25**, 475–478.
Blood, R. O., Jr. and Wolfe, D. M.
    1960   *Husbands and Wives: The Dynamics of Family Living.* New York: Free Press.
Blumstein, P. and Schwartz, P.
    1983   *American Couples.* New York: William Morrow.
Bohannon, Paul
    1970   *Divorce and After.* Garden City: Doubleday.
Bonacich, Edna
    1972   "A theory of ethnic antagonism: The split labor market. *American Sociological Review* **37**, 547–549.
    1976   "Advanced capitalism and black-white relations in the U.S.: A split labor market interpretation. *American Sociological Review* **41**, 34–51.
Booth, A.
    1977   "Wife's employment and husband's stress: A replication and refutation." *Journal of Marriage and the Family* **39**, 645–650.
Bouvier, Leon F.
    1980   *America's Baby Boom Generation: The Fateful Bulge.* Washington, D.C.: Population Reference Bureau.
Bowles, Samuel and Gintis, Herbert
    1976   *Schooling in Capitalist America: Educational Reform and the Contradictions of Economic Life.* New York: Basic Books.
Brumberg, Richard and Modigliani, Franco
    1962   "Utility analysis and the consumption function." *In* K. K. Kurihara (ed.), *Post-Keynesian Economics.* Princeton, New Jersey: Princeton University Press.
Burke, R. and Weir, T.
    1976   "Relationship of wives' employment status to husband, wife, and pair satisfaction and performance. *Journal of Marriage and the Family* **38**, 279–287.
Burr, W.
    1970   "Satisfaction with various aspects of marriage over the life cycle: A random middle class sample." *Journal of Marriage and the Family* **32**, 29–37.
Burstein, Paul
    1979   "Equal employment opportunity legislation and the income of women and nonwhites." *American Sociological Review* **44**, 367–391.
    In   *Discrimination, Jobs, and Politics: The Struggle for Equal Employment*
    press   *Opportunity in the United States Since the New Deal.* Chicago: Chicago University Press.
Butz, William P. and Ward, Michael P.
    1977   *The Emergence of Countercyclical U.S. Fertility.* R-1605-NIH. Santa Monica, Calif.: Rand Corp.
    1979a   "The emergence of countercyclical U.S. fertility." *American Economic Review* **69**, 318–327.
    1979b   "Will U.S. fertility remain low? A new economic interpretation." *Population and Development Review* **5**, 663–688.

Campbell, A., Converse, P., and Rodgers, W.
    1976   The Quality of American Life. New York: Russell Sage.
Caplow, T., Bahr, H., Chadwick, B., Hill, R., and Williamson, M.
    1982   Middletown Families: Fifty Years of Change and Continuity. Min-
            neapolis: University of Minnesota Press.
Card, Josefina J. and Wise, Lauress L.
    1978   "Teenage mothers and teenage fathers: The impact of early childbear-
            ing on the parents' personal and professional lives." Family Planning
            Perspectives 10, 199–205.
Carmichael, H. Lorne
    1983   "The agent-agents problem: Payment by relative output." Journal of
            Labor Economics 1, 50–65.
Chafetz, Janet S.
    1984   Sex and Advantage. Totowa, N.J.: Rowman and Allanheld.
Cherlin, Andrew J.
    1978   "Remarriage as an incomplete institution." American Journal of
            Sociology 84, 634–650.
    1981   Marriage, Divorce, Remarriage: Social Trends in the United States.
            Cambridge, MA: Harvard University Press.
Chodorow, Nancy
    1978   The Reproduction of Mothering. Berkeley, CA: University of Califor-
            nia Press.
Clogg, Clifford C.
    1982   "Cohort analysis of recent trends in labor force participation." De-
            mography 19, 459–480.
Coale, A. and Hoover, E.
    1958   Population Growth and Economic Development in Low-Income
            Countries. Princeton: Princeton University Press.
Coggswell, Betty E. and Sussman, Marvin B.
    1979   "Family and fertility." In W. Burr, R. Hill, F. I. Nye, and I. L. Reiss
            (eds.), Contemporary Theories About the Family, pp. 180–202. New
            York: The Free Press.
Corcoran, M. and Duncan, G. J.
    1979   "Work history, labor force attachment, and earnings differences be-
            tween the races and sexes." Journal of Human Resources 14, 3–20.
Corcoran, Mary, Duncan, G. J., and Ponza, M.
    1984   "Work experience, job segregation, and wages." In B. F. Reskin (ed.),
            Sex Segregation in the Workplace: Trends, Explanations, Remedies,
            pp. 171–191. Washington, D.C.: National Academy Press.
Cott, Nancy F.
    1977   The Bonds of Womanhood: "Women's sphere" in New England,
            1780–1835. New Haven, CT: Yale University Press.
Coverman, Shelly
    1983   "Gender, domestic labor time, and wage inequality." American
            Sociological Review 48, 623–637.
    In   "Explaining husbands' participation in domestic labor." Sociological
    press   Quarterly.
Cramer, James C.
    1980   "Fertility and female employment: Problems of causal direction."
            American Sociological Review 45, 397–432.

Daymont, T. and Statham, A.
  1983   "Occupational atypicality: Changes, causes, and consequences." *In*
            L. B. Shaw, (ed.), *Unplanned Careers: The Working Lives of Middle
            Aged Women*, pp. 61–76. Lexington: D.C. Heath.
DeTray, Dennis N.
  1973   "Child quality and the demand for children." *Journal of Political
            Economy* **81,** S70–S95.
Doeringer, P. and Piore, M.
  1971   *Internal Labor Markets and Manpower Analysis*. Lexington, MA: D.C.
            Heath.
Downs, Anthony and Gilberto, S. M.
  1981   "How inflation erodes the income of fixed-rate lenders." *Real Estate
            Review* **11,** 43–51.
Duncan, Beverly
  1979   "Change in worker/nonworker ratios for women." *Demography* **16,**
            535–547.
Duncan, Beverly and Duncan, Otis Dudley
  1978   *Sex Typing and Social Roles: A Research Report*. New York: Academ-
            ic Press.
Duncan, G. J.
  1984   *Years of Poverty, Years of Plenty*. Ann Arbor: Institute for Social
            Research.
Duncan, O. D., Featherman, D. L., and Duncan, B.
  1972   *Socioeconomic Background and Achievement*. New York: Seminar
            Press.
Dunlop, John T.
  1958   *Industrial Relations Systems*. New York, N.Y.: Holt, Rinehart and
            Winston.
Durkheim, Emile
  1895   *The Rules of Sociological Method*. (English Ed., 1938.) New York, NY:
            The Free Press.
Easterlin, R.
  1961   "The American baby boom in historical perspective." *American
            Economic Review* **51,** 869–911.
  1968   *Population, Labor Force, and Long Swings in Economic Growth*. New
            York: Columbia University Press.
  1978   "What will 1984 be like? Socioeconomic implications of recent twists
            in age structures." *Demography* **15**(4), 397–432.
  1980   *Birth and Fortune: The Impact of Numbers on Personal Welfare*. New
            York: Basic Books.
Elder, Glen H., Jr.
  1974   *Children of the Depression: Social Change in Life Experience*. Chica-
            go, Ill.: University of Chicago Press.
Elkin, F. and Handel, G.
  1978   *The Child and Society: The Process of Socialization*, 3rd ed. New York
            Random House.
England, Paula
  1981   "Assessing trends in occupational sex segregation, 1900–1976." *In*
            Ivar Berg (ed.), *Sociological Perspectives on Labor Markets*, pp. 273–
            295. New York: Academic Press.

1982   "The failure of human capital theory to explain occupational sex segregation." *Journal of Human Resources* **17,** 358–370.

1984a   "Socioeconomic explanations of job segregation." *In* H. Remick (ed.), *Comparable Worth and Wage Discrimination: Technical Possibilities and Political Realities.* Philadelphia: Temple University Press.

1984b   "Wage appreciation and depreciation: A test of neoclassical economic explanations of occupational sex segregation." *Social Forces* **62,** 726–749.

In   "Occupational segregation: Rejoinder to Polachek." *Journal of Human Resources.*
press

England, Paula and McLaughlin, Steven

1979   "Sex segregation of jobs and male-female income differentials." *In* R. Alvarez, K. Lutterman, and Associates (eds.), *Discrimination in Organizations,* pp. 189–213. San Francisco: Jossey Bass.

England, Paula and Norris, Bahar

In   "Comparable worth: a new doctrine of sex discrimination." *Social Science Quarterly.*
press

England, Paula, Kuhn, Alice, and Gardner, Teresa

1981   "The ages of men and women in magazine advertisements." *Journalism Quarterly* **58,** 468–471.

England, Paula, Chassie, Marilyn, and McCormack, Linda

1982   "Skill demands and earnings in female and male occupations." *Sociology and Social Research* **66,** 147–168.

Ericksen, J. A., Yancey, W. L., and Ericksen, E. P.

1979   "The division of family roles." *Journal of Marriage and the Family* **38,** 301–313.

Espenshade, Thomas J.

1979a   "The economic consequences of divorce." *Journal of Marriage and the Family* **41,** 615–625.

1979b   *The Value and Cost of Children.* Washington, D.C.: Population Reference Bureau.

Farkas, George

1974   "Specification, residuals, and contextual effects." *Sociological Methods and Research* **2**(3), 333–363.

1976   "Education, wage rates, and the division of labor between husband and wife." *Journal of Marriage and the Family* **41,** 473–483.

1977   "Cohort, age, and period effects upon the employment of white females: Evidence for 1957–1968." *Demography* **14,** 33–42.

Farkas, George and England, Paula

In   "Integrating the sociology and economics of employment, compensation and unemployment." *In* Richard Simpson and Ida Simpson (eds.),
press   *Research in the Sociology of Work, Vol. 3: Unemployment.* Greenwich, CT.: JAI Press.

Farkas, George and Olsen, Randall J.

1983   "Fertility and poverty—Data from a large experiment." Grant proposal funded by the National Institute of Child Health and Human Development.

Featherman, David and Hauser, Robert

1978   *Opportunity and Change.* New York: Harcourt, Brace, Jovanovich.

Ferber, Marianne
  1982   "Labor market participation of young married women: Causes and effects." *Journal of Marriage and the Family* **44,** 457–468.
Ferree, Myra
  1976   "Working class jobs: Housework and paid work as sources of satisfaction." *Social Problems* **23,** 431–441.
Fienberg, Stephen E. and Mason, William M.
  1979   "Identification and estimation of age-period-cohort models in the analysis of discrete archival data." *Sociological Methodology.* San Francisco, CA: Jossey-Bass.
Filer, Randall Keith
  1981   "The influence of affective human capital on the wage equation." *In* R. G. Ehrenberg (ed.), *Research in Labor Economics* **4,** pp. 367–416. Greenwich, Conn.: JAI Press.
Fisher, Charles R.
  1980   "Differences by age groups in health care spending." *Health Care Financing Review* **1,** 89.
Flanagan, R. J., Smith, R. S., and Ehrenberg, R. G.
  1984   *Labor Economics and Labor Relations.* Glenview, Ill.: Scott, Foresman and Company.
Folbre, Nancy
  1983   "Of patriarchy born: The political economy of fertility decisions." *Feminist Studies* **9,** 261–281.
Freedman, Deborah and Thornton, Arland
  1979   "The long-term impact of pregnancy at marriage on the family's economic circumstances." *Family Planning Perspectives* **11,** 6–11.
Freeman, Richard B.
  1980   "The evolution of the American labor market, 1940–80." *In* M. Feldstein (ed.), *The American Economy in Transition,* pp. 349–396. Chicago: University of Chicago Press.
Freeman, Richard B. and Medoff, James L.
  1984   *What Do Unions Do?* New York: Basic Books.
Freeman, Richard B. and Wise, David A.
  1982   *The Youth Labor Problem: Its Nature, Causes and Consequences. National Bureau of Economic Research Conference Report.* Chicago: University of Chicago Press.
Friedman, Milton
  1957   *A Theory of the Consumption Function.* Princeton, N.J.: Princeton University Press.
Fuchs, Estelle
  1977   *The Second Season: Life, Love and Sex—Women in the Middle Years.* Garden City, N.Y.: Anchor Press/Doubleday.
Fuchs, Victor
  1974   "Women's earnings: Recent trends and long-run prospects." *Monthly Labor Review* **97,** 23–36.
  1983   *How We Live.* Cambridge: Harvard University Press.
Furstenberg, F. and Allison, P.
  1984   Unpublished results from their analysis of the National Survey of Children.

Furstenberg, F. and Seltzer, J. A.
1983   "Divorce and child development." Presented at the American Ortho-psychiatric Association Panel on Current Research in Divorce and Remarriage, April 8, Boston.

Gans, Herbert J.
1962   *The Urban Villagers.* New York: The Free Press.
1967   *The Levittowners: Ways of Life and Politics in a New Suburban Community.* New York: Random House.

Gecas, V.
1976   "The socialization and child care roles." *In* F. I. Nye (ed.), *Role Structure and Analysis of the Family,* pp. 35–59. Beverly Hills: Sage.
1979   "The influence of social class on socialization." *In* W. Burr, R. Hill, F. I. Nye, and I. L. Reiss (eds.), *Contemporary Theories About the Family,* pp. 365–404. New York: The Free Press.

Geerken, Michael and Gove, Walter R.
1983   *At Home and At Work: The Family's Allocation of Labor.* Beverly Hills, CA: Sage.

Gersick, Kelin
1979   "Fathers by choice: Divorced men who receive custody of their children." *In* G. Levinger and O. Moles (eds.), *Divorce and Separation: Context, Causes, and Consequences,* pp. 307–323. New York: Basic Books.

Giddens, Anthony
1971   *Capitalism and Modern Social Theory.* London: Cambridge University Press.

Gilligan, Carol
1982   *In a Different Voice: Psychological Theory and Women's Development.* Cambridge, MA: Harvard University Press.

Glenn, Norval D.
1975   "Psychological well-being in the post-parental stage: Some evidence from national surveys." *Journal of Marriage and the Family* **37,** 105–110.

Glenn, Norval D. and Weaver, Charles
1977   "The marital happiness of remarried divorced persons." *Journal of Marriage and the Family* **39,** 331–337.
1978   "A multivariate, multisurvey study of marital happiness." *Journal of Marriage and the Family* **40,** 269–282.

Glick, Paul C. and Norton, Arthur J.
1979   *Marrying, Divorcing, and Living Together in the U.S. Today* (updated reprint). Washington, D.C.: Population Reference Bureau.

Glueck, S. and Glueck, E.
1957   "Working mothers and delinquency." *Mental Hygiene* **41,** 327–352.

Goetting, Ann
1981   "Divorce outcome research: Issues and perspectives." *In* A. Skolnick and J. Skolnick (eds.), *Family in Transition,* pp. 367–387. Boston: Little, Brown.

Goldman, Noreen, Westoff, Charles F., and Hammerslough, Charles
1984   "Demography of the marriage market in the United States." *Population Index* **50,** 5–25.

Goode, William
    1979   *World Revolution and Family Patterns.* (1st ed., 1963). New York:
            Free Press.
Goode, William, Hopkins, Elizabeth, and McClure, Helen
    1971   *Social Systems and Family Structure.* Indianapolis, IN: Bobbs-Merrill.
Gordon, David M.
    1972   *Theories of Poverty and Unemployment.* Lexington, MA: D.C. Heath.
Gover, D.
    1963   "Socio-economic differentials in the relationship between marital
            adjustment and wife's employment status." *Marriage and Family
            Living* **25,** 452–458.
Granovetter, Mark
    1973   "The strength of weak ties." *American Journal of Sociology* **78,**
            1360–1380.
    1974   *Getting a Job.* Cambridge: Harvard University Press.
    1981   "Toward a sociological theory of income differences." *In* Ivar Berg
            (ed.), *Sociological Perspectives on Labor Markets,* pp. 11–47. New
            York: Academic.
Green, Gordon
    1983   "Wage Differentials For Job Entrants, by Race and Sex." Ph.D. dis-
            sertation, Department of Economics, George Washington University.
Greenberger, Ellen and Steinberg, Laurence
    1983   "Sex differences in early labor force experience: Harbinger of things
            to come." *Social Forces* **62,** 467–487.
Grinker, W., Cooke, D., and Kirsch, A.
    1970   *Climbing the Job Ladder: A Study of Employee Advancement in
            Eleven Industries.* New York: Shelley.
Gurin, G., Veroff, J., and Feld, S.
    1960   *How Americans View Their Mental Health.* New York: Basic Books.
Hakel, Milton and Dunnette, Marvin
    1970   *Checklists for Describing Job Applicants.* Minneapolis: Industrial Re-
            lations Center, University of Minnesota.
Hamermesh, Daniel and Grant, James
    1979   "Econometric studies of labor–labor substitution and their im-
            plications for policy." *Journal of Human Resources* **14,** 518–542.
Hanushek, E.
    1981   "Throwing money at schools." *Journal of Policy Analysis and Man-
            agement* **1,** 19–41.
Harpham, Edward J.
    1984   "Fiscal crisis and the politics of social security reform." *In* A. Cham-
            pagne and E. J. Harpham (eds.), *The Attack on the Welfare State,* pp.
            9–36. Prospect Heights, Ill.: Waveland Press.
Hartmann, Heidi I.
    1981   "The family as the locus of gender, class and political struggle: The
            example of housework." *Signs* **6,** 366–394.
Hauser, Robert M.
    1970a   "Context and consex: A cautionary tale." *American Journal of Sociol-
            ogy* **75,** 645–664.
    1970b   "Reply to Barton." *American Journal of Sociology* **76,** 517–520.
    1974   "Contextual analysis revisited." *Sociological Methods and Research*
            2, 365–375.

Havighurst, R. J., Munnichs, J., Neugarten, B., and Thomae, H.
    1969   *Adjustment to Retirement: A Cross-National Study.* Assen, The Netherlands: Van Gorcum and Company.
Heer, David
    1958   "Dominance and the working wife." *Social Forces* **36,** 341–347.
    1963   "The measurement and bases of family power: An overview." *Journal of Marriage and the Family* **25,** 133–139.
Hendershott, Patric
    1980   "Real user costs and the demand for single-family housing." Brookings Papers on Economic Activity **2.**
Hendrick, C. and Hendrick, S.
    1983   *Liking, Loving, and Relating.* Monterey: Brooks/Cole.
Herzog, E. and Sudia, C. E.
    1973   "Children in fatherless families." *In* B. Caldwell and H. Ricciuti (eds.), *Child Development and Social Policy.* Chicago: University of Chicago Press.
Hetherington, E. M.
    1979   "Divorce: A child's perspective." *American Psychologist* **34,** 851–858.
Hetherington, E. M., Camara, K. A., and Featherman, D. L.
    1983   "Achievement and intellectual functioning of children in one-parent households." *In* J. T. Spence (ed.), *Achievement and Achievement Motives,* pp. 205–284. San Francisco, W. H. Freeman and Co.
Hetherington, E. M., Cox, M., and Cox, R.
    1977   "The aftermath of divorce." *In* J. H. Stevens and M. Mathews (eds.), *Mother-Child, Father-Child Relations.* Washington, D.C.: National Association for the Education of Young Children.
    1978   "The aftermath of divorce." *In* J. H. Stevens Jr. and M. Mathews (eds.), *Mother-Child, Father-Child Relations,* pp. 146–176. Washington, D.C.: National Association for the Education of Young Children.
    1979   "Play and social interaction in children following divorce." *Journal of Social Issues* **35,** 26–49.
Hicks, John R.
    1966   *The Theory of Wages,* 2nd. ed. New York: St. Martins Press.
Hildebrand, George H.
    1980   "The market system." *In* E. R. Livernash (ed.), *Comparable Worth: Issues and Alternatives,* pp. 79–106. Washington, D.C.: Equal Employment Advisory Council.
Hill, M. S.
    1983   "Trends in the economic situation of U.S. families and children: 1970–1980." *In* R. R. Nelson and F. Skidmore (eds.), *American Families and the Economy,* pp. 9–58. Washington, D.C.: National Academy Press.
Hill, Charles T., Rubin, Zick, and Peplau, Letitia Anne
    1979   "Breakups before marriage: The end of 103 affairs." *In* G. Levinger and O. Moles (eds.), *Divorce and Separation,* pp. 64–82. New York: Basic Books.
Hill, D. and Hoffman, S.
    1977   "Husbands and wives." *In* G. J. Duncan and J. N. Morgan (eds.), *Five Thousand American Families,* Vol. 5, pp. 29–70. Ann Arbor: Institute for Social Research.

Hirshleifer, Jack
   1976   *Price Theory and Applications.* Englewood Cliffs: Prentice-Hall.
Hite, Shere
   1976   *The Hite Report.* New York: Macmillan.
   1981   *The Hite Report on Male Sexuality.* New York: Knopf.
Hochschild, A.
   1983   *The Managed Heart.* Berkeley: University of California Press.
Hodson, Randy
   1978   "Labor in the monopoly, competitive and state sectors of production."
             Politics and Society **8,** 429–480.
   1983   *Worker's Earnings and Corporate Economic Structure.* New York:
             Academic Press.
   1984   "Companies, industries, and the measurement of economic
             segmentation." *American Sociological Review* **49,** 335–348.
Hodson, Randy and England, Paula
   In   "Industrial structure and sex differences in earnings." *Industrial Rela-*
   press   *tions.*
Hodson, Randy and Kaufman, Robert L.
   1982   "Economic dualism: A critical review." *American Sociological Re-*
             view **47,** 727–739.
Hofferth, Sandra L. and Moore, Kristin A.
   1979   "Early childbearing and later economic well-being." *American
             Sociological Review* **44,** 784–815.
Hoffman, L. W.
   1975   "The value of children to parents and the decrease in family size."
             Proceedings of the American Philosophical Society **119,** 430–438.
Hoffman, L. W. and Hoffman, M. L.
   1973   "The value of children to parents." *In* J. T. Fawcett (ed.), *Psychological
             Perspectives on Population,* pp. 19–76. New York: Basic.
Hoffman, L. W. and Manis, J. D.
   1979   "The value of children in the United States: A new approach to the
             study of fertility." *Journal of Marriage and the Family,* pp. 538–596.
Hoffman, L. W., Thornton, A., and Manis, J. D.
   1978   "The value of children to parents in the United States." *Population:
             Behavioral, Social and Environmental Issues* **1,** 91–131.
Hoffman, Saul
   1977   "Marital instability and the economic status of women." *Demography*
             14, 67–76.
Hogan, Dennis P., Astone, Nan M., and Kitagawa, Evelyn
   1984   "The impact of social status, family structure, and neighborhood on
             contraceptive use among black adolescents." Mimeographed, Pop-
             ulation Research Center, University of Chicago.
Hohm, Charles
   1975   "Social security and fertility: An international perspective." *Demogra-*
             phy **12,** 629–644.
Horan, Patrick
   1978   "Is status attainment research atheoretical?" *American Sociological
             Review* **43,** 534–541.
Horan, Patrick, Beck, E. M., and Tolbert, Charles II
   1980   "The market homogeneity assumption: On the theoretical founda-
             tions of empirical knowledge." *Social Science Quarterly* **61,** 278–
             292.

Hout, Michael
    1978   "The determinants of marital fertility in the United States, 1968–70: Inferences from a dynamic model." *Demography* **15,** 139–160.
Huber, J. and Spitze, G.
    1980   "Considering divorce: An expansion of Becker's theory of marital instability." *American Journal of Sociology* **86,** 75–89.
    1981   "Wife's employment, household behaviors, and sex-role attitudes." *Social Forces* **60,** 150–169.
Jacobs, Jerry A.
    In   "Trends in sex-segregation in American higher education, 1948–
    press   1980," *Women and Work* **1.**
Jencks, C. et al.
    1972   *Inequality: A Reassessment of the Effect of Family and Schooling in America.* New York: Basic Books.
Johnson, Ralph E.
    1970   "Extramarital sexual intercourse: A methodological note." *Journal of Marriage and the Family* **32,** 279–82.
Kalleberg, Arne, Wallace, Michael, and Althauser, Robert
    1981   "Economic segmentation, worker power, and income inequality." *American Journal of Sociology* **87,** 651–683.
Kanter, Rosabeth
    1977   *Men and Women of the Corporation.* New York: Basic Books.
Kellam, S., Ensminger, M., and Turner, R.
    1977   "Family structure and the mental health of children." *Archives of General Psychiatry* **34,** 1012–1022.
Kerckhoff, Alan C.
    1972   *Socialization and Social Class.* Englewood Cliffs: Prentice-Hall.
Kessler, R. C. and McLeod, J. D.
    1984   "Sex differences in vulnerability to undesirable life events." *American Sociological Review* **49,** 620–631.
Kessler, R. C., McLeod, J. D., and Wethington, E.
    In   "The costs of caring: A perspective on the relationship between sex
    press   and psychological distress." *In* I. Sarason and B. Sarason (eds.), *Social Support: Theory, Research, and Applications.* The Hague: Martinus Nijhof.
Kligler, D.H.
    1954   "The effects of the employment of married women on husband and wife roles. Ph.D. dissertation, Department of Sociology, Yale University.
Kohlberg, Lawrence
    1966   "A cognitive developmental analysis of children's sex-role concepts and attitudes." *In* E. E. Maccoby (ed.), *The Development of Sex Differences,* pp. 82–173. Stanford, CA: Stanford University Press.
Kohlberg, Lawrence and Zigler, Edward
    1967   "The impact of cognitive maturity on the development of sex-role attitudes in the years 4 to 8." *Genetic Psychology Monographs* **75,** 89–165.
Kohn, Melvin
    1969   *Class and Conformity* (2nd. ed., 1977). Homewood, Ill.: Dorsey.
Kohn, Melvin and Schooler, Carmi (with J. Miller, K. Miller, and R. Schoenberg)
    1983   *Work and Personality: An Inquiry into the Impact of Social Stratification.* Norwood, New Jersey: Ablex.

Komarovsky, Mirra
  1953   *Women in the Modern World: Their Education and Their Dilemmas.*
          Reprinted Dubuque, Iowa: Brown Library Publishing Company.
  1962   *Blue-Collar Marriage.* New York: Random House.
Kramarae, Chris
  1980   *The Voices and Words of Women and Men.* Oxford, England: Per-
          gamon Press.
Krueger, Anne O.
  1963   "The economics of discrimination." *Journal of Political Economy* **71,**
          481–486.
Lazear, Edward
  1972   Econometric appendix for "On the shadow price of children," by R. T.
          Michael and E. P. Lazear. Unpublished memorandum, University of
          Chicago.
  1979   "Why is there mandatory retirement?" *Journal of Political Economy*
          87, 1261–1284.
Lazear, Edward and Moore, Robert
  1984   "Incentives, productivity, and labor contracts." *Quarterly Journal of
          Economics* **99,** 275–296.
Lazear, Edward and Rosen, Sherwin
  1981   "Rank-order tournaments as optimum labor contracts." *Journal of
          Political Economy* **89,** 841–864.
Lee, R.
  1972   "Population growth and the beginnings of sedentary life among the
          Kung Bushmen." *In* B. Spooner (ed.), *Population Growth: An-
          thropological Implications,* Chap. 14. Cambridge, MA: MIT Press.
Leibenstein, Harvey
  1963   *Economic Backwardness and Economic Growth.* New York: Wiley.
Leibowitz, Arleen
  1974   "Home investments in children." *Journal of Political Economy* **82,**
          S111–S131.
  1977   "Parental inputs and children's achievement." *Journal of Human
          Resources* **12,** 242–251.
Leijonhufvud, Axel
  1981   *Information and Coordination: Essays in Macroeconomic Theory.*
          New York: Oxford University Press.
Lesthaeghe, R.
  1983   A Century of Demographic and Cultural Change in Western Europe. A
          Sociological Interpretation. Brussels: Unpublished manuscript, Vrije
          Universiteit.
Levin-Epstein, Michael D.
  1984   Primer of Equal Employment Opportunity, 3rd ed. Washington, D.C.:
          Bureau of National Affairs.
Levinson, Richard
  1975   "Sex discrimination and employment practices: An experiment with
          unconventional job inquiries." *Social Problems* **22,** 533–543.
Levy, Frank and Michel, Richard
  1985   "Are Baby-Boomers Selfish?" Urban Institute Working Paper.

Lewin, Peter and England, Paula
 1982 "Reconceptualizing statistical discrimination." Presented at the Annual Meetings of the Southwestern Social Science Association.
Lin, Nan, Ensel, Walter, and Vaughn, John
 1981 "Social resources and strength of ties: structural factors in occupational status attainment." *American Sociological Review* **46**, 393–405.
Lindert, Peter H.
 1977 "Sibling position and achievement." *Journal of Human Resources* **12**, 198–219.
 1978 *Fertility and Scarcity in America*. Princeton, N. J.: Princeton University Press.
Lindsay, Cotton Mather
 1980 "Equal pay for comparable work: An economic analysis of a new antidiscrimination doctrine." Occasional paper of the Law and Economics Center, University of Miami, Coral Gables, Florida.
Lippman, Steven and McCall, John J.
 1976 "The economics of job search: A survey." *Economic Inquiry* **14**, 155–189.
Lloyd, Cynthia and Niemi, Beth
 1979 *The Economics of Sex Differentials*. New York: Columbia University Press.
Looft, W.
 1971 "Sex differences in the expression of vocational aspirations by elementary school children." *Developmental Psychology* **5**, 366.
Lord, George, III and Falk, William
 1982 "Hidden income and labor market segmentation." *Social Science Quarterly* **63**, 208–224.
Lopata, Helen Znaniecki
 1971 *Occupation: Housewife*. New York: Oxford University Press.
Lowenthal, M. F. and Weiss, L.
 1976 "Intimacy and crises in adulthood." *The Counseling Psychologist* **6**, 10–15.
Lowenthal, M. F., Thurnher, M., and David, C.
 1975 *Four Stages of Life—A Comparative Study of Women and Men Facing Transitions*. San Francisco: Jossey-Bass.
Lynd, Robert S. and Lynd, Helen Merrell
 1929 *Middletown: A Study in American Culture*. New York: Harcourt and Brace.
 1937 *Middletown in Transition: A Study in Cultural Conflicts*. New York: Harcourt and Brace.
Maas, Henry S. and Kuypers, Joseph A.
 1975 *From Thirty to Seventy—A Forty-Year Longitudinal Study of Adult Life Styles and Personality*. San Francisco: Jossey-Bass.
Maccoby, Eleanor E. and Jacklin, Carol N.
 1974 *The Psychology of Sex Differences*. Stanford, CA: Stanford University Press.

McGee, Jeanne and Wells, Kathleen
    1978   "Life-span model of gender role identity." Presented at the Annual
            Meetings of the Gerontological Society.
McLanahan, S.
    1983   "Family structure and the reproduction of poverty." Discussion paper
            720-83, Institute for Research on Poverty, University of Wisconsin.
McLaughlin, Steven
    1982   "Differentials in female labor force participation surrounding the first
            birth." Journal of Marriage and the Family 44, 407–420.
Madden, Janice F.
    1973   The Economics of Sex Discrimination. Lexington, MA: Lexington
            Books.
    1975   "Discrimination—A manifestation of male market power?" In C.
            Lloyd (ed.), Sex, Discrimination, and the Division of Labor, pp.
            146–174. New York: Columbia University Press.
Malcolmson, James M.
    1984   "Work incentives, hierarchy, and internal labor markets." Journal of
            Political Economy 92, 486–507.
Malkiel, B. F. and Malkiel, J. A.
    1973   "Male-female pay differences in professional employment." Amer-
            ican Economic Review 63, 693–705.
Manser, Marilyn and Murray Brown
    1979   "Bargaining analyses of household decisions." In C. Lloyd, E. An-
            drews, and C. Gilroy (eds.), Women in the Labor Market, pp. 3–26.
            New York: Columbia University Press.
Marini, Margaret Mooney and Brinton, Mary C.
    1984   "Sex typing in occupational socialization." In Barbara F. Reskin (ed.),
            Sex Segregation in the Workplace: Trends, Explanations, Remedies,
            pp. 192–232. Washington, D.C.: National Academy Press.
Marshall, Alfred
    1923   Principles of Economics, 8th ed.: London: Macmillan.
Masnick, George and Bane, Mary Jo
    1980   The Nation's Families. Boston: Auburn.
Mason, K. O., Mason, W. M., Winsborough, H. H., and Poole, W. K.
    1973   "Some methodological issues in cohort analyses of archival data."
            American Sociological Review 38, 242–258.
Mayer, Thomas
    1972   Permanent Income, Wealth and Consumption. Berkeley: University of
            California Press.
Mayhew, Bruce H.
    1980   "Structuralism versus individualism: Part I, Shadowboxing in the
            dark." Social Forces 59, 335–375.
    1981   "Structuralism versus individualism, Part II, Ideological and other
            obfuscations." Social Forces 59, 627–648.
Medoff, James and Abraham, Katherine
    1980   "Experience, performance, and earnings." Quarterly Journal of Eco-
            nomics 95, 703–736.
    1981   "Are those paid more really more productive? The case of experi-
            ence." Journal of Human Resources 16, 186–216.

Merrill, Sally
    1984   "Home equity and the elderly." *In* H. J. Aaron and G. Burtless, (eds.), *Retirement and Economic Behavior*, pp. 197–228. Washington, D.C.: The Brookings Institution.

Michel, A.
    1970   "Wife's satisfaction with husband's understanding in Parisian urban families." *Journal of Marriage and the Family* **32,** 351–360.

Miller, B. C.
    1976   "A multivariate developmental model of marital satisfaction." *Journal of Marriage and the Family* **38,** 643–657.

Miller, Joanne and Garrison, Howard H.
    1982   "Sex roles: The division of labor at home and in the workplace." *Annual Review of Sociology* **8,** 237–262.

Millman, Sara and Hendershot, Gerry
    1980   "Early fertility." *Family Planning Perspectives* **12,** 139–149.

Mincer, Jacob
    1958   "Investment in human capital and personal income distribution." *Journal of Political Economy* **66,** 281–302.
    1963   "Market prices, opportunity costs, and income effects." *In* C. F. Christ et al. (eds.), *Measurement in Economics*. Stanford, CA: Stanford University Press.
    1974   *Schooling, Experience, and Earnings*. New York: National Bureau of Economic Research.

Mincer, Jacob and Polachek, Solomon
    1974   "Family investments in human capital: Earnings of women." *Journal of Political Economy* **82,** S76–S108.

Moore, K. A., Peterson, J. L., and Furstenberg, F. F. Jr.
    1984   "Starting early: The antecedents of early, premarital intercourse." Presented at the Annual Meetings of the Population Association of America.

Mott, Frank L. and Moore, Sylvia
    1983   "The tempo of remarriage among young American women." *Journal of Marriage and the Family* (May), pp. 427–436.

Murnane, Richard
    1981   "Interpreting the evidence on school effectiveness." *Teachers College Record* **83,** 19–35.

Murnane, Richard J., Maynard, Rebecca A., and Ohls, James C.
    1981   "Home resources and children's achievement." *Review of Economics and Statistics*, pp. 369–377.

Nalebuff, Barry and Zeckhauser, Richard
    1981   "Involuntary unemployment reconsidered: Second-best contracting with heterogeneous firms and workers." Discussion paper 675–681, Institute for Research on Poverty, University of Wisconsin–Madison.

Namboodiri, N. K.
    1981   "On factors affecting fertility at different stages in the reproductive history: An exercise in cohort analysis." *Social Forces* **59,** 1114–1129.

National Center for Health Statistics
    1980   Advance Data, no. 58. "Remarriages of Women 15–44 Years of Age Whose First Marriage Ended in Divorce: United States, 1976."

Nemerowicz, Gloria Morris
  1979   *Children's Perceptions of Gender and Work Roles.* New York: Praeger.
Neugarten, Bernice L.
  1968   *Middle Age and Aging.* Chicago: University of Chicago Press.
  1970   "Dynamics of transition of middle age to old age." *Journal of Geriatric Psychology* **4,** 71–87.
  1974   "The roles we play." In American Medical Association, (ed.), *The Quality of Life: The Middle Years.* Acton, MA: Publishing Sciences Group.
Neugarten, Bernice L. and Datan, Nancy
  1974   "The middle years." In S. Arieti (ed.), *American Handbook of Psychiatry,* 2nd ed. New York: Basic Books.
Nilsen, S.
  1984   "Recessionary impacts on the unemployment of men and women." *Monthly Labor Review* **107,** 21–25.
Nordhaus, William
  1984   "Comments on papers by George Perry and Thomas Sargent." *American Economic Review* **74,** 419–421.
Norton, R. D.
  Forth- "Industrial policy and American renewal." *Journal of Economic Literature.*
  coming *ature.*
Norton, Arthur J. and Glick, Paul C.
  1979   "Marital instability in America: Past, present, and future." In G. Levinger and O. C. Moles (eds.), *Divorce and Separation: Context, Causes, and Consequences.* New York: Basic Books.
Okun, Arthur
  1981   *Prices and Quantities: A Macroeconomic Analysis.* Washington, D.C.: Brookings.
Olneck, Michael and Wolfe, Barbara L.
  1980   "Intelligence and family size: Another look." *Review of Economics and Statistics* **62,** 241–247.
O'Neill, June
  1985   "The trend in the male-female wage gap in the United States." *Journal of Labor Economics* **3,** S91–S116.
Oppenheimer, Valerie
  1970   *The Female Labor Force in the United States.* Berkeley: University of California Institute of International Studies.
Parcel, Toby L. and Mueller, Charles W.
  1983   *Ascription and Labor Markets.* New York: Academic Press.
Parsons, T.
  1949   "The social structure of the family." In R. Anshen (ed.), *The Family: Its Function and Destiny,* pp. 173–201. New York: Harper and Row.
  1955   "The American family: its relations to personality and to the social structure." In T. Parsons and R. F. Bales (eds.), *Family, Socialization and Interaction Process,* pp. 3–33. New York: Macmillan.
Parsons, T. and Bales, R. F.
  1955   *Family Socialization and Interaction Process.* New York: Free Press.
Pearlin, L. and Johnson, J.
  1977   "Marital status, life-strains, and depression." *American Sociological Review* **42,** 704–715.

Perrucci, Carolyn G., Pottes, Harry R., and Rhoads, Deborah C.
    1978   "Determinants of male family-role performance." *Psychology of Women Quarterly* **3**, 53–66.
Pfeiffer, John
    1985   "Girl talk-Boy talk." *Science* **85**, 58–63.
Phelps, Edmund
    1972   "The statistical theory of racism and sexism." *American Economic Review* **64**, 59–61.
Piore, Michael
    1979   *Unemployment and Inflation: Institutionalist and Structuralist Views.* White Plains: M.E. Sharpe.
Polachek, Solomon
    1975   "Discontinuous labor force participation and its effects on women's market earnings." *In* Cynthia Lloyd (ed.), *Sex, Discrimination, and the Division of Labor,* pp. 90–122. New York: Columbia University Press.
    1979   "Occupational segregation among women: Theory, evidence, and a prognosis." *In* Cynthia Lloyd (ed.), *Women in the Labor Market,* pp. 137–157. New York: Columbia University Press.
    1981   "Occupational self-selection: A human capital approach to sex differences in occupational structure." *Review of Economics and Statistics* **58**, 60–69.
    In   "Occupational segregation: A defense of human capital predictions."
    press   *Journal of Human Resources.*
Pratt, William, *et al.*
    1984   *Understanding U.S. Fertility: Findings from the National Survey of Family Growth, Cycle III.* Washington, D.C.: Population Reference Bureau.
Preston, Samuel H.
    1984   "Children and the elderly: Divergent paths for America's dependents." *Demography* **21**, 435–458.
Preston, Samuel H. and McDonald, John
    1979   "The incidence of divorce within cohorts of American marriages contracted since the civil war." *Demography* **16**, 1–25.
Pullum, T. W.
    1980   "Separating age, period and cohort effects in white U.S. fertility, 1920–1970." *Social Science Research* **9**, 225–244.
Rabban, Meyer L.
    1950   "Sex role identification in young children in two diverse social groups." *Genetic Psychological Monographs* **42**, 81–158.
Raiffa, Howard
    1982   *The Art and Science of Negotiation.* Cambridge, MA: Harvard University Press.
Rainwater, Lee
    1970   *Behind Ghetto Walls.* New York: Aldine.
Raschke, Helen and Vernon Raschke
    1979   "Family conflict and children's self-concepts: A comparison of intact and single-parent families." *Journal of Marriage and the Family* **41**, 367–374.
Reid, John
    1982   *Black America in the 1980s.* Washington, D.C.: Population Reference Bureau.

Renne, Karen
    1970   "Correlates of dissatisfaction in marriage." *Journal of Marriage and the Family* **32,** 54–67.
    1971   "Health and marital experience in an urban population." *Journal of Marriage and the Family* **33,** 338–350.
Remick, Helen
    1984   "Comparable worth and wages: Economic equity for women." Industrial Relations Center, University of Hawaii–Manoa.
Richman, Judith
    1977   "Bargaining for sex and status: The dating service and sex-role change." *In* P. Stein, J. Richman, and N. Hannon (eds.), *The Family: Functions, Conflicts, and Symbols,* pp. 158–165. Reading, MA: Addison-Wesley.
Rindfuss, Ronald R. and Sweet, James A.
    1977   *Postwar Fertility Trends and Differentials in the United States.* New York: Academic Press.
Robinson, John P.
    1980   "Housework technology and household work." *In* S. F. Berk (ed.), *Women and Household Labor,* pp. 53–68. Beverly Hills: Sage.
Rogers, Gayle T.
    1980   "Pension coverage and vesting among private wage and salary workers, 1979: Preliminary estimates from the 1979 survey of pension plan coverage." Working paper 16, Office of Research and Statistics, Social Security Administration.
Rollins, B. C. and Cannon, K. L.
    1974   "Marital satisfaction over the family life cycle: A re-evaluation." *Journal of Marriage and the Family* **36,** 271–282.
Rollins, B. C. and Feldman, H.
    1970   "Marital satisfaction over the family life cycle." *Journal of Marriage and the Family* **32,** 20–28.
Roos, Patricia A. and Reskin, Barbara F.
    1984   "Institutional factors contributing to sex segregation." *In* Barbara F. Reskin (ed.), *Sex Segregation in the Workplace: Trends, Explanations, Remedies,* pp. 235–260. Washington, D.C.: National Academy Press.
Rosen, Benson
    1982   "Career progress of women: Getting in and staying in." *In* H. J. Bernardin (ed.), *Women in the Work Force,* pp. 70–99. New York: Praeger.
Rosen, B. and Jerdee, T. H.
    1974a   "Effects of applicant's sex and difficulty of job on evaluations of candidates for managerial positions." *Journal of Applied Psychology* **59,** 511–512.
    1974b   "Sex stereotyping in the executive suite." *Harvard Business Review* **52,** 45–58.
    1978   "Perceived sex differences in managerially relevant behavior." *Sex Roles* **4,** 837–843.
Rosenbaum, James
    1979   "Organizational career mobility: promotion chances in a corporation during periods of growth and contraction." *American Journal of Sociology* **85,** 21–48.
    1984   *Career Mobility in a Corporate Hierarchy.* New York: Academic.

Ross, Heather L. and Sawhill, Isabel V.
  1975   *Time of Transition: The Growth of Families Headed by Women.*
          Washington, D.C.: The Urban Institute.
Rossi, Alice
  1977   "A biosocial perspective on parenting." *Daedalus* **106,** 1–31.
  1984   "Gender and parenthood." *In* A. Rossi (ed.), *Gender and the Life
          Course,* pp. 161–191. New York: Aldine.
Rubin, Lillian B.
  1976   *Worlds of Pain.* New York: Basic Books.
  1979   *Women of a Certain Age.* New York: Harper and Row.
  1983   *Intimate Strangers.* New York: Harper and Row.
Russell, Louise B.
  1982   *The Baby Boom Generation and the Economy.* Washington, D.C.:
          Brookings.
Rutter, M. and Madge, N.
  1976   *Cycles of Disadvantage.* London: Heinemann.
Sales, Esther
  1977   "Women's adult development." *In* I. Frieze, *et al.* (eds.), *Women and
          Sex Roles: A Social Psychological Perspective.* New York: W. W.
          Norton.
Saluter, Arlene
  1983   *Marital Status and Living Arrangements: March 1982.* Current Popula-
          tion Reports, series P-20, No. 380. Washington, D.C.: U.S. Govern-
          ment Printing Office.
Sanday, Peggy Reeves
  1981   *Female Power and Male Dominance.* Cambridge: Cambridge Univer-
          sity Press.
Sandell, Steven H. and Shapiro, David
  1978   "A re-examination of the evidence." *Journal of Human Resources* **13,**
          103–117.
Scanzoni, John
  1970   *Opportunity and the Family.* New York: Macmillan.
  1972   *Sexual Bargaining.* Englewood Cliffs: Prentice-Hall.
  1975   "Sex roles, economic factors, and marital solidarity in black and white
          marriages." *Journal of Marriage and the Family* **37,** 130–145.
  1977   *The Black Family in Modern Society: Patterns of Stability and Security,*
          enlarged edition. Chicago: University of Chicago Press.
  1979a   "A historical perspective on husband-wife bargaining power and
          marital dissolution." *In* G. Levinger and O. Moles (eds.), *Divorce and
          Separation,* pp. 20–36. New York: Basic Books.
  1979b   "Social processes and power in families." *In* W. R. Burr, R. Hill, F. I.
          Nye, and I. L. Reiss (eds.), *Contemporary Theories About the Family,*
          Vol. 1. New York: The Free Press.
Scanzoni, L. D. and Scanzoni, J.
  1981   *Men, Women, and Change,* 2nd. ed. New York: McGraw-Hill.
Scherer, F. M.
  1980   *Industrial Market Structure and Economic Performance,* Rev. ed.
          Chicago: Rand McNally.
Schervish, Paul
  1983   *The Structural Determinants of Unemployment.* New York: Academ-
          ic.

Schotter, Andrew and Schwodiauer, Gerhard
   1980   "Economics and the theory of games: A survey." *Journal of Economic Literature* **18,** 479–527.
Schram, R. W.
   1979   "Marital satisfaction over the family life cycle: a critique and proposal." *Journal of Marriage and the Family* **41,** 7–12.
Schultz, T. Paul
   1981   *The Economics of Population.* Reading, MA: Addison-Wesley.
Schultz, T. W.
   1960   "Capital formation by education." *Journal of Political Economy* **68,** 571–583.
   1961   "Investment in human capital." *American Economic Review* **51,** 1–17.
   1963   *The Economic Value of Education.* New York: Columbia University Press.
   1974   *Marriage, Family Human Capital, and Fertility* (ed.). Supplement to the Journal of Political Economy 82.
   1981   *Investing in People.* Berkeley: University of California Press.
Seyfried, B. A. and Hendrick, C.
   1973   "When do opposites attract? When they are opposite in sex and sex-role attitudes." *Journal of Personality and Social Psychology* **25,** 15–20.
Shapiro, David and Mott, Frank
   1979   "Labor supply behavior of prospective and new mothers." *Demography* **16,** 199–208.
Simon, Julian
   1974   "Interpersonal welfare comparisons can be made—And used for redistribution decisions." *Kyklos* 27.
   1977   *The Economics of Population Growth.* Princeton, N.J.: Princeton University Press.
Simpson, Ida Harper and England, Paula
   1981   "Conjugal work roles and marital solidarity." *In* J. Aldous (ed.), *Two Paychecks: Life in Dual-Earner Families,* pp. 147–172. Beverly Hills: Sage.
Slocum, W. L. and Nye, F. I.
   1976   "Provider and housekeeper roles." *In* F. I. Nye (ed.), *Role Structure and Analysis of the Family,* pp. 81–99. Beverly Hills: Sage.
Smith, D. P.
   1981   "A reconsideration of Easterlin cycles." *Population Studies,* pp. 247–264.
Smith, James P. and Ward, Michael P.
   1980   "Asset accumulation and family size." *Demography* **17,** 243–260.
   1984   *Women's Wages and Work in the Twentieth Century.* R-3119-NICHD. Santa Monica: Rand.
Smith, James P. and Ward, Michael P.
   1985   "Time-series growth in the female labor force." *Journal of Labor Economics* **3,** S59–S90.
Soldo, Beth J.
   1980   *America's Elderly in the 1980s.* Washington, D.C.: Population Reference Bureau.

Sontag, Susan
    1972   "The double standard of aging." *Saturday Review* **55,** 29–38 (September 23).
Spanier, Graham B., Lewis, Robert A., and Cole, Charles L.
    1975   "Marital adjustment over the family cycle: The issue of curvilinearity." *Journal of Marriage and the Family* **37,** 263–275.
Spence, A. Michael
    1974   *Market Signaling.* Cambridge: Harvard University Press.
Stack, Carol
    1974   *All Our Kin.* New York: Harper and Row.
Stafford, Rebecca, Backman, Elaine, and Dibona, Pamela
    1977   "The division of labor among cohabiting and married couples." *Journal of Marriage and the Family* **39,** 43–54.
Stevenson, Mary
    1975   "Relative wages and sex segregation by occupation." *In* C. Lloyd (ed.), *Sex Discrimination and the Division of Labor.* New York: Columbia University Press.
Stewart, Alison Clark and Fein, Greta
    1983   "Early childhood programs." *In* P. Mussen (ed.), *Handbook of Child Psychology, 4th ed.,* Vol. II: Infancy and Developmental Psychobiology, pp. 917–999. New York: Wiley.
Stigler, George
    1961   "The economics of information." *Journal of Political Economy* **69,** 213–225.
    1962   "Information in the labor market." *Journal of Political Economy* **70,** Suppl., p. 70.
Stockard, Jean and Johnson, Miriam M.
    1980   *Sex Roles: Sex Inequality and Sex Role Development.* Englewood Cliffs: Prentice-Hall.
Stone, L.
    1982   "The historical origins of the modern family." The Fifth Annual O. Meredith Wilson Lecture in History. Published by the Department of History, University of Utah, Salt Lake City.
Summers, G., Evans, S., Clements, F., Beck, E. M., and Minkoff, J.
    1976   *Industrial Invasion of Nonmetropolitan America.* New York: Praeger.
Sweet, James A., and Rindfuss, Ronald R.
    1981   "Those ubiquitous fertility trends: United States, 1945–1979." Working paper 81-28, Center for Demography and Ecology, University of Wisconsin–Madison.
Szinovacz, M. E.
    1977   "Role allocation, family structure and female employment." *Journal of Marriage and the Family* **39,** 781–791.
Taubman, Paul
    1977   *Kinometrics.* Amsterdam: North-Holland.
Thibaut, John W. and Kelley, Harold H.
    1959   *The Social Psychology of Groups.* New York: Wiley.
Thorne, Barrie and Henley, Nancy
    1975   *Language and Sex: Difference and Dominance.* Rowley, MA: Newbury House.

Thornton, Arland
    1983   "Changing attitudes toward divorce with children: Evidence from an intergenerational panel study." Presented at the Annual Meetings of the Population Association of America.
Thornton, Arland and Freedman, Deborah
    1983   *The Changing American Family*. Washington, D.C.: Population Reference Bureau.
Tiebout, Charles M.
    1956   "A pure theory of local expenditures." *Journal of Political Economy* **64,** 416–424.
Tolbert, Charles II, Horan, Patrick, and Beck, E. M.
    1980   "The structure of economic segmentation: A dual economy approach." *American Journal of Sociology* **85,** 1095–1116.
Treiman, Donald J. and Hartmann, Heidi I.
    1981   *Women, Work, and Wages: Equal Pay for Jobs of Equal Value*. Washington, D.C.: National Academy Press.
Treiman, D. J. and Terrell, K.
    1975   "Women, work, and wages—Trends in the female occupational structure since 1940." *In* K. Land and S. Spilerman (eds.), *Social Indicator Models*. New York: Russell Sage.
U.S.A. Today
    1984   "Kids and divorce: No long-term harm." December 20, 1984.
U.S. Bureau of the Census
    1983   *Child Support and Alimony: 1981* (Advance Report). Current Population Reports, Special Studies. Series P-23, No. 124.
    1984   *Money Income of Households, Families, and Persons in the United States: 1982*. Current Population Reports, Consumer Income. Series P-60, No. 142.

U.S. Department of Labor
    1950   *Employment and Training Report of the President*. Washington, D.C.: U.S. Government Printing Office.
    1979   *Employment and Training Report of the President*.Washington, D.C.: U.S. Government Printing Office.
    1982   *The Female-Male Earnings Gap: A Review of Employment and Earnings Issues*. Report 673, Bureau of Labor Statistics. Washington, D.C.: U.S. Government Printing Office.
    1983a   *Employment and Earnings* (January). Washington, D.C.: U.S. Government Printing Office.
    1983b   *Time of Change: 1983 Handbook on Women Workers*. Bulletin 298. Washington, D.C.: U.S. Government Printing Office.
    1984   *Employment Patterns of Minorities and Women in Federal Contractor and Noncontractor Establishments, 1974–1980: A Report of the Office of Federal Contract Compliance Programs*. In xerox, Employment Standards Administration.

Vaillant, George E.
    1977   *Adaptation to Life*. Boston: Little, Brown.

van de Walle, Etienne and Knodel, John
    1980   *Europe's Fertility Transition: New Evidence and Lessons for Today's Developing World*. Washington, D.C.: Population Reference Bureau.

Vanek, Joann
 1974   "Time spent in housework." *Scientific American* **231,** 116–120.
Wachter, Michael and Williamson, Oliver
 1978   "Obligational markets and the mechanics of inflation." *Bell Journal of Economics* **6,** 250–278.
Waite, Linda J.
 1981   *U.S. Women at Work.* Washington, D.C.: Population Reference Bureau.
Waite, Linda J. and Stolzenberg, Ross M.
 1976   "Intended childbearing and labor force participation of young women: Insights from nonrecursive models." *American Sociological Review* **41,** 235–252.
Walker, K. E. and Woods M.
 1976   *Time Use: A Measure of Household Production of Family Goods and Services.* Washington, D.C.: American Home Economics Association.
Waller, Willard
 1937   "The rating-dating complex." *American Sociological Review* **2,** 727–735.
 1951   *The Family.* (Original edition, 1938.) Revised by Reuben Hill. New York: Dryden Press.
Wallerstein, Judith S. and Kelly, Joan Berlin
 1980   *Surviving the Breakup: How Children and Parents Cope with Divorce.* New York: Basic Books.
Weingarten, Kathy
 1978   "The employment pattern of professional couples and their distribution of involvement in the family." *Psychology of Women Quarterly* **3,** 43–52.
Weiss, Robert S.
 1975   *Marital Separation.* New York: Basic Books.
Welch, Finis
 1979   "Effects of cohort size on earnings: The baby boom babies' financial burst." *Journal of Political Economy* **87,** S65–S97.
White, Lynn
 1979   "Sex differentials in the effect of remarriage on global happiness." *Journal of Marriage and the Family* **41,** 869–876.
Williamson, Oliver, Wachter, Michael, and Harris, Jeffrey
 1975   "Understanding the employment relationship: The analysis of idiosyncratic exchange." *Bell Journal of Economics* **6,** 250–278.
Willis, Robert J.
 1973   "A new approach to the economic theory of fertility behavior." *Journal of Political Economy* **81,** S14–S64.
Wilson, John
 1983   *Social Theory.* Englewood Cliffs: Prentice-Hall.
Winch, R. F.
 1958   *Mate-Selection: A Study of Complementary Needs.* New York: Harper.
Wolf, Douglas A. and Levy, Frank
 1984   "Pension coverage, pension vesting, and the distribution of job tenures." *In* H. J. Aaron and G. Burtless (eds.), *Retirement and Economic Behavior,* pp. 23–64. Washington, D.C.: Brookings.

Wray, J.
  1971   "Population pressure on families: family size and child spacing." *In* R.
              Revelle (ed.), *Rapid Population Growth: Consequences and Policy
              Implications.* Baltimore: Johns Hopkins University Press.
Wright, J. D.
  1978   "Are working women really more satisfied? Evidence from several
              national surveys." *Journal of Marriage and the Family* **40,** 301–313.
Wright, E. O. and Perrone, Luca
  1977   "Marxist class categories and income inequality." *American
              Sociological Review* **42,** 32–55.
Zellner, Harriet
  1975   "The determinants of occupational segregation." *In* C. Lloyd (ed.),
              Sex, Discrimination, and the Division of Labor, pp. 125–145. New
              York: Columbia University Press.
Zelnik, M. and J. F. Kantner, 1980
  1980   "Sexual activity, contraceptive use and pregnancy among metropoli-
              tan area teenagers: 1971–1979." *Family Planning Perspectives* **12,**
              230–237.
Zill, Nicholas
  1978   "Divorce, marital happiness and the mental health of children: Find-
              ings from the FCD national survey of children." Presented at the
              NIMH Workshop on Divorce and Children, Bethesda, Maryland.

AUTHOR INDEX

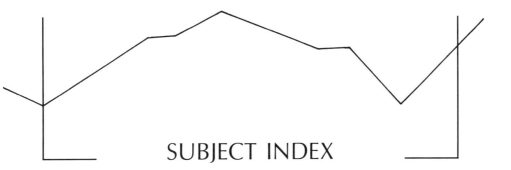

SUBJECT INDEX